Conflict in Caledonia

Law and Society Series
W. Wesley Pue, General Editor

The Law and Society Series explores law as a socially embedded
phenomenon. It is premised on the understanding that the
conventional division of law from society creates false dichotomies in thinking, scholarship, educational practice, and social life.
Books in the series treat law and society as mutually constitutive
and seek to bridge scholarship emerging from interdisciplinary
engagement of law with disciplines such as politics, social theory,
history, political economy, and gender studies.

A list of titles in the series appears at the end of the book.

Conflict in Caledonia

Aboriginal Land Rights
and the Rule of Law

LAURA DeVRIES

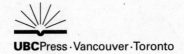

UBCPress · Vancouver · Toronto

21 20 19 18 17 16 15 14 13 12 11   5 4 3 2 1

Printed in Canada on FSC-certified ancient-forest-free paper
(100% post-consumer recycled) that is processed chlorine- and acid-free.

Library and Archives Canada Cataloguing in Publication

DeVries, Laura, 1982-
    Conflict in Caledonia : Aboriginal land rights and the rule of law / Laura DeVries.

(Law and society series, ISSN 1496-4953)
Includes bibliographical references and index.
Also issued in electronic format.
ISBN 978-0-7748-2184-1

    1. Caledonia Land Claim Dispute, Caledonia, Ont., 2006-. 2. Iroquois Indians –
Ontario – Caledonia – Claims. 3. Native peoples – Legal status, laws, etc. – Canada.
I. Title. II. Series: Law and society series (Vancouver, B.C.)

F1668.X39 2011   282'.52   C2010-907361-4

Canadä

UBC Press gratefully acknowledges the financial support for our publishing program
of the Government of Canada (through the Canada Book Fund), the Canada Council
for the Arts, and the British Columbia Arts Council.

This book has been published with the help of a grant from the Canadian Federation
for the Humanities and Social Sciences, through the Aid to Scholarly Publications
Program, using funds provided by the Social Sciences and Humanities Research
Council of Canada.

Printed and bound in Canada by Friesens
Set in Myriad and Sabon by Artegraphica Design Co. Ltd.
Copy editor: Stacy Belden
Proofreader: Carrie Villeneuve

UBC Press
The University of British Columbia
2029 West Mall
Vancouver, BC V6T 1Z2
www.ubcpress.ca

Contents

Acknowledgments

I am profoundly grateful to Terre Satterfield for all of her invaluable support, both for encouraging me to write this book in the first place and for generously offering crucial feedback, advice, and support whenever needed (which was often). Deepest appreciation also goes to Juanita Sundberg and Susan Hill for their essential guidance and encouragement in the initial research and writing process, to Anna-Marie Bick and Brad Williamson for their thoughtful and valuable advice on the first draft, and to Lara Hoshizaki for generously lending her formidable mapping skills to the effort. Matthew Kudelka is an editing genius and my effusive thanks go to him for his swift and excellent work on the manuscript. Many thanks to Allan Lissner for permission to use his photograph on the cover of this book. It was difficult to find the right cover image for this book, and this photograph captures some of the complexity of the situation in Caledonia. British and Canadian flags have been planted on disputed land for many decades, and both groups have staked poignant and controversial claims to territory throughout the dispute. I would also like to thank the many members of Six Nations and Caledonia communities who provided practical assistance during the research phase as well as those who frankly shared their opinions and insights on the subject at hand. Financial support for research came from the Social Sciences and Humanities Research Council of Canada (SSHRC) as well as from the University of British Columbia's Martha Piper Research Fund.

More generally, my parents have supported me in everything I have ever attempted to do.

Conflict in Caledonia

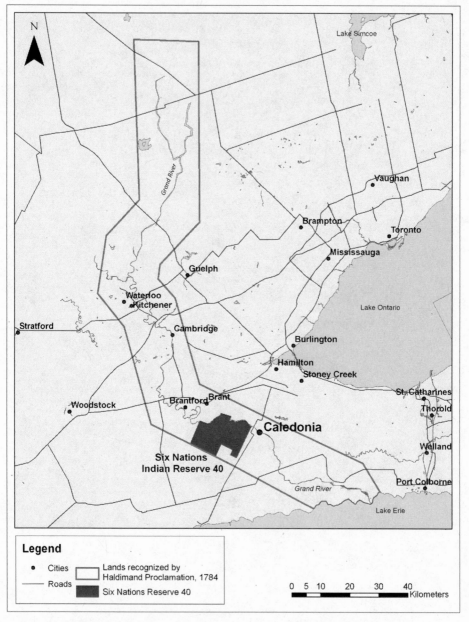

· Geography of the Six Nations' Grand River Territory in southern Ontario. The dispute on which this book centres is located in the town of Caledonia, indicated in larger type (map created by Lara Hoshizaki and used with permission).

Introduction

Many centuries ago, six nations united to form the Haudenosaunee Confederacy. Representatives from each of the nations – Mohawk, Seneca, Cayuga, Onondaga, Tuscarora, and Oneida – formed the Confederacy Council, a political structure that allowed for national and individual autonomy if consensus could not be reached on a particular course of action. The Haudenosaunee decided that their lands would be united: a "dish with one spoon" for each to use responsibly and with an eye to future generations. They were extremely successful in war and were a force to be reckoned with, both by other First Nations and by the Europeans who eventually arrived on Turtle Island, which they had renamed North America.

These Europeans – initially the Dutch and later the French and British, in turns – eagerly sought trading and military alliances with the Haudenosaunee Confederacy, which they referred to as the League of the Iroquois. At first, the settlers were few, and the treaties, both in word and in outcome, were mutually agreeable. The British and the Haudenosaunee decided on a relationship that was best symbolized by two boats travelling down the same river – together but independent. Years of interdependence in economy and battle culminated in the Haudenosaunee providing assistance to the British during the American War of Independence. However, treaties that were increasingly broken by the British eventually compelled a large number of Haudenosaunee, led by Joseph Brant, to migrate from what had just become the United States of America to a more northern part of their traditional territory in what is now southern Ontario. They had become wary of European promises, the latest being a pledge by the British to compensate them for any losses of land they might suffer as a result of their alliance in the American War of Independence. It appeared, however, that the British intended to see this promise through. In 1784, Lieutenant Governor Frederick Haldimand issued a proclamation – expressed in terms that reflected the new arrivals' ways of noting ownership – that recognized a stretch of land along the Grand River, from source to mouth, totalling about one million acres, as Haudenosaunee territory.

Although this area was only a tiny fraction of their original land, the Haudenosaunee believed that with this recognition the covenant of alliance with the British would be restored and the settlers' incursions would cease. Unable to pursue their traditional mix of farming and hunting due to the reduction in their territory and the increasing presence of immigrants, the Haudenosaunee decided to lease some of their land to generate monetary income for themselves and their descendants. Despite promises to the contrary, however, and even despite further military assistance to the British during settler uprisings, the Haudenosaunee found that many European squatters were settling on their land without property title or permission from either Six Nations or the colonial government. This squatting was illegal under British law, but the government in London was unable or unwilling to ensure that local colonial officials enforced this law. Many squatters were eventually given title to the land by the colonial government, and many of the land leases were somehow treated as sales, even though payments never appeared in Six Nations' trust fund accounts. Over time, through fraud, neglect, and outright theft, the Haudenosaunee of the Grand River Territory once again found themselves hemmed in on all sides. Settler societies were constantly growing, and the Haudenosaunee generally got the short end of the legal stick. At the same time, options for physical resistance were limited.

The British and subsequent Canadian governments have long maintained that in 1841 they succeeded in solving the problem once and for all by arranging a "general surrender" of land from Six Nations. This adjustment reduced the Grand River Territory to a postage-stamp-sized reserve. Six Nations has contested this surrender ever since. At first, opposition consisted of petitions, letters, delegations to colonial governments, both local and in London, and the like. Later, in the 1970s, Six Nations was among the first Native groups to press its land claims through official Canadian channels. Six Nations has also submitted twenty-eight claims of fraud, theft, and non-payment for lands ranging from the town plot of Brantford to those acres flooded during the building of the Welland Canal. One of these claims has been settled, in favour of Six Nations, and the others either are still in process or are yet to be addressed. While the disputes are stalled, Ontario has continued steadily to sell land to settlers, who now hold title under Canadian property law and have built farms, villages, towns, and cities on what Six Nations considers its own sovereign lands.

The Haudenosaunee have never agreed to be part of Canada but have been forced over the years to at least pay lip service to its laws and customs. All the while, Six Nations' trust funds have been diverted to support Canadian projects. In 1924, the RCMP raided the Confederacy council house and, supported by a small minority of Six Nations people, installed a new "elected" band council approved by the *Indian Act* in place of the Confederacy.[1] Until 1960, it was illegal for Natives to raise money for the purpose of litigation against the Crown. In the 1970s, when the government finally introduced a land claims process, hopes for fairer dealings glimmered, but this process has proved to be largely ineffectual.

The Six Nations Reserve is located between the town of Caledonia and the city of Brantford (which, ironically enough, is named after Joseph Brant). Both places are now thoroughly entangled in Canada's dispute with Six Nations. In February 2006, a contingent of Haudenosaunee physically occupied a half-built housing development in Caledonia called Douglas Creek Estates, halted construction, and renamed the land Kanonhstaton, "the protected place." The land developers, Don and John Henning of Henco Homes, found themselves painfully enmeshed in an unresolved land dispute. At the local courthouse in Cayuga (a town named for one of the six nations), the Hennings sought and received an injunction against the protesters. The protesters refused to obey it and leave the property. In April, the Ontario Provincial Police were sent in to remove them, but this effort failed. Indeed, the attempt motivated the protesters to block the main road through Caledonia as well as the highway bypass skirting the town – a serious obstruction to all who lived there as well as to anyone driving south. Negotiations to address the unresolved claim commenced, with the Confederacy Council recognized as the representative of Six Nations. Soon afterwards, the barricades were removed, and the Ontario government purchased the land from the developers. Only a nominal contingent of protesters remains on Douglas Creek Estates.

Five years after this particular land-related protest was launched (there have been others involving Six Nations over the years), negotiations seem to be on semi-permanent hold. Protests and construction stoppages have spread south from Caledonia to the town of Hagersville and west to Brantford. The Elected Band Council of Six Nations has resumed litigation against Canada, demanding a formal and complete accounting of land leases, sales, and trust fund monies that were to have been held for Six Nations. The Confederacy Council continues to seek resolution through negotiation, but momentum has waned on all sides.

Why is it essential to make sense of this moment? Why present this land dispute as especially important to Canada? Why maintain that the conversations echoing throughout are crucial to our understanding of law and society in this country? Some might contend that Six Nations should forget about it – that what is done is done – while others argue that ownership simply needs to be resolved by checking the records, and others might go slightly further (as I initially did) and suspect that clashing conceptions of land ownership are complicating the dispute. The first attitude is essentially a modern-day version of the racist *terra nullius* or "empty land" doctrine to which the arriving Europeans resorted in order to delegitimize other civilizations; the second relies too heavily on the accuracy and fairness of documents written and managed by the colonial government; and to move toward the third is to comprehend only one small part of the differences between Haudenosaunee and Canadian ideas about society, law, and territory.

We stand at a critical juncture. Disputes such as this one have enormous power to shape the country that Canada is still becoming, at a time when First Nations across the continent are asserting their rights to land and self-government. The contest over this piece of land in Caledonia – a charming small town like so many others in southern Ontario – tells us things we need to face about our past and offers insights, even illuminations, into what might yet be. I argue in this book that the things we say about the world – the claims we stake and the truths we make – are more than mere words. They shape both legal and physical landscapes.

In the following chapters, I will be exploring in depth the story I have just summarized. It is a powerful and fascinating one, and I have elected to use it as the backbone of my argument (though not always chronologically), hoping to satisfy those readers who want to learn more about what happened during the dispute. The tale is gripping regardless of one's level of interest in (or indifference to) the accompanying discussion, which will apply insights from activists, scholars, lawyers, and philosophers of various stripes. Quite simply, I find the story of the dispute, as well as others' ideas about various aspects of the history, law, people, and geography involved, to be captivating. I may perhaps be predisposed toward fascination because of my upbringing on the original Haldimand Tract. However, I also believe that the issues raised in what appears to be a contest over land speak powerfully not only to Canadian relationships with First Nations more broadly (to which many, if not most, people in Canada can relate) but also to familiar discourses regarding national identity, multiculturalism, law, and human rights. In delving into this dispute, I learned a lot about who I am and how I see the world, about the cultural milieu in which I find myself, and – by extension – about how the parties involved in this dispute are motivated and informed by the societal and cultural conversations in which they have been raised to participate.

If only for the insights that we can glean about ever-mesmerizing human behaviour and culture and how these translate into histories, societies, and law, the story is an absorbing one. Importantly, however, I believe it is one that primarily offers Canadians reasons to think about things differently rather than to congratulate themselves. I also consider it extremely important to try to understand how things have happened – that is, the mechanisms of law and action or inaction by which injustice was enabled – thus, to better understand our country and to better equip ourselves for transformative change. Having had the privilege of spending two years learning about the moment in which we find ourselves, I wanted to be part of the ongoing dialogue about how we humans shape our societies. My aim has not been to write a destructive book, to provide a laundry list of problems, or to propose impossible changes to life in this country. Rather, it has been to offer a closer look at Canadian society from the perspective of the uncommon ground in Caledonia. The words exchanged during and about this dispute reveal injustice and denial, which are major components of the founding of Canadian law and society, and point to a new way forward. I describe how the shaping of our society by old ideas and clichés, translated into law, continues to this day, although often sneaking in just below the surface of events, and I show that this process is neither natural, inevitable, nor acceptable. Neither Canada nor Six Nations is inherently bad or intrinsically virtuous – to simplify either entity in this manner would be to make caricatures of both of them. Human societies, being comprised of wondrously complex and inventive human beings, are neither predetermined nor simple. Our history is messy and still happening, and *we are part of it* – this is the ever-crucial positive side of the coin of critique.

The "rule of law" is a concept dearly held by many Canadians, whether they would articulate it using that phrase or not. However, these three words are often invoked insensibly of the context in which they exist, ignoring the ways that "the law" came to be and the people whose own laws were ignored in the process. The "rule of law" cannot be a self-justifying phrase, so that anything decreed "by law" is unquestioningly also taken to be "right" or "good." The Supreme Court of Canada has interpreted the phrase to mean that all exercises of legitimate public power must have a source in law and that every state official or agency is subject to the constraints of the law. Over time, the Court has fleshed out these ideas more specifically, most recently describing three principles. First, the law is supreme over government as well as individuals. Second, the rule of law requires the creation of an actual system of law that preserves and embodies the more general principle of normative order. Finally, relationships between the state and individuals must be regulated by law.[2] One of the main themes of this book is an exploration of how people on both sides of the dispute in Caledonia have used the phrase "rule of law" and how the idea of "the law" has been historically developed and applied. Law does not emerge in a vacuum.

Given the stated values of this country – peace, order, and good government – Canada can and must pay more attention to the divide between its principles and its actions. Surprisingly, I have learned that the historical events on which this dispute turns are often surprisingly absent in recognized and passed-on accounts of Caledonia. Geography, meanwhile, bears evidence of history – we can literally see its workings on the land. Kanonhstaton, "the protected place," was first snatched from a future as the Douglas Creek Estates by a handful of protesters. I use the two names interchangeably because its future, which is as yet undetermined, serves as a powerful proxy for the undecided, but inevitably intertwined, futures of Canada and Six Nations. The story of this moment and how it came to be is the foundation for my argument, and the fascinating people involved serve to illuminate it. To smooth the path for those less saturated by the events of the past four years in Caledonia, I have included in the appendices both a timeline of events and an index of the key persons.

In Chapter 1, I set out the reasons for the title of this book while introducing some of the pivotal events, characters, and ideas in the dispute, explaining how the term "rule of law" has come to be used on both sides as justification and explanation for actions and stances. Chapter 2 explores the significance of land in national imaginations and identities, demonstrating that Canada's development has been predicated on legislations of dispossession that to this day reverberate tenaciously in land management policy – legislations that inspired the Caledonia occupation. Chapter 3 delves into Canadian multiculturalism as it plays out in this small town, showing how notions of normalcy and rationality, which are assumed to be properties of Caledonia and Canada but not of Six Nations or of other First Nations asserting their land rights, are mobilized in support of prejudicial governance and non-functioning claims systems. In Chapter 4, I juxtapose Haudenosaunee ideas about land ownership and sovereignty with an exploration of how ideas about political legitimacy and the right to interpret history have been contested in this dispute. These lines of questioning are continued in

Chapter 5, which examines the differing visions for justice in this dispute as well as the possibilities for achieving a mutually satisfactory resolution both in Caledonia and in conflicts elsewhere. Possibilities for rethinking sovereignty over land and law are introduced in Chapter 6, which examines the opportunities for change that are inherent in the Canadian Constitution. I wrap up both story and argument in the conclusion.

"Rule of Law"

The Ontario Provincial Police (OPP) had an unusual assignment on 20 April 2006. Almost two months earlier, a group of protesters from the Six Nations Reserve had occupied a housing development site in the small but growing town of Caledonia. Asserting that the land belonged to the Haudenosaunee people and describing their actions as a "reclamation," the protesters, led by two young women named Dawn Smith and Janie Jamieson, had shut down work on this latest expansion of suburbia and were refusing to leave the contested site until the land dispute had been addressed by the federal government. The task facing the police was to "remove" them. They stormed the site shortly after 4:30 that morning and at first succeeded in pushing back the occupants. However, calls for help soon brought many hundreds of Six Nations people to the site, and in the end the police themselves retreated from Douglas Creek Estates. This literal battle for ground would play an immeasurably formative role in the dispute. In material terms, it would shape the actions taken later, including the construction of barricades blocking entry to the site and the physical confrontations between the protesters and the citizens of Caledonia. In discursive terms, it would structure dialogue patterns by reinforcing both sides' earlier viewpoints and by creating space for new narratives to emerge.

A popular view of history is that it is over and done, so that all that is left from it is for us to accept and live out its legacies. The events of the past are indeed powerfully reflected in this dispute – but there is also an opportunity to shape the future through our words and actions. I turn to these opportunities for change in the last chapters of this book. However, it is first crucial to understand how yesterday's stories are retold, referred to in shorthand, and reinvented to become the events of today, which is perhaps part of the reason why we have the eerie feeling that this dispute is "nothing new." And it is also important to ask why events of this kind seem so sticky, tangled, and persistent.

Contrasting stories of the attempted removal of the protesters, as told by those involved, serve as a launch pad for our search for answers. Although the provincial and federal governments were reluctant to publicly refer to the "Caledonia situation" as a dispute over land, their reticence was not shared by the OPP, who assumed the right to step in when "objective" law demanded it.[1] The OPP's post-raid press release began with an emphasis on success, noting that the police had arrested and removed sixteen protesters: "At approximately 4:30 a.m. today, teams of officers trained in the safe orderly removal of protesters attended the Douglas Creek Estates, Caledonia and removed the protesters. Officers were required to use the least amount of force that was necessary in order to affect some of the arrests."[2] This description avoided characterizing the amount of force that actually *was* used to "remove" the protesters. The press release continued: "The site was secured, however a short time later the site was re-occupied. During this time three OPP officers were injured and required medical attention. Our officers showed tremendous restraint while confronted by the protesters with weapons which included axes, crowbars, rocks and a various assortment of make-shift batons."

These statements conjure up notions of violence, militancy, and the deviance of those acting beyond the law. Indeed, Six Nations protesters and the hundreds of supporters mobilized from the reserve after the OPP arrived did deviate from Canadian law when resisting the officers. Their views about the need for the reclamation, however, differed from those of the police. In praising its officers for their "restraint," the OPP was suggesting that other options had been available. The officers could have responded, presumably, by fighting the protesters to the death using the automatic weapons they had stashed in nearby vans, or they could have given orders for the snipers hiding behind bushes to shoot, instead of merely pepper spraying, tasering, and kicking protesters and striking them with batons. In concluding with the statement: "We ask everyone to work with us in restoring calm," the OPP was dodging responsibility for disrupting the peace that had largely prevailed prior to the raid. In effect, the police action was an assertion of Canada's claim to the (battle)ground and to the sovereignty and legitimacy of the Canadian nation-state.

The idea of "land as battleground" was stated much more explicitly by Six Nations representatives – after all, the land and their efforts to reclaim it were thoroughly implicated in their existence (and recognition) as a sovereign people. The raid conjured up memories of two previous police actions. In 1924, the RCMP had taken over the Six Nations' council house, deposed the traditional hereditary Confederacy Council, and installed the Elected Band Council in its place. A 1959 attempt by supporters of the Confederacy to retake the council house was similarly quelled by the RCMP. This 2006 raid heightened the distrust of the police felt by many at Six Nations, who viewed it as a declaration of war and as a manifestation of continuing attempts at cultural (and thus literal) genocide.[3]

The protesters declared that police intervention – which the OPP had promised not to initiate without warning – had disturbed a previously peaceful occupation. Some angry protesters set fire to piles of tires and dropped a van from a nearby highway overpass to the road below. Ruby Montour, a vocal protester who later became a much recognized figure at protests on building sites beyond Caledonia, highlighted the significance of the raid and the attention paid to the reclamation and Six Nations' political rights after the roadblocks had gone up. "It's history in the making," she contended: "It's the first time we've been listened to."[4] Confederacy Chiefs Allen MacNaughton and Leroy Hill were disgusted with the unexpected police action, which occurred almost immediately after they had finished talking with government officials late into the night. Hill, however, pointed out that at least the failed raid and resulting blockades would grab the government's attention: "We come from a long tradition of diplomacy and using a good mind and resolving things at the table. We predict they'll be listening to us a little better [at meetings]."[5]

Before the raid, entry to the disputed site had been blocked only at its front gate. Soon afterwards, protesters erected barricades blocking Argyle Street, the Highway 6 bypass, and the nearby Canadian National railway line, asserting that their safety was at risk. This chronology – OPP raid, *then* barricades that inconvenienced Caledonia – is often neglected in recollections of the occupation. The raid still echoed strongly on its first anniversary. Hazel Hill, another prominent Six Nations voice, compared it again to the 1924 imposition of the Elected Band Council, a "forced armed invasion of the RCMP against the Haudenosaunee on the direction of the Crown,"[6] and asserted that it was proof that the Crown intended to deprive Six Nations people of their collective future.[7]

For many Six Nations people, the raid and the reclamation have re-emphasized the common bond they have outside of Canada. Although not all Six Nations citizens agreed with the occupation strategy, many viewed the reclamation effort as a crucial time in Six Nations' ongoing, still-being-created history.[8] The injured bodies of protesters and officers, the weapons used on both sides of the skirmish, the fires burning along the railway tracks, and the barricades erected on the roads around the site proved to be powerful images for those who supported the reclamation as well as for those who did not. A pictorial history of the raid clearly depicts a battle, referring to "lines of defence," "war," OPP "sharpshooters" hidden in the bushes, "our nation under attack," and Caledonia "under siege" by blockades.[9] Cayuga Chief Cleve General said he "never thought I would live to see the day we would stand up for who we are."[10] As Janie Jamieson summarized it, "we were fighting for our existence."[11] For the protesters, the landscape was firmly tied to identity and future. However, the OPP's effort equally marked the space as one of rights and belonging, sovereignty and law – in short, as a territorial battleground.

What do these different stories tell us? How does what is said (or left unsaid) about the police operation enlighten us as to the roots of this dispute? And what does it tell us about the possibility of resolution? Would the police have been called to take action if politicians had not described the occupation so emphatically as criminal? Indeed, the OPP's failure to oust the protesters seems to have strengthened the emphasis on the "rule of law" by inflaming already aggrieved protesters. Once the barricades were up, Caledonians' frustrations were directed toward what was perceived to be neglect of the rule of law. As the title of this book suggests, these three small words have the power to conjure up entire ways of being.

A Common Tale?

The police raid propelled the protest into local and national public awareness. In fact, the occupation had been launched two months earlier, on 28 February 2006, with broadcasters reporting on a strategically planned "occupation" by Haudenosaunee protesters of a half-finished forty-hectare housing development in Caledonia called Douglas Creek Estates.[12] The protesters had (re)claimed the land as their own, asserting that it had never been surrendered to the Crown to be sold to third parties and that action was necessary, following years spent waiting for Canada's land claims system to address major thefts and fraudulent "sales" of land.[13] Many non-First Nations Caledonians and other Canadians across the country reacted with shock and feelings of betrayal. In their view, Canadian land title meant ownership and the fact that the developing company had paid for the property "fair and square." What might it signify if First Nations people could invade and seize land at will, apparently without consequences?

Yet should the events really have been surprising? Physical and discursive expressions of First Nations' "land claims" in the forms of demonstrations, declarations, and scholarship on the subject have been mounting in frequency and are an ever-increasing presence in the Canadian political landscape, forcefully disrupting Canadian cultural imaginations based in history long past and harmony in diversity predicated on the ongoing denial of First Nations' rights.[14] Years after the beginning of this protest, negotiations between Canada and Six Nations drag on without appreciable progress, when they are held at all. Why are the two sides so unable to resolve the issue? Is it possible that they have such differing perceptions of the dispute? The word "reality" assumes singularity, but when we pay attention to the past and present historical, geographical, and cultural accounts provided by those contending for the land, we notice that possibilities for more than one "reality" exist. What circumstances underpin this conflict? How are its origins shaping its outcome?

In this book, I argue that this publicly conducted dispute over land exposes ongoing historical erasures in Canada as well as many easy assumptions that we have made about Canadian law and society. Explicitly or otherwise, Canada and Six Nations concur that the land at issue in Caledonia is not simply land. It is bound up in the imaginations and realities of each party's identity, economy, societal organization, and legal regime – indeed, in the status of both Canadians and Haudenosaunee as externally legitimated cultures and nations. What is not held in common, however, is the recognition afforded to each party. The conflict calls into question Canada's self-image – its very identity as a just nation – thereby exposing obstacles to honourable and honest relations with the First Nations within its borders. It highlights the imperative for a new approach to dispute resolution – indeed, a new relationship – since the ability to sustain Canadian society now depends on our ability to rearticulate what this society actually is. The story to be told – and *we are all telling stories* – could begin at any number of places. I will be telling this story while gradually unmapping the histories and discourses surrounding the dispute, exposing, examining, and questioning the "common place" assumptions and imaginaries that delineate Canadian geographical and political spaces both past and present.[15]

Framework
Since much of this book touches on cultural identity, it is only fair to open this section by delineating my own. I am the product of several generations of American-Dutch immigrants on my mother's side, and I am two Canadian generations from the Netherlands on my father's. I was born in Hamilton in 1982, a few months after Queen Elizabeth II signed the *Canada Act* that brought our newly minted Constitution into effect, and I have always claimed

my Canadian-ness unabashedly.[16] My world was Dutch Reformed: I was peered by fellow grandchildren of immigrants steeped in the theology of Calvin, the politics of conservatism, and an ethic championing family values and honest hard work. In terms of geography, my family's postal address was Caledonia (which lay twelve kilometres southeast of our rural home), our phone number was listed in the directory for Ancaster (ten kilometres northeast), and we voted and paid taxes in Brantford (fifteen kilometres west).

Officially, I grew up very nearly centred between these three places, while attending school in Hamilton and church in Ancaster. In actuality, though, we were just a few kilometres north of the Six Nations Indian Reserve. Yet when I was growing up, I "knew" very little about Six Nations. Walking in the fields behind our house, we would find sharpened stones that my father would identify as arrowheads, so I was aware that other people used to live there. From the years before status cards were regularly checked, I remember occasionally filling the car's tank with tax-free gas at the Six Nations Reserve, so I knew that the rules were different. It is not that negative things were said about Six Nations; it is just that, generally speaking, my world paid very little attention to the nearby reserve.

Beginning in secondary school and as I entered university, I grew more aware of the complexities of Canada's history of, and relations with, the nations that first inhabited North America (previously known as Turtle Island). By the time the long-fused bomb of Six Nations' unaddressed land-related disputes with Canada finally detonated in 2006, I was beginning to suspect that there was more to the story than was commonly acknowledged. Deep-rooted differences between "us" and "them" were palpable, and I was becoming curious about the possibilities for mutually satisfactory resolution. It is understandable that Six Nations' conceptions of the dispute differ from those of the surrounding settler societies, but given two hundred years or so of "shared" history, why do such strong disparities persist? How do history and geography intertwine to form the spaces and ideas that we now perceive as "commonplace"?

Cultural frameworks such as the one I have described earlier – those that my settler-descended peers and I take for granted – are in fact crucial to how Canada's political and physical spaces have been demarcated. Beliefs that reaffirm national imaginaries of innocent multiculturality, individual rights, progressive development, and "peace, order, and good government" through the "rule of law" also infer particular definitions of "normalcy" – definitions that exclude those who dare challenge what is perceived as normal. These societal conversations (that is, discourses) do not arise independently, but, rather, are shaped by long histories of entanglement and difference, legal and moral justificatory regimes, and physical practices that stake claims to land and rights. Canada's ongoing debate over First Nations' rights is an intensely public one in many ways. Most people have an opinion on the subject, and many hold strong views. We base our opinions on information and world views gleaned from our personal experiences and identity, from the opinions of acquaintances, friends, and reporters, and from what is said publicly both about, and as part of the debate among, those involved.

Discourse does not merely reflect different perspectives shaped by identity and power situations. It represents possible worlds and is inevitably tied to projects for change in particular directions.[17] Words are not simply words – for example, how people use language to classify things, events, or people as "normal" or "abnormal," "acceptable" or "unacceptable," has powerful real-world consequences because "discourses help to produce the very categories, facts and objects that they claim to describe."[18] In legislating, policing, and imposing borders, rendering judgments, and setting negotiation constraints; in ascribing "lawlessness" and "abnormality" to Six Nations; and in myriad other ways of classifying what is "normal" and "acceptable" in Canadian terms, Canada has imposed the ground rules for the dispute over Douglas Creek Estates. These ways of describing and dealing with the dispute serve ongoing colonial agendas that have set the dispute's "shape" and that have prioritized Western frameworks for individual (property) rights, economic growth, and development. These frameworks are then legitimated by injecting the language of tolerance, multiculturality, progress, objective law, and other "imaginaries."

When people communicate – be it through spoken or written words, advertisements, photographs, or videos – they are constantly envisioning a project, which can be to entertain, inform, or propagate a viewpoint. It does not matter whether their intentions are conscious or unconscious, explicitly stated or only implied. The crucial point is that the context of the communication is inseparable from the communication itself. Norman Fairclough maintains that to understand the importance of discourse we need to see the cycle involved.[19] Discourse is conditioned by society, and, in turn, it constitutes society.[20] Struggles between opposing persons or groups, then, consist at least in part of claims to a universal status for opposing representations of the world – claims expressed both through what is said and what is left unsaid.[21] Discourse analysis can take many forms, from detailed linguistic breakdowns to broader characterizations of frame, tone, assumptions, and message. My work falls into the latter category. This book dissects the public communications and negotiations that were generated by the Caledonia dispute and examines the common sense "logics" implicated in the impasse.

I began my research with two questions in mind: How have Canadian and Haudenosaunee values regarding land been acted upon, and publicly elucidated, in the communications and negotiations of the Douglas Creek Estates land dispute; and what insights can be generated from this dispute for the relationship between Canada and Six Nations? I found more than just the "simple" cultural, economic, or spiritual differences in their ways of viewing land. Although these differences were visible throughout the conflict, ongoing conversations deliberately invoking or muffling historical contexts of relationship, sovereignty, law and order, and orderly society were at least as loud and clear.

Given that the Caledonia dispute is still "hot" and given as well the growing urgency of First Nations' land and resource issues across the country, I will be treating my analysis as a launching point from which to discuss Canadian-First Nations relationships more generally. Caledonia serves as an ideal case study. The (apparently) bounded geography of the lands under dispute, the long history of interactions with Six Nations, and the considerable size and influence of Six Nations itself, work together to highlight land and resource issues in a powerful way. The discourses enacted around this dispute are illuminative not only in terms of what has made the Caledonia conflict so fractious but also as an illustration of the erasures and omissions that have shaped the geography and politics of the Canadian nation.

To chart the discourses that have established the parameters of the dispute, I have worked from unclassified texts such as newspapers, press releases, information pamphlets and posters, official position statements, letters, legislation, jurisprudence, "advocacy" texts, and statements of claim – materials that any interested party will have already seen or can easily find. This approach was chosen for several reasons. First, the public face of communication and negotiations is the one that is primarily used in shaping public opinion, which, in turn, can or cannot provide impetus to address Aboriginal-Canadian differences. Second, the Haudenosaunee people in general, and especially Six Nations, have been studied by anthropologists, historians, and legal experts for centuries. Although some of these research relationships have had positive aspects, many Six Nations people are understandably wary of possible misrepresentation and appropriation of their cultural and intellectual property. In addition, in-depth interviews with select individuals in the Caledonia and Six Nations communities would have simplified personal agenda-pushing on both "sides," making a candid analysis more difficult. Finally, for this study of the public discourses constituting a dispute over the resource of land, a much broader informational scope was appropriate than that which would have been possible to generate from interviews limited by time constraints and availability, willingness, and especially the "representativeness" of the possible informants. Although I was given unfettered access by various community members to many less public documents, most notably meeting minutes for the negotiations between Canada and Six Nations, I have chosen not to directly utilize these texts in my analysis. However, they have provided insights that confirm the more public face of the deliberations.

Stories and Labels

I begin the story in February 2006 when the protest first began and end the main body of my investigation in December 2007, by which time communications had plateaued both in tone and volume. My protagonists are "Canada" and "Six Nations" – each a heterogeneous people with a unique history and perspective, working together to build a group identity and discourse. My account gives voice to both official and unofficial spokespersons: for Canada, these include various municipal, provincial, and federal officials as well as the OPP; on Six Nations side, we hear from the on-the-ground protesters and their spokespersons, the Confederacy Council, elders and clan mothers, and the elected band chief.[22] I do not try to delineate the positions of the "majority" of either the Canadian or Six Nations people but, rather, those of the official stakeholders (and sometimes gatekeepers). Whether, for instance, individual government officials privately believe that Six Nations has been wronged or not becomes less important than the messages they publicly propagate. These are the meanings conveyed to the public – the messages that affect public opinion and that in some cases inspire individual grassroots action and reaction. Internal differences of opinion within various arms of the Canadian state or within Six Nations, while sometimes strategically highlighted, can also be suppressed in crucial ways. Caledonia, Six Nations, other indigenous nations, and Canada are not homogenous entities – indeed, memberships can be confusingly mixed by blood, by habitat, and by loyalty – and they contain both supporters and opponents of the reclamation, each for its own reasons. More importantly, although many of these people have clearly stated viewpoints in this dispute, I have not accorded them positions of representativeness. Many of these figures, however, will be introduced along the way, as the discourses built around, and responding to, their activities and identities are revelatory in their own right. Likewise, in using the labels "Canada" and "Six Nations," I do not seek to conceal divergences of viewpoint. Indeed, I will argue that the ways in which political difference is mobilized are important expressions of both parties' identities and, it follows, their approaches to the dispute.

Contesting visions of the land and its (re)claimants are starkly evidenced in the referents Kanonhstaton and Douglas Creek Estates; protesters and protectors; reclamation and occupation; reserve and territory; and settler and Natives, First Nations, indigenous peoples, Haudenosaunee, Iroquois, and Six Nations of the Grand River Territory. These competing names, heavily weighted with truth claims, are easily noted by casual observers. In the end, I seek to chart public characterizations of the dispute by the parties directly involved because these characterizations are evidence of a competition over the land itself – and, it follows, of the terms by which law and society operate: its terms of ownership, its history, its markings through stories and symbols, and its place in the mobilizations of relationships, cultures, citizenship, politics, values, and justice. All of my analyses are, of course, open to further discussion and dispute.[23] My intention is to write a "counter-story" that challenges Canadian imaginaries of objective law and order, of a nation, and of a land shaped by immigrants. According to Richard Delgado, "stories, parables, chronicles, and narratives are powerful means for destroying mindset – the bundle of presuppositions, received wisdoms, and shared understandings against a background of which legal and political discourse take place ... Ideology – the received wisdom – makes current social arrangements seem fair and natural ... Stories can shatter complacency and challenge the status quo."[24] My deeply implicated position in this dispute makes me want to go further, in the belief that "we participate in creating what we see in the very act of describing it."[25] I seek to tell a story that shows how this dispute over land in Caledonia, Ontario, is very much about the right to shape both political and physical landscapes – to show that "the law" does not exist outside of societal influence but, instead, both reflects and influences Canadian societal trajectories.

It is easy to first assume, as I did, that the dispute is about differing cultural visions over the piece of land and the means of its possession. This is certainly one aspect of the dispute. However, Kanonhstaton, "the protected place," stands for more than just land in general. The discourses surrounding the dispute tie together justice, law, nature, Six Nations, indigeneity, Canada, history, geography, economy, culture, and identity in powerful ways. I argue that the ways in which the Canadian government has dealt with the dispute are working to erase Six Nations as a rightful actor in the past, present, and future of the Grand River landscape and to form a discursive and physical space that is helping to extend colonial history and law into the present.

"Rule of Law"

Colonial legal forms continue to shape Canadian society according to settler norms, which still largely ignore First Nations' land rights. One result is that the Canadian government has created a literal and figurative battleground on which third parties such as the Henning brothers, owners of Henco – the developers of Douglas Creek Estates – have been placed between Six Nations and the Crown. Labelling the reclamation "illegal" has made the equation with "wrong" an easy (albeit illogical) leap, and, as a result, the protesters' actions were quickly constructed as immoral. Haldimand County had given Six Nations notice of the subdivision plan, and the land was privately owned. According to Canadian law, there was no problem. Indeed, there was every logical reason for Henco to proceed with construction despite the outstanding land claim, especially considering the past record of government inaction on issues of disputed title. Six Nations again cautioned both Henco and Haldimand County Council several months beforehand that the ownership of the Douglas Creek Estates lands was in dispute. Yet provincial and municipal land policy meant that the developers were in the right as the possessors of provincial title. Haldimand Mayor Marie Trainer's early comment neatly summarized local sentiments: "Somehow we have to get back to the rule of law in Haldimand County ... It's so upsetting to everyone. It just seems a disrespect for the laws and Canada."[26]

The physical occupation of Douglas Creek Estates had begun on 28 February with the arrival of the Six Nations Land Claims Awareness Group, headed by Dawn Smith and Janie Jamieson, although, as detailed in later chapters, Six Nations' attempts to gain attention for their unresolved land claims had begun much, much earlier. At Henco's request, an interim injunction was issued against the protesters a few days later on 3 March, and the injunction was confirmed by Ontario Superior Court Judge David Marshall a week after that. Owner Don Henning correctly pointed out: "We're sympathetic to Six Nations and some of their historical causes [but] *we* have done nothing wrong or illegal. The real dispute is with the federal government."[27] In a 16 March hearing that confirmed the initial injunction, Justice Marshall stated that "the question of the ownership of the land is not the essence of why we are here today. We are looking at the issue of contempt and the right of the owner to access his land."[28] Haldimand County Council felt similarly. As Councillor Buck Sloat put it (with unintended irony): "The longer this goes on the harder it will be to resolve. They are breaking the law. The occupation of someone else's land is illegal."[29] After the government issued a moratorium on construction at Kanonhstaton, the Hennings' lawyer commented: "My clients are law abiding. Clearly these protesters are breaking the law and at the end of the day, the government is capitulating. And that makes my client furious."[30]

Six Nations would often rearticulate this "rule of law" discourse, pointing out that the Haudenosaunee had their own system of law and that Canada was breaking its own law by failing to pay for lands, by continuing to develop on disputed lands and by failing to consult First Nations in resource management decisions. Ipperwash Park, a land dispute involving the Ojibway of Stoney Point in 1995, during which protester Dudley George was shot by an OPP sniper, undoubtedly cast a shadow over the reclamation. When the Ipperwash Inquiry concluded in August 2006, Mayor Trainer grumbled: "Two-hundred per cent, it's affected us. It's why everyone is so afraid to enforce the rule of law for everyone, because of what happened there. They don't want to see it happen here."[31] As Sloat put it,

> I don't believe a resolution will ever be accomplished by more and more long, drawn-out negotiations with the protesters ... We are constrained in our freedom to express ourselves or act resolutely by the sensitivities of those who are politically correct or endlessly patient ... I want to be sure that the laws applied to them are the same laws, which would penalize me – or anyone else on Canadian soil – if I committed such outrageous acts.[32]

The "rule of law" was also one of the preferred tropes of Toby Barrett, Conservative Haldimand member of provincial parliament (MPP), when it came to criticizing the Ontario Liberals:

> When faced with difficult issues, government must always remember that the rule of law is not negotiable. The rule of law is of particular interest along the Grand River and across sand country. Illegal land seizures, the illegal tobacco trade, and the burden of government regulation have done more than cripple our area's economy – they have caused many to wonder whether we are all governed by the same set of laws ... Last summer, after purchasing the occupied land at Caledonia, Premier McGuinty sent taxpayer-funded lawyers to court to then legalize the land occupation ... Aboriginal people have many legitimate grievances [but] government should pursue civil remedies against those who lead protests that cross the line between free speech and disregard for public safety and the rule of law ... It's time for all elected representatives to view the rule of law as non-negotiable – and to keep that in mind when confronting new issues as they arise.[33]

In placing the apparently inflexible "rule of law" above consideration, Barrett was displaying a surprising lack of awareness of Six Nations' frequent assertions that, in fact, they do *not* believe themselves to be governed by Canada's laws. While this logic does not excuse any violent actions taken by some who have affiliated themselves with the protest (many of whom were not from Six Nations), it is nonetheless important to recognize the distinction between *illegal* and *immoral*. Some actions taken by protesters, and some taken by Caledonians, were both illegal and wrong by anyone's measure. On the other hand, the protest itself, while unquestionably illegal according to Canadian law, must be understood in light of the history that has led up to it as well as the fact that there would be no chance of Six Nations regaining title once the disputed land was developed into homes, even if land claims processes one day found that their claim was legitimate. Barrett's comments also fail to consider that Canadian law also requires payment for purchases of land – a requirement that has not been followed in most cases of Aboriginal land seizure.

There have been occasional limits to local politicians' tolerance of these statements. When John Tory, the leader of the provincial Conservatives, declared that he wanted to have a "friendly but firm chat" with the leaders of Six Nations, saying that "we cannot have a situation like that, where people take the law into their own hands," Brant County MPP Dave Levac (whose riding includes Six Nations) retorted: "I believe that John Tory is trying to make a false accusation that there is not one law ... In fact, there have been charges laid and Native people jailed. There is one law and it is being respected." Lloyd St. Amand, Brant federal member of parliament, pointed out that "the phrase 'friendly but firm' ... smacks of the parental, paternalistic approach by some public figures which has advanced nothing whatsoever ... This is adult to adult, people to people."[34] Often, however, the law has been invoked as its own justification, without regard to its history and construction or whether it reflected principles of justice. For instance, the federal response to the Confederacy's account of the history of the Douglas Creek lands professed to be "bound by our understanding of Canadian law,"[35] and Ontario negotiator Jane Stewart declared that "Ontario stands behind its land and property management system."[36] These were circular arguments in that they did not account for how the law had been shaped. The government was insisting that its hands were tied – but who else is responsible for the law?

After issuing repeated injunctions and arrest warrants for the protesters, Justice Marshall delivered a lengthy ruling on 8 August 2006.[37] It opened: "Ladies and gentlemen we speak of the Rule of Law. This case deals with an issue that is arguably the pre-eminent condition of freedom and peace in a democratic society. It is upheld wherever in the world there is liberty." He later continued: "The citizens of Caledonia may well ask why – why should I pay a fine which a judge has ordered when, on Douglas Creek Estates, the protesters do not have to obey the court's order? To that person, this court has no teeth. To that person, this is not a court at all." Still later, he declared:

> It is common knowledge that the people of Caledonia, after 5 months of occupation, have seen security in their town replaced by lawlessness; protestors in battle fatigues, police officers in riot gear, and uncertainty of their future. Their property values reduced, racial relations with the neighbouring native people destroyed after many years of peaceful co-existence. It is a sad, sad result on both sides but one that might be avoided in future by proactive, quick settlement of land claims and, as well, by the crown and the police responding quickly to this court's reasoned orders.

Justice Marshall called for a suspension of negotiations "until the barricades are removed from Douglas Creek Estates and the rule of law restored to that property."[38] The judgment sparked an immediate reaction from protesters, who moved a downed hydro tower close to Highway 6 and threatened to pull it over the road should the government heed the judge's order,[39] declaring that "Marshall has no jurisdiction. This is a federal issue and he is an Ontario court judge."[40]

The Ontario Court of Appeal later ruled the occupation legal. Ontario had by this time bought the property from the Hennings, who then attempted to drop their injunction. Justice Marshall vowed to continue, however, arguing that "the dissolving of the injunction doesn't deal with the matter of contempt and the rule of law in Caledonia."[41] To Hazel Hill, however, Justice Marshall was "trying to hang onto some fictional power over this whole land reclamation when common sense should tell him that his part was over the day Henco was bought out, and when you really look at it, the OPP did enforce his injunction on April 20th." She also hinted at a possible conflict of interest, in that Justice Marshall lived on land falling within the Haldimand Tract: "Perhaps it is not the foundation of society that he is worried about, but something a little more personal."[42] In response to these and other criticisms, Justice Marshall contended: "The land I own was acquired through the legal system ... It's the only legal system we have here."[43]

The Ontario Court of Appeal definitively overturned Justice Marshall's orders in December 2006, pointing out that the Supreme Court of Canada had repeatedly recommended negotiation over litigation "to reconcile the claims of our aboriginal communities with the rights of the Crown" and that "many considerations are at play beyond the obligation to enforce the law," including Aboriginal and treaty rights, constitutional rights, property rights, the right to protest, and the government's obligation to consult and accommodate in cases of unresolved land title.[44] The court concluded that "the immediate enforcement and prosecution of violations of the law may not always be the wise course of action or the course of action that best serves the public interest."[45] The court also pointed out that Justice Marshall had placed the onus on the OPP to play judge and jury in deciding which demonstrators were in contempt of court, so that the protesters were found guilty of criminal contempt merely by virtue of arrest, with no opportunity to contest their conviction.[46] In response to the appeal court's final ruling, Mayor Trainer declared: "It's illegal. It shows two rules of law – you and I couldn't stay there illegally but they apparently can. That's what's irritating for everyone."[47]

Six Nations, however, repeated that it had its own system of law. Janie Jamieson had, in fact, begun the occupation under the assumption that Canadian law did not apply to the protesters: "Ontario Provincial Police officers mean nothing to us. We are governed only by the Great Law. It is only out of respect that we allow them to be here."[48] When presented with the first injunction, Dawn Smith asserted: "I am an ally to you, not a subject."[49] The papers were burned in a campfire at the protest site,[50] and the protesters refused to leave.[51] Following contempt-of-court orders at the end of March, Jamieson repeated: "That's the Canadian court system, that's not us. That just has no bearing on why we are here."[52] She also called attention to what she viewed as Justice Marshall's hypocrisy. In his 2002 local history book, he had acknowledged the existence of the Haudenosaunee people's organized system of law when the Europeans arrived.[53] Allen MacNaughton pointed out that though the imposition of the Elected Band Council in 1924 implied that Six Nations must adhere to Canada's Constitution, "we're not for that. We are our own people. We have our own constitution."[54] Hazel Hill put it more bluntly in one of her newsletters: "JURISDICTION. What part of WE ARE NOT CANADIAN, is it they don't understand. And how do you get it through their thick skulls that the laws of Canada do not apply. We are a Sovereign Nation."[55]

Reclamation leaders also pointed out that "under that Great Law, we have a duty, we are obligated to protect the land. We're not obligated to uphold that provincial law, that injunction."[56] They recognized, though, that Six Nations' laws and beliefs, such as the Dish with One Spoon wampum that includes rights and responsibilities to protect the land, create direct conflict with Canadian law.[57] Six Nations negotiators were at the table only out of respect for alliances made with the British Crown by their ancestors, "so when they talk about their policies needing to be followed, and only their policies, that doesn't bode well for the future of these negotiations."[58] The Confederacy Council's position on its land rights is perhaps best addressed in its land rights statement, which was adopted in council on 4 November 2006, affirming its historical ties with the Grand River Territory, the relationship between Six Nations and the Crown, and a desire to return to the relationship of respect that existed in the early years of foreign settlement.[59] Six Nations also maintained that Canada was and had been breaking its own "rule of law." In the land rights statement, the Confederacy Council explains:

> We want the land that is ours. We are not interested in approving fraudulent dispossessions of the past. We are not interested in selling land. We want the Crown to keep its obligations to treaties, and ensure all Crown governments – federal, provincial, and municipal – are partners in these obligations. We want an honourable relationship with Canada.
>
> That relationship, however, must be based on the principles that were set in place when our original relationship with the Crown was created. *That is the rule of law that we seek.* It involves the first law of Canada – the law that Canada inherited from both France and Britain. It is the law of nations to respect the treaties, to not steal land, or take advantage of indigenous peoples by legal trickery. As the Supreme Court of Canada has frequently stated, where treaties are involved, the honour of the Crown is always at stake.
>
> We seek to renew the existing relationship that we had with the Crown prior to 1924. That relationship is symbolized by the *Tehontatenentson-terontahkwa* ("The thing by which they link arms") also known as the Silver Covenant Chain of Peace and Friendship. Our ancestors met repeatedly to repolish that chain, to renew its commitments, to reaffirm our friendship and to make sure that the future generations could live in peace, and allow the land to provide its bounty for the well-being of all the people. The Covenant Chain symbolizes our treaty relationship, also symbolized by *Tekani Teyothata'tye Kaswenta* (Two Row Wampum) which affirms the inherent sovereignty and distinctness of our governments. An essential part of this relationship is our commitment to resolve matters through good-faith negotiation between our governments, including consultation on any plans which might affect the other government or its people.[60]

The various claims that were lodged asserted that over the past two hundred years not only had much of the land purchased or leased from Six Nations not been paid for, but much of it had also been outright stolen and that the funds that did accrue had been fraudulently managed. Contraventions were repeated every time Canada failed to consult and accommodate First Nations with lands under claim. Information pamphlets circulated to raise awareness of Six Nations' land claims referenced the Supreme Court of Canada's decisions in *Haida Nation v. British Columbia, Taku River Tlingit First Nation v. British Columbia,* and *Mikisew Cree First Nation v. Canada,* which mandate consultation and accommodation of First Nations when development is proposed on land where an unresolved land claim exists.[61] As the protesters saw it, consultation and accommodation were not courteous gestures. Rather, they were required under Canadian law for any project on disputed land, be it a mine, a highway, or a housing development such as Douglas Creek Estates.[62] The complications of the Supreme Court of Canada jurisprudence on this subject, and the fact that the disputed land was no longer owned by the Crown, were not viewed by the protesters as good enough reasons to refrain from taking a stand at Douglas Creek Estates. Another information pamphlet, calling for a moratorium on development on disputed Six Nations' lands until resolution was achieved, detailed the significant efforts made by Six Nations to have its land rights addressed, including a request for an accounting of lands and assets from the Crown, litigation, and exploratory talks.[63]

These differing ideas of the meaning of "rule of law" also meant that each group viewed the physical manifestations of the other's beliefs as aggression toward itself. For Canada, Six Nations' flags, protests, and picket signs constituted direct action against both the developers and the laws of Canada. For Six Nations, the continued issuance of building permits signalled a denial of its own nationhood, law, and land rights as well as a need for places to grow. They repeatedly pointed out the Crown's responsibility to stop municipalities from issuing illegal development permits on disputed land while land claims processes were stalled.[64] Allen MacNaughton has called attention to the irony that "Canada and Ontario see the civil actions our people take against development on our lands as direct action that threatens the talks. However, they do not see that their developers are committing the same kind of action on our lands."[65] Elected Band Chief Bill Montour observed that direct action seemed to be the only way to be noticed by the provincial and federal governments: "Even though they say they don't want to negotiate over barrels of guns and barricades and stuff like that, they keep on with development and it's just a farce."[66] Likewise, the Caledonia Citizens Alliance also noticed that playing "hardball" was the only surefire way of gaining the government's attention.[67] As Confederacy Chief Arnie General put it, the sooner "the citizens of Caledonia would start to realize that they are on native land ... I think we would have, we would have a better understanding of each other's ways. I mean, we're not here to kick them out, I think that's the farthest thing from our minds."[68] Differing concepts of what "the law" demands, however, resulted in continuing conflict over development that spread beyond Caledonia.[69] Even in the early days of the Caledonia protest, General had acknowledged that the protesters might not be able to stop the Douglas Creek Estates development, but added: "I'm not saying there aren't other developments we can stop." Six Nations' land was being stolen "all up and down the Grand River ... and the government will not sit down and talk with us."[70] Neighbouring municipalities and towns, especially nearby Brantford, were immediately aware of the implications of Six Nations' protest at Kanonhstaton. Discussing an upcoming city planning meeting in June 2006, a Brantford city councillor pointed out that "if the focus is on land, notification and development, I don't know why we wouldn't invite our neighbours at Six Nations. The Confederacy and the elected council should be at the table. If I was them I'd be upset. We're all members of the Grand River family. We all share the same space. We need to hear all the perspectives."[71]

Some kilometres upriver, the city of Kitchener's chief administrative officer recommended stopping work on environmental assessments for projects until First Nations' communities had been consulted. A councillor visiting from Haldimand County, however, advised that there was no need to stop development: "This would close the door on a lot of projects. Where does it end? Where does it stop?" The proposal was turned down by a show of hands.[72] In Haldimand, too, there was concern about the potential for further disputes with Six Nations. At a county meeting in late July 2006, one of the councillors, discussing a letter from the Six Nations Elected Band Council regarding possible land rezoning for another development in Caledonia, asked: "I'm a little concerned about just ignoring it. Are we setting the developer up to get into a Douglas Creek type situation?" Another individual noted that, although the Haldimand County Council would back the developers, recent months had shown that the county must have a paper trail for every decision. It was agreed that "all we're trying to do is protect the interests and residents of the county."[73]

The question "Where will it end?" might well have been asked by Six Nations, which was wondering whether development on disputed lands would ever cease. In Caledonia, Kitchener, and Brantford, at least, it appeared that concern was not strong enough to warrant actually changing "the law." Although the councillors' concern at times appeared genuine, it became clear that the needs of Six Nations were being considered only when solutions were simple and convenient. Echoing sentiments expressed in Caledonia, Brantford Mayor Mike Hancock called Six Nations "neighbours" and "friends," and he cited "many common interests and priorities such as tourism and economic development." He also hoped to see "land claims and treaty issues dealt with and resolved to provide certainty in our relationship."[74] The bottom line, however, was that efforts to "consult and accommodate" had better not actually stop projects from going ahead. The non-binding 1996 Grand River Notification Agreement, which asked that parties in the "Notification Area" inform one another of projects, had proved inadequate.[75] Increasingly common, protest signs put up by Six Nations people in Brantford were a clear sign of frustration over unaddressed land disputes and illegal development. As Leroy Hill explained, "the fact of the matter remains that most of Brantford is Six Nations' Land (except for the 50 acres that has been paid for)."[76]

In the spring of 2007, when protesters forced work to stop on a development site in Hagersville, a small town south of Caledonia, Six Nations' spokesperson Clyde Powless pointed out that "we're not against development, but we should be consulted, especially when we say we're negotiating on the very lands that are being developed. That's a slap right in the face." The developer, Dan Valentini, sounded oddly like Henco had a year earlier: "I can't blame the natives because if they have a claim, clearly something exists. They've been trying to reach out to the government to settle this and it hasn't been settled. I'm caught in the middle. But I think as Canadians, we're all caught in the middle." Dawn Smith was coy when asked whether the protesters' actions had been sanctioned by the Elected Band Council or by the Confederacy Council: "They didn't tell us not to."[77] Citing "lawlessness" and "unacceptable behaviour [that] will not be tolerated," Ontario Minister Responsible for Aboriginal Affairs David Ramsay called a temporary halt to negotiations.[78] Mayor Trainer took the protest as a sign that Six Nations planned to cause a ruckus across Canada, claiming that "all of Canada is on their radar screen"[79] and calling Caledonia a "pilot project for Natives to see what they can get in occupations across the country."[80]

Despite repeated letters to local councils explaining how Six Nations' land rights had been ignored,[81] and despite meetings with developers to explain issues of disputed land,[82] development continued in Caledonia. The Canadian government's position as to the law regarding disputed lands placed developers in direct conflict with frustrated Six Nations protesters.[83] One awful result was a violent altercation at another development site in Caledonia. Builder Sam Gualtieri was severely beaten, with lasting repercussions to his health and ability to work, by several people insisting that the land on which he was building a house for his daughter belonged to them. Three youths were arrested for the attack, and Gualtieri cited the incident as evidence that Native children "are growing up hating us."[84] The violence was quickly and rightly denounced publicly by Six Nations' Elected Band Council and Confederacy Council as well as by the Ministry of Aboriginal Affairs. This incident is much more complicated than any one explanation can account for – and the violence can never be justified. The attack is deeply troubling not only for its brutality but also because the actions of these youths were, inevitably, used to justify claims of the general lawlessness of Native people, the illegitimacy of the protest, and so on, thus perpetuating a cycle of simplistic responses. These actions could have occurred whether or not the attackers were simply "bad apple" opportunists looking for trouble (as no one will likely ever know), their attack was truly motivated on some level by concerns over land rights, their own lives had been marred by violence or other circumstances, or any combination of these possibilities. Hazel Hill, for her part, maintained that Canadian policies were creating divisions within Six Nations as to the most appropriate way to address continuing encroachment.[85]

Demonstrations also began in Brantford. In August 2007, a group of about ten Six Nations protesters stood with placards and banners at a busy corner while city trucks hauled fill material from the area. "It's contempt of court to develop on land where a claim exists," Jamieson explained again. Holding up placards, which stated, for example, "Break a Treaty, Break a Law" and "We Are Not Terrorists," they repeated their worn refrain. One pamphlet distributed at various demonstrations explained: "The government is not telling people that they're involved in land that's under claim. They're trying to hoodwink their own people. We tried to tell them in Haldimand-Norfolk but they didn't listen and it's developing into the same situation here. Brant County is known for its farmland and the government is set to destroy it. Once that land is gone, there's no getting it back."[86]

The expansion of protests to locations other than Douglas Creek Estates has been the unmistakable result of fundamentally clashing perspectives on what the "rule of law" calls for. Ontario property law is at odds with Haudenosaunee ideas of law as well as with Supreme Court of Canada decisions. Six Nations' "rule of law" discourse highlights several things: first, the continuing violation by Canadians of their own law; second, a call for justice and the "right thing"; and, third, the direct conflict between regional planning on the one hand and, on the other, the need to resolve Six Nations' land claims according to Canadian law. These ideas are often explicated more simply on placards with messages such as: "You Cry Rule of Law so Honour our Treaties and Leases!!"[87] The issue of law is also tightly linked to the perception that the Canadian government is trying to permanently undermine Six Nations' culture and subjugate it as a nation. As one protester put it, "they want us to go away, but we won't. We can't. To us, it's black and white. We're not going to win in the white man's courts, because it's the white man's law."[88]

Canada's account, meanwhile, both discursively and physically consigns Six Nations and the Douglas Creek Estates occupation to outside "the" (Canadian) law, again in furtherance of Canadian projects and values. This dispute over unsurrendered land is also a dispute over the legitimacy of Haudenosaunee law – a dispute that in turn revolves around questions about (un)surrendered sovereignty. Genuine dialogue is complicated by these opposing ideas about what "lawlessness" and the "rule of law" actually mean. The material consequences of this clash are everywhere: handcuffs and bodily injuries on defiant protesters (both Six Nations and Caledonian), zoning changes from Brant County to Brantford city land, and ever-expanding suburbia.

A Cautionary Tale

"Rule of law," indeed – which law is to be recognized? How did such different pictures of "the" law come to be? What do these vastly dissimilar discourses say about the dispute and about Canadian-First Nations relationships? And how might we go about searching for peace and resolution in this clash and in others like it? I have written this book to try to answer these questions. But how did the prospects for mutually agreeable solutions look at first glance? The federal government's "fact finder," Michael Coyle, was speedily dispatched for a preliminary investigation of the dispute and issued his eerily predictive report on 7 April 2006, less than six weeks after the reclamation began.[89] He opened his report by outlining his perceptions of the positions of the various "stakeholders" involved: the protesters at the site, the Confederacy chiefs and clan mothers, Henco, the Elected Band Council, the OPP, and the provincial and federal governments. Advancing his views as to what should or could be done to resolve the dispute, he titled the first option – continuing to urge an end to the protest and relying on existing processes to address Six Nations' land grievances – "Maintaining the Status Quo." His predictions as to the likely failure of this approach proved prescient:

> This approach might be embraced by those who believe that the government should not be seen to reward those involved in unlawful actions. Such a concern is understandable, but offering no response to the continuing occupation means that the police may soon have no choice but

to intervene. As two recent enforcement actions in relation to native occupations show, police intervention poses a risk to human lives, both for the occupiers and the police. If the occupation ends in police intervention without any prior constructive response to Six Nations' concerns from Canada, the atmosphere for future discussions and community consideration of settlement proposals could be jeopardized.

Finally, pursuing such an approach would not directly address the underlying grievances, either in connection with the Plank Road lands or Six Nations' claims generally ... Failure to quickly address Six Nations' land grievances leaves the likelihood of future occupations near Six Nations. Equally important, disputes over Six Nations' land rights have festered unresolved for a very long time. Neither litigation nor the Specific Claims process has proved capable thus far of resolving any of the claims, much less resolve them quickly. The exploratory discussions appear positive, but under this route alone the bulk of Six Nations' claims will remain unresolved for a further decade or more. *The present situation offers the opportunity to adopt fresh approaches.*[90]

The second option, which Coyle clearly advocated, was titled a "Commitment to Enhanced Dialogue." It included suggestions to expand the mandate of the discussions; to investigate the possibility of addressing Six Nations' claims comprehensively and at the same time, rather than individually; to develop formal mediation processes to assist in negotiations; to address Six Nations' land base concerns with flexible regulations governing additions to reserve lands; and to renew the relationship between the Crown and Six Nations. Despite the "risk" of being viewed as catering to "illegal" protesters, he called for recognition and restoration of the Haudenosaunee-Crown alliance relationships.[91] He concluded: "In the end, of course, the success of any dialogue will depend on the ability of all parties to listen with respect and work to become 'at one mind' – a concept familiar to the traditions of all parties."[92] In short, Coyle was asking the parties to recognize one another's differing discourses and "rules of law." He correctly foresaw that without such mutual respect, resolution of the dispute would prove elusive.

Places to Grow

2

To uninformed observers, the reclamation of Douglas Creek Estates must have seemed to come out of nowhere. To those removed from the histories, geographies, politics, and policies of the area, the protesters had apparently dropped onto the land merely to foment trouble in a peaceful town. The terrain of the dispute, however, had been tattooed with history long before Six Nations protesters claimed the construction site by inhabiting it. The town of Caledonia, which is named for its Scottish settlers' heritage, is located in Haldimand County, named after Lieutenant Governor Sir Frederick Haldimand, whose 1784 proclamation would play such a key role in this story. Adjacent to the electoral riding and county of Haldimand is Brant County, which is named for Six Nations' own historical giant, Joseph Brant, and which encompasses the Six Nations Reserve. The names of all six nations of the Haudenosaunee are sprinkled throughout the area: Haldimand's county seat is the downriver town of Cayuga; I grew up in Onondaga Township; and Indian Line Road runs south and east from Brantford (originally Brant's Ford) along the contemporary Six Nations' border. These names both expose and render commonplace the area's complex history.

In similarly overlooked ways, the fight for Kanonhstaton/Douglas Creek Estates is the result of decades and centuries of Canadian history and policy – a legacy of legislation that continues to shape space and place. The management of land according to settlers' priorities continues with the *Places to Grow Act*, passed in June 2005 by the Ontario Ministry of Energy and Infrastructure.[1] Promising "Better Choices, Brighter Future,"[2] the legislation is a telling précis of the paradigm of prosperity, economic growth, and population management within which the province and the country operate. The legislation purports to represent what *is*, rather than what is *intended*: "The Government of Ontario recognizes that in order to accommodate future population growth, support economic prosperity and achieve a high quality of life for all Ontarians, planning must occur in a rational and strategic way."[3] Assuming an all-knowing rationality; apparently eschewing intangibles such as emotional, traditional, and moral values; claiming to "recognize" what "must" occur in order to manage apparently inevitable population growth for the benefit of "all Ontarians"[4]; and providing economic and population justifications, the 2005 legislation offers a backgrounder on the land where this development must occur and the people whose lives will be affected by the prescribed "growth."[5] The blurring of fact and prediction in the *Places to Grow Act* conceals the alternative futures posited by those who have different priorities or who do not wish to fall under the "all Ontarians" umbrella raised by the ministry. Crucially, the act also ignores the ways in which its predictions are self-fulfilling.[6] In identifying "where and how growth should occur"[7] and providing "population projections and allocations,"[8] it takes as its justification the very growth that it is legislating into place. We can also safely question the inclusiveness of Ontario's "public," which is unlikely to include First Nations except as regulated by provincial law.

In the spring of 2006, the Ontario government followed up on the *Places to Grow Act* by releasing its *Growth Plan for the Greater Golden Horseshoe* (GGH) area of southern Ontario, where Six Nations and Haldimand and Brant Counties are located.[9] The plan promises to "create a clearer environment for investment decisions and will help secure the future prosperity of the GGH" and to reflect "a shared vision amongst the Government of Ontario, the municipalities of the GGH and its residents."[10] Central to the plan is its designation of urban growth centres, complete with population and job density targets. Haldimand and Brant Counties have been designated "growth areas," with Haldimand County's population predicted to grow from 46,000 in 2001 to 56,000 in 2031 and Brant County/Brantford from 129,000 to 173,000 over the same period.[11] Neither the act nor the plan mention Six Nations or any other First Nation living in the geographical area of the GGH, even though Six Nations predicts that its on-reserve population of 11,300 in 2005 will increase to 19,200 by 2025 and to 41,600 by 2055 – growth that also needs a "place."[12] At the time the plan was disseminated, Six Nations was already well aware of pressure on its lands. Once the development was actually legislated, it was necessary – indeed, painfully easy – to point out the disregard for the Supreme Court of Canada rulings that had mandated consultation and accommodation where land title is disputed as well as the crucial need for Haudenosaunee places to grow.

Making Native Space[13]

An account of how the once extensive territories of the Haudenosaunee were reduced to the current postage stamp reserve will shed considerable light on Six Nations' present resistance to further development on disputed land. When European settlers began to arrive in waves, various treaties establishing friendship, trading, and military alliances were negotiated between the British and the powerful Iroquois Confederacy (as the Haudenosaunee Confederacy was known), whose territory comprised an enormous swath from the Hudson River in the east to Lake Erie in the northwest, including what is now northern Pennsylvania.[14] The outbreak of the American War of Independence in 1775 put these alliances to the test. Final decisions whether to join in the fighting were left to the individual nations within the Confederacy. Most of them initially tried to stay neutral, but as the revolution dragged on many Haudenosaunee fought with distinction (often not for the first time) alongside their British allies.[15] This alliance would have disastrous and far-reaching effects.

The eight-year war destroyed many Haudenosaunee villages.[16] Furthermore, the international boundary imposed by the Treaty of Paris at the war's close placed many Haudenosaunee lands within the American republic, despite earlier British promises that this would not happen.[17] After the American victory, the Haudenosaunee's status as British allies – and enemies to the newly independent Americans – required that around 5,000 of them retire from their traditional lands to the Niagara River near what is now Lewiston, New York. The possibility of defeat had been foreseen, however. Fearing an uprising, Governor Haldimand, who presided over what is now Quebec and Ontario, had twice offered the Haudenosaunee compensatory lands – first in 1775 and again in 1779 – in the event of a British loss. Joseph Brant, a key Mohawk military leader, journeyed from Niagara after the war to claim these promised lands. Although not a hereditary Confederacy chief, Brant had served as a Confederacy spokesperson by virtue of his personal abilities, extensive education, and familiarity with the British.[18] Brant selected land along the Grand River, within the traditional western and northern Beaver Hunting Grounds of the Haudenosaunee, partly in order to remain close to kin who had chosen to remain in the United States. The Haldimand Proclamation of 25 October 1784 declared:

> In Consideration of the early Attachment to his Cause manifested by the Mohawk Indians, & of the loss of their Settlement they thereby sustained

that a convenient Tract of Land under His Protection should be chosen as a Safe & Comfortable Retreat for them & others of Six Nations who have either lost their Settlements within the Territory of the American States, or wish to retire from them to the British ... I do hereby in His Majesty's name authorize and permit the said Mohawk Nation, and such other of Six Nations Indians as wish to settle in that Quarter to take Possession of, & Settle upon the banks of the River commonly called Ours or Grand River, running into Lake Erie, allotting to them for that purpose Six Miles Deep from each Side of the River beginning at Lake Erie, & extending in that Proportion to the head of the said River, which them & their Posterity are to enjoy for ever.[19]

In light of their important role in the American War of Independence, the Haudenosaunee maintain that they have a special status among the First Nations of Canada as allies, not subjects, and that the Grand River lands were recognized as their territory on this basis.[20] The disorderliness of early Canadian law, however, was to have deep and direct effects on the migrants who accompanied Brant to found Six Nations Grand River community as well as on their descendants.[21]

The tract was six miles wide on each side of the river from source to mouth – in all, about 1,200 square miles.[22] In terms of terrain, soil characteristics, and animal and plant life, the lands were quite similar to the home territories of Six Nations. They were also familiar, having long been traditional hunting grounds.[23] Even so, the move from Niagara was difficult, for the migrants had few provisions and little time to prepare the land for settlement, and had been traumatized by the losses they had incurred during the war.[24] The initial settlement included distinct clearings and forested lands, twelve national or sub-national villages, and national rather than individual plots of land, which were settled under the guidance of specific leaders.[25]

In Brant's view, the Haldimand Proclamation simply recognized long-standing Haudenosaunee control over these lands and conferred uninhibited "fee simple" title in the settlers' introduced legal system of "ownership" so that the lands were "absolutely" theirs to use, manage, or dispose of as they saw fit for the benefit of their people.[26] However, Crown-appointed trustees of Six Nations concluded that the Haldimand Proclamation had left legal title vested in the Crown.[27] Presumably, Six Nations either failed to notice the racism that differentiated their title from that of the white Loyalists resettled by the Crown (who held conventional fee simple rights to their land) or they chose to ignore it.[28] Other issues arose quickly. Haldimand had apparently not used the appropriate government seal on the document, and the land had not been properly surveyed.[29] The Simcoe Patent, which was issued in 1793 by Upper Canada's first lieutenant governor, John Graves Simcoe, confirmed the Haldimand Proclamation, as well as the Crown's pre-emptive right to the land, and sought to deny Six Nations the right to sell any part of their territory without Crown approval.[30] It also designated 300,000 fewer acres than its predecessor by failing to note the headwaters of the river as part of the tract[31] – a fact immediately noted and protested by Six Nations through various statements of claim, journeys to the Colonial Office in Britain,[32] and formal claims processes that continue to this day.[33] It is possible that both Haldimand and Simcoe sought to placate the still powerful Six Nations with an ambiguous grant that sounded like a deed but lacked the key language required for a fee simple deed according to British law.[34] After all, as early as 1785, the Grand River Six Nations numbered more than 1,800 – a significant power base in the young colony. Brant himself was respected as a leader and war chief.[35]

Retorting that Six Nations was fully capable of protecting their own interests and that Six Nations' law governed the disposition of the lands, Brant began in 1796 to exercise the power of attorney granted to him to act on Six Nations' behalf, leasing large acreages and investing the proceeds.[36] This history is complicated by the thorny personality of Brant himself, who was comfortable in both European and Haudenosaunee settings from youth, a powerful and famous warrior, and a chosen spokesperson and advocate for Six Nations and the Confederacy Council, but who was perhaps driven too hard by personal egotism and by his own vision for his people, so that he occasionally overstepped the authority accorded to him by the council.[37] Asserting that the area was too small for the traditional hunting-gardening economy of Six Nations and that it was certain to be encroached on by further waves of settlers and squatters, Brant worked to bridge the gap between the expectations of the Haudenosaunee and British law and property systems, hoping to ensure the future welfare of Six Nations by establishing annuities from a permanent fund created by leasing the land.[38]

The Crown's agents often maintained that by selling lands, Six Nations would be assured a perpetual income.[39] Many in the community, however, spoke out against leasing or selling Six Nations' land, concerned that it would lead to eventual loss[40] or feeling that land is "not a commodity which can be conveyed."[41] Indeed, many settlers capitalized on the disorder and moved onto Six Nations' lands,[42] and Brant sometimes sold more land than he had been authorized to do.[43] Some Six Nations individuals leased areas of land on 999-year terms or alienated land on other terms without community approval.[44] Sales of about 350,000 acres from what had once been nearly one million acres under the original Haldimand Proclamation were formally sanctioned by the Crown in February 1798. Local authorities, including Peter Russell, Simcoe's replacement as Upper Canada's lieutenant governor, had good reason to fear trouble with Six Nations, and they agreed to register the sales, reinforcing Brant's view that the lands of the Haldimand Proclamation fully belonged to Six Nations: "As to the Title I believe there's no danger now."[45] However, the government also often confirmed grants of land larger than those that had been released by Six Nations.[46]

Meanwhile, Caledonia's story began to intertwine with that of Six Nations.[47] The first non-Native settlers in the vicinity of what would become Caledonia were friends of Joseph Brant, fellow refugees from the American War of Independence. They were allotted land in Seneca and Oneida Townships, and other settlers soon followed, though they were not necessarily in possession of title given by Six Nations or the colonial government. With the passing of a bill in 1832 that authorized canal and lock building on the Grand River, the Grand River Navigation Company was formed. In addition, the Crown approached Six Nations in the early 1830s about building a plank road from Hamilton (north of Caledonia) to Hagersville (to the south), and they eventually agreed to lease the land for the road as well as for some developments alongside it.

One of Caledonia's founding figures, Ranald McKinnon, arrived in 1835 in what was still viewed largely as a "wilderness" area. That same year, the Grand River Navigation Company launched full operations, and Caledonia began to grow more rapidly, which escalated problems with squatters on Six Nations' land. By 1846, Six Nations' villages of Seneca and Oneida had been subsumed by Caledonia. Seven years later, canal traffic had more than doubled, and with it the town grew in size and prosperity, stabilizing at a population of around 1,250 between 1852 and 1881. The town newspaper, the *Grand River Sachem*, began publishing in 1856; the town hall opened for its first meeting in 1858; and various factories and sawmills opened in the 1860s. After the railway came, the navigation company collapsed, and Caledonia's population slumped to a low of 801 in 1901. By 1941, though, it had increased again to about 1,400.

Haudenosaunee society at this time was deeply shaped by the visions of Handsome Lake, the Seneca Confederacy chief and prophet,[48] who outlined ways to adjust to post-Contact life within the traditional cultural framework and who encouraged the Haudenosaunee to actively "remake their world"[49] in the face of changes resulting from European incursions, especially land loss and threats of assimilation.[50] Focusing primarily on a return to traditional principles, he also declared that it was now appropriate, due to changes in the balance between hunting and farming, for men to till the fields (previously worked mainly by women). He encouraged new house-building technologies – thereby perpetuating a shift from larger to smaller longhouses that had begun before Contact – as well as the keeping of livestock to compensate for the loss of wild game.[51] At the same time, however, Handsome Lake warned against too much involvement in the white man's wars and affairs, emphasizing the incorporation of new ideas only as appropriate to the Haudenosaunee ways of life and duties to Creation. Haudenosaunee versions of Christianity that adopted over time served as pragmatic responses to the massive changes occurring in the 1800s both at Six Nations and in other Haudenosaunee communities,[52] although the traditional longhouse religion remained strong.[53]

Settler world views prizing individual rights and hierarchical government contrasted starkly with Haudenosaunee laws of communal ownership and balanced leadership.[54] These differences played out dramatically over the next centuries when it came to issues of land "ownership." Canadian prosperity is, after all, tied to an extractive economy and an expanding frontier of essentially free natural resources, while these resources, in turn, have "been the cause and result of social and legal discrimination against Aboriginal peoples."[55] The Haudenosaunee have traditionally held with other First Nations a concept of land that is markedly at odds with Western ideas about individual ownership. The leaders of the Six Nations democratic societies were accountable to their people, which meant that sharing the land was first and foremost a participatory process.[56] When hordes of settlers arrived, the spirit and letter of the alliances were severely tested as Six Nations' land became increasingly desirable. Canada's ruling class leaned heavily on British constitutional concepts: on the "rule of law," which provided a justifying discourse for taking over other people's lands, and for rules to which everyone was subject; and on "parliamentary sovereignty," which was later inscribed in the preamble to the *Constitution Act, 1867.*[57] The ideas expressed in the 2005 *Places to Grow Act* are, in fact, nothing new.

Sidney Harring explains that two main factors influenced the outcome of land title disputes on the Grand River lands: an essentially unenforced formal system for land acquisition by settlers; and a colonial Native land policy still in the making, poorly understood by Upper Canadian officials, and deliberately hedged in communications with Six Nations. Although regulating an influx of nearly one million people between 1800 and 1851 would have been difficult with even the best of intentions, "the government's professed inability to protect Indian lands from squatters belies both logic and reality, a fact Six Nations pointed out at the time."[58] The result was chaos that never seemed to favour Six Nations, thanks to the political repercussions that would have resulted from rooting out "innocent settlers" who were increasingly squatting on Six Nations' lands and isolating their settlements that stretched out along the Grand River.[59] It is impossible to believe that settlers in the Upper Canada of the 1840s could have been ignorant of the rules for obtaining written patents to obtain land. Indeed, squatters relied on the colonial government's unwillingness to remove them and assumed that eventually they would get legal title to their lands – a case of unwritten policy running counter to official law.[60]

The transfer of power from imperial Britain to provincial authorities made it even easier to separate the Haudenosaunee from their land. The Indian Department under Samuel Jarvis was known for its fraudulent accounting and for its theft of First Nations' trust funds.[61] Tales abound of the honoured founders of Brantford and Caledonia fraudulently obtaining land, often directly depriving Six Nations families and community of promised income as a result.[62] Six Nations surrendered land for the town plot of Brantford in 1829, but as Brantford and Caledonia grew other land was increasingly taken without payment.[63] As mentioned earlier, much of this land remains under formal claim today.[64] Further complicating the issue were the distinctions often made, without legal basis, between "deserving" and "undeserving" squatters, whereby those who immediately built houses and fences were rewarded with legal title, while those who merely stole timber or kept bawdy houses on the land were not.[65]

A great deal of Six Nations' land was gradually stolen over time. Moreover, even when monies from land sales actually made it into the trust funds, it was managed by white Indian Department officials who did not consult the Confederacy Council. For instance, thousands of dollars from Six Nations' trust funds were secretly invested in the Grand River Navigation Company, whose main purpose was to bring in more settlers, even as the system of locks and canals directly flooded Six Nations' lands and ruined their fishery. When the company went bankrupt, nearly all of Six Nations' annuity funds were wiped out with it.[66] The British also ended the "present-giving" ceremonies that had marked their indebtedness to the First Nations for sharing their lands. Six Nations resented the termination of this expression of its distinct status in colonial society – a decision signifying that the Crown relied less on Six Nations as military allies than they had when settler populations were low.[67] Yet despite British betrayals of the Covenant Chain – the formal agreement by which the Haudenosaunee and the British had pledged alliance alongside independence – Six Nations mobilized hundreds of warriors in support of the Crown during the War of 1812 as well as during the 1837-38 colonial uprising, and they suffered heavy casualties as a result. Such loyalties indicate how great an importance Six Nations' placed on alliance with the Crown, which was in large part a military alliance.[68]

By 1836, the Colonial Office in London had been forced to conduct the first of many inquiries into failing Native policies in the colonies, prompted by reports of widespread squatting on, and theft of, Native lands as well as the often violent removal of the people living there.[69] The ensuing report recommended that official colonial policy actually be implemented overseas – that the indigenous people be accorded full land "rights" according to the British definition and that the generosity of "British justice" be extended to them just as it had been to white settlers. Further reports in 1840 and 1844 confirmed that the reserves had been overrun with squatters, that thousands of dollars of Native trust funds had disappeared, and that complaints from Native people abounded. It would seem that for all intents and purposes they had been abandoned by their former allies.[70]

Yet despite decades of documented complaints by Six Nations, the settlers made further inroads. Coinciding with Caledonia's boom years, the government communicated to Six Nations its inability (read "refusal") to protect their lands and proposed that Six Nations dispose of most of the remainder of their land and consolidate from their separate communities a compact "reserve" along the Grand River.[71] In as many words, Samuel Jarvis, chief superintendant of the Department of Indian Affairs, explained that the government could not be expected to evict 2,000 European squatters.[72] Most of Six Nations saw through this abandonment to the government's goal of forced land sales. Jarvis, however, propped up the small minority that favoured selling lands.[73]

Protests against a purported "general surrender" of land on 18 January 1841, which was signed in Kingston without the full Six Nations Confederacy Council's authority, began immediately. Many Six Nations members maintained that the small group of chiefs that had agreed to the sale had been coerced, deceived, and intimidated by the government. Petitions were immediately sent to government authorities, prompting an inquiry commissioned by the governor general in 1843, which held for the surrender of Six Nations' lands, thereby reducing them to about 5 percent of the original Haldimand Tract.[74] Challenges to the legitimacy of this surrender continue today, figuring hugely in the Caledonia land dispute. According to Six Nations' website,

> On January 18, 1841, the Crown purported to take a surrender from Six Nations even though this document contained only six Chief Signatures and did not identify any specific lands. Immediately after the surrender, beginning on February 4, 1841, then again on July 7, 1841 and June 24, 1843, Six Nations sent petitions disputing the surrender ... On December 18, 1844, the Crown purported to take surrender from Six Nations ...

After 1845, despite the clear wishes of Six Nations not to sell the land, the Plank Road and surrounding lands were patented in fee simple and sold to third parties. Six Nations did not consent to any sale of the lands on or surrounding the Hamilton Port-Dover Plank Road.[75]

The reserve that was eventually confirmed in 1847 forced Six Nations to abandon their separate communities, cleared fields, and buildings along the river and to consolidate on 22,000 acres on the south side of the Grand River. This was a difficult exercise, given opposition from within Six Nations and occupation by squatters who initially refused to leave. It cost Six Nations tens of thousands of dollars to pay for "improvements" that had been made to the land by squatters even after eviction notices had been posted, and the economic sacrifice of homes and villages along the river was considerable.[76] Hundred-acre allotments were made to each family, although lands continued to be communally owned and governed, as were resources such as timber, sand, sulphur springs, gravel, prey animals, and fish.[77] The new settlement also included some white, mixed-marriage, and black families with friendship and kinship ties to Six Nations, in keeping with traditional land-sharing values.[78] The distribution of individual plots was also seen as a way of proving Six Nations' ownership to colonial authorities.[79] Yet a "unified reserve identity" increasingly thickened due to the international quality of the smaller reserve lands,[80] and the Haudenosaunee at Six Nations adjusted to the new environment by making a variety of social, political, and economic adaptations to their clan system of kinship.[81]

Where to Grow?

As the events described earlier detail, the occupation in Caledonia followed on the heels of many attempts by Six Nations to gain recognition of its land rights issues over the years. Petitions, letters, and delegations had been dispatched, though all had been ignored. According to *Indian Act* policy, Natives had also been prevented from raising funds to file grievances against Canada for many years. When Canada established its Office of Native Claims in 1974, Six Nations created its own Land Claims Research Office.[82] Extensive research on the terms of the Haldimand Proclamation and other treaties, the unlawful alienation of much of Six Nations' land, the frequent non-payment for land that was lawfully surrendered, and the mismanagement of the financial assets that resulted from sales and leases resulted in the submission of twenty-nine claims to Canada's specific land claims process between 1980 and 1995. Only one of these claims has been resolved. One of the twenty-eight unresolved files – the Hamilton-Port Dover Plank Road claim – encompasses the land on which Douglas Creek Estates was half-built in 2006.

Over the years, it became clear that the specific land claims process would not provide resolution. In 1995, in *Six Nations of the Grand River Band v. The Attorney General of Canada and Her Majesty the Queen in Right of Ontario,* Six Nations filed legal action demanding a full accounting of all leases, sales, and monies.[83] The lawsuit progressed extremely slowly, and Six Nations decided to put the litigation in abeyance in 2005 in favour of attempting negotiations outside both the specific land claims process and the courtroom. Also in 2005, the *Places to Grow Act* was passed, and with it came official plans in 2006 to intensify development on the very lands that had been at the centre of the stalled land claims process for so long. Finally, Dawn Smith and Janie Jamieson, the initial leaders of the reclamation effort, decided that the development of forty more hectares into yet another housing development at the borders of the burgeoning community of Caledonia and on the doorstep of the boxed-in Six Nations Reserve was too much.[84] The farmland on which Douglas Creek Estates was to be built was known by local old-timers to be subject to an unspoken "gentlemen's agreement," according to which Six Nations would cause no fuss about plough-deep agricultural uses of land waiting in the claims process.[85] However, development on lands pending resolution in the claims process had continued apace for years, and previous protests had resulted only in the Grand River Notification Agreement, a rubber-stamp, non-binding process favouring Canada and developers.

Smith and Jamieson organized Six Nations Land Claims Awareness Group in 2005 as the municipal governments of Caledonia and Brantford continued to issue building permits. All the while, Ontario continued to sell disputed land to developers. As reclamation spokesperson Hazel Hill would write in one of her frequent missives updating supporters and the public about the occupation and negotiations: "They hurry up and try to develop as much land as possible so they can say they can't return it to Six Nations."[86] According to dedicated protester Ruby Montour,

> we sat back while they built Canadian Tire and other plazas on our land. This is Six Nations land. We're not backing up any more. They've pushed us into this position. They're encroaching on our land more and more. Where are our children going to live? That's not Douglas Creek Estates. That's Six Nations land. Six miles on either side of the Grand River is Six Nations territory and everybody is living on it except for us.[87]

Although long-term residence on the building site began in February 2006, Smith and Jamieson had begun to push back on 25 October 2005, when their small group halted construction at Douglas Creek Estates for one day. The day after that, Six Nations' Elected Council Chief Dave General wrote to Don Henning, co-owner of Henco Homes, the developer of the Douglas Creek project, warning him against continuing the development: "As you may be aware, you are not the first proponent within the Grand River Tract to have experienced peaceful protest by Six Nations members."[88] On 16 November, Six Nations' volunteers handed out information pamphlets to a few thousand drivers on the highway bypass near the site, asking people to "honour Six Nations' land claims: Do not buy or sell unsettled land."[89] "How can the Haudenosaunee people prosper if there are no lands left for their families to grow?" they asked.[90] General wrote to Haldimand County officials on 4 January 2006, explaining that "Six Nations is concerned about the cumulative effect of [Douglas Creek] and impending growth in the Caledonia area on the Grand River Tract and the Grand River Basin."[91] His appeal, which clearly referenced the *Places to Grow Act* and the *Growth Plan for the Greater Golden Horseshoe*, was ignored. Another information pamphlet, calling for a moratorium on development on disputed Six Nations' lands until resolution had been achieved, detailed the efforts taken by Six Nations to have its land rights addressed – efforts that included litigation, exploratory talks, and a request for an accounting of lands and assets from the Crown. The same pamphlet noted that Ontario's *Places to Grow Act* "has chosen to ignore the Supreme Court ruling, in direct violation of Canadian law." It concluded that "the only just and right thing to do is to *place a moratorium on ALL DEVELOPMENT within the Haldimand Tract* until fair and just compensation and resolution is achieved."[92]

The physical-space-shaping objectives of Ontario's *Places to Grow Act* are obvious. Less apparent is how that act and the growth plan work to erase Six Nations from history and landscape. On the government-produced map accompanying the plan, Six Nations' territory is literally blanked out: all of the immediately surrounding areas are coloured beige, indicating that they have been earmarked for increased development, but the territory itself is white and unlabelled – by implication, it is separate but not worth pointing out. In a less visible way, Ontario's legislation continues on the same societal and spatial trajectory that earlier colonial laws and practices had initiated. Canadian space has been moulded according to prerogatives and property laws defined by settlers, and Six Nations has been denied recognition as a legitimate people with the right to influence the shaping of landscapes according to its own values and needs.

Upriver from Caledonia, Brantford city councillors were well aware of the consequences of the *Places to Grow Act*.[93] Meetings of the Brant Riding Intergovernmental Committee, which included Mayor Mike Hancock, Brant Member of Provincial Parliament David Levac, County Mayor Ron Eddy, Member of Parliament Lloyd St. Amand, and Six Nations' Elected Council

Chief Dave General, briefly attempted to outline protocols for consultation with Six Nations. Meanwhile, expansions of Brantford's borders in accordance with the *Places to Grow Act* were approved,[94] with Brantford contending that land ownership and claims issues with provincial and federal governments were separate from municipal boundary issues.[95] Attempts to focus on economic and development unity between Brantford and Six Nations were encouraging at first.[96] However, the underlying assumptions were unchanged: development was to continue; economic growth was to be the priority; the *Places to Grow Act* would be the basis for planning; and Six Nations would be only included in the process as one stakeholder among several.

Six Nations' response to Brantford's presentation explaining the need for more land to accommodate densification and population increases as mandated by the *Places to Grow Act* was largely incredulous. "You've talked about more expansion and growth in Brantford," one woman put it, "but what about growth at Six Nations? Where are we going to put our people? People who want a house on the reserve can't get one. What about what we need?"[97] As Arnie General put it, "you are in violation of constitutional law. We are the ones upholding the law ... They call it Places to Grow? Well, I call it Places to Destroy."[98] What law was Arnie General talking about? After centuries of dispossession, theft, and legalized discrimination against First Nations across North America, the Canadian courts, at least, were beginning to move toward changing the status quo. For example, the split decision at the Supreme Court of Canada in *Calder v. British Columbia (Attorney General)*, the 1973 case that addressed Nisga'a land title in British Columbia, suggested that Aboriginal title existed prior to the colonization of North America and was not derived from Canadian law – that it existed at the time of the Royal Proclamation.[99] Crucially, the Court also held that the *manner* of sovereign territory acquisition was not immune to review by the courts.[100] And Canada, in its patriated Constitution of 1982, was among the first of the English settler countries to formally recognize the rights of indigenous peoples, principally in section 35(1): "The existing aboriginal and treaty rights of the aboriginal peoples of Canada are hereby recognized and affirmed." The addition of the word "existing," however, was a last-minute addition intended to win support from those hoping that the 1982 act would reduce rights to those actually being enjoyed in 1982.[101]

By enshrining rights without defining them, the *Constitution Act* launched a procession of jurisprudence, which, though gradually closing in on justice for First Nations, remains hazy in its final effects. No longer can the judiciary avoid assessing Aboriginal rights and title: legal positivism, which emphasizes the letter of the law rather than moral ideas or contextual circumstances, holds that "whether Aboriginal people enjoy a unique constitutional relationship with the Canadian state depends solely on whether the text and structure of the constitution as interpreted by the judiciary support such a claim."[102] Surely, there must be some substance to the rights or there would be no reason to include the text in the Constitution.[103]

Canadian courts, perhaps simply reflecting their mandate, often seem to approach the resolution of Aboriginal title as a "lawful obligation" rather than on the basis of justice or morality.[104] Moreover, although the law as defined by the Supreme Court of Canada may have recognized continuing Aboriginal title to land in hopeful ways, it remains for the Canadian government and society to act on the overarching idea of Aboriginal title and work out the details, as the Court has often pointed out. For instance, the rights included in section 35(1) were implicated in both the Meech Lake Accord, which would have recognized Quebec's demands for distinct nation status but ignored similar Aboriginal aspirations, and the Charlottetown Accord, which proposed to recognize Aboriginal right to self-government.[105] Both accords were defeated.

Another step forward came in 1984, when the Supreme Court of Canada held in *Guerin v. the Queen* that the basis for Native title originates in pre-Contact Native society and legally mentioned for the first time the fiduciary trust relationship between Canada and Aboriginal peoples – a relationship that finds its roots in the Royal Proclamation of 1763 and the treaties that followed.[106] In *Simon v. the Queen*, the Court concluded that treaties are neither contracts nor international agreements but, instead, *sui generis* agreements conveying the unique status of Aboriginal peoples and, as such, that they require liberal interpretation of the intentions of both parties at the time of the treaty.[107] In *R. v. Sparrow*, the Supreme Court of Canada decided that section 35 provides a strong legal foundation for the recognition of Aboriginal rights, including an examination of the history involved in the rights[108] and a requirement for any law interfering with the exercise of Aboriginal rights to meet a strict test of justification.[109] However, the Court also reaffirmed the standard colonial view that sovereignty, legislative authority, and underlying title to Aboriginal lands were all vested in the Crown. It could have used *Sparrow* to give Aboriginal peoples absolute power over Aboriginal and treaty rights, but it did not, fearing the legal vacuum that might occur if section 35 were interpreted as excluding all federal regulatory power.[110] *Sparrow* determined that unlike other government actions that violate the Constitution, those that contravene Aboriginal treaty rights may be rationalized and permitted.[111]

Yet in the landmark decision *Delgamuukw v. British Columbia*, the Supreme Court of Canada rendered the most liberal interpretation of Aboriginal title the common law world has yet seen.[112] For example, it recognized, at least in theory, full communal property ownership, the right to participate in activities currently integral to Aboriginal society (as long as the said activities are not irreconcilable with historical attachments to lands), and constitutional protection for Aboriginal territorial interests.[113] This decision called for political accommodation and compromise.[114] However, "the goal of negotiations was 'the reconciliation of the pre-existence of aboriginal societies with the *sovereignty* of the Crown.'"[115] The decision actually defines Aboriginal rights and title in terms of the common law, not on its own terms. In purporting to absorb Aboriginal law into the common law, and protecting Aboriginal rights as of 1982 when they were constitutionally enshrined, the decision is in many ways a classic example of continuing colonial and hegemonic assertions of sovereignty. In other words, Canadian governments may still infringe on Aboriginal rights and title in pursuit of a pressing public objective (which is not defined by the Aboriginal group in question but, rather, on Canadian terms). On the one hand, the Supreme Court of Canada's recognition of Aboriginal oral histories as legitimate courtroom evidence toward Aboriginal rights and title is an overt attempt to shed some of the Euro-centric ways of viewing history, and its understanding of Aboriginal title to land is quite broad, though still limited. On the other hand, no doubt conscious of questions surrounding the power of appointed courts in a democratic society, the Court has been walking a delicate and shifting line between what "the law" says about Aboriginal rights and what is politically possible in Canada today. In *Delgamuukw*, Chief Justice Antonio Lamer openly called for negotiated, rather than litigated, solutions, pointing out that ultimate reconciliation of the pre-existence of Aboriginal societies with the sovereignty of the Crown will have to be achieved through negotiated settlements. He concluded: "Let us face it, we are all here to stay."[116] In many judgments since then, Canadian courts have reiterated the importance of political recognition of the importance of Aboriginal rights and negotiation of new agreements and relationships.

A milestone in this direction was the forging of the Nisga'a Final Agreement (NFA) in 2000 between British Columbia and the Nisga'a people, who gained fee simple title (the most familiar and broadest form of ownership recognized by the common law) – not reserve title as defined by the *Constitution Act, 1867* – to 8-9 percent of their traditional lands. They also gained paramount legislative sovereignty over federal and provincial laws in many aspects of self-government, including the management of lands, constitution, and language, through a Nisga'a Lisims government and Nisga'a

Village governments. The Supreme Court of British Columbia held that the formation of Canada in 1867 did not extinguish the right of Aboriginal peoples to govern their own societies.[117] The NFA appeared to contravene the long-held principle that all legislative authority is exhausted by the federal and provincial governments, and it also made it more possible to allow for three levels of government.[118] As Emily MacKinnon explains, although the NFA explicitly states that it does not alter the Constitution of Canada, it has resulted in a shift in the distribution of powers: "If the Nisga'a government chooses to exercise its legislative powers in areas where Nisga'a laws are paramount, federal and provincial legislation ceases to apply to the extent of any conflict." She argues that the Nisga'a government is a new kind of federal entity possessing "characteristics of both subordinate and coordinate authority [that] has given rise to a new asymmetrical Canadian federation."[119] The Crown holds underlying title to the land, but agreements over legal supremacy have left the Nisga'a with subordinate powers in some areas and paramountcy in others, though even its paramount legislation may be infringed upon if the *Sparrow* test of justification is met.

Finally, and most crucially to our story in Caledonia, a series of cases, notably *Haida Nation v. British Columbia, Taku River Tlingit First Nation v. British Columbia,* and *Mikisew Cree First Nation v. Canada,* rendered judgments requiring the government to "consult and accommodate" First Nations on issues that may impact their lands and rights, even when land is currently held up in the formal claims process.[120] Absent consultation and accommodation, First Nations may eventually win title to lands that, in the meantime, have been developed, deforested, or otherwise depleted in value. In *Haida Nation,* the Supreme Court of Canada ruled that the government cannot avoid its duty to consult and accommodate by passing it off to third parties such as, in that case, a logging company. While the government may delegate procedural aspects of its responsibility to industry proponents seeking a particular development, the Crown alone remains legally responsible for the consequences of its actions and interactions with third parties that affect Aboriginal interests: "The honour of the Crown cannot be delegated."[121] The courts are increasingly issuing wider-ranging interpretations of Aboriginal and treaty rights under the Constitution. Questions of land title and sovereignty surface over and over. In practice, while First Nations do not have a legal veto over development, when they feel that the government has failed to meet its responsibility to consult and accommodate on development where land title is unresolved, the reality is often direct protest, sometimes accompanied by litigation, with developers caught in the middle. Mining and forestry industries, especially, have escalated pre-development discussions with local First Nations and have often formed "partnership" agreements with them, although the actual benefits accruing to First Nations under these arrangements remain largely unstudied.

Kanonhstaton is one of a number of land parcels hanging in the balance between legislation such as the *Places to Grow Act* and court rulings directing consultation and accommodation. The land at issue is now held privately and is no longer Crown land, causing many people to question whether the requirements to consult and accommodate even apply. However, projects such as Douglas Creek Estates or other developments encouraged under the *Places to Grow Act* preclude even the possibility of receiving undeveloped land in any possible future settlements. Six Nations people have been protesting the 1841 purported general surrender since 1841. However, it was not until 2006, with the start of the reclamation, that the resulting Hamilton-Port Dover Plank Road claim, which was filed in June 1987 under Canada's specific claims process, was to be addressed.[122] Continuing development on the Plank Road lands was weakly noted by the non-binding 1996 Grand River Notification Agreement, in which Six Nations and local, provincial, and federal governments agreed to inform one another of actions that might affect the environment within the "Notification Area."[123] This agreement, however, had no power to stop development pending resolution of Six Nations' claims. Douglas Creek Estates was a last straw for Six Nations protesters tired of seeing lands gobbled up while claims languished in Canada's backlogged system. The protesters encouraged the developers themselves to join the protest, since the problems stem from federal inaction and affect Six Nations and the surrounding settler societies. Kanonhstaton, "the protected place," awaits decisions that have been long promised through the process of negotiation.

Land and Society

The preceding account of the *Places to Grow Act* and of the discourses and conflicts over the land in Caledonia is not a singular tale. Conversations at Caledonia draw from, and rearticulate, explicitly and implicitly, common space-shaping projects across the country and the continent and around the world. Those speaking and writing about this dispute reinvent complex arguments, discourses, and identities to fashion both physical and political landscapes. Physical space both carries and reinforces uneven social relations. By examining actual landscapes, we can see how place is implicated in abstract political, social, and economic processes.[124] We can read the land: "If history is lifeless without topography, so, too, are topographies without history."[125] The *Places to Grow Act* is not simply a piece of legislation setting out those areas in southern Ontario that are to be more developed and those that are to be maintained at lower population densities – it expresses economic priorities, historical processes, and cultural identity. By its very omission of Six Nations, Ontario's planning mechanisms betray assumptions about sovereignty and right of way. There is a relationship between the way we see the world and our location in specific "*topos* of territory, native soil, city, body," which combine to create history and identity.[126] The fertile Grand River valley that so pleased Joseph Brant also inspired the Europeans who followed, given its rich Carolinian forests, its fertile soils, and the scenic and resource-filled river itself. Had the land not been so bountiful, its future would have been shaped differently. When on approach the Grand River lands come into view, we should see not only the managed landscapes of farms, homes, towns, parks, dams, and forests but also the ways in which conflicting visions for – and rights to – the land have contoured the area's topography.

The ancestors of the Haudenosaunee had weighty ties to these lands and their hunting grounds since "time immemorial," and the Ohswe:kenhronon formed this most recent settlement along the Grand River in 1784.[127] They, along with the settler communities that put down roots starting in the 1800s, identify intensely with the land and with the outcomes of the human labour that have mixed with it over millennia, centuries, and decades. However, these identifications result not only from personal interactions with the land – both Caledonia and Ohsweken, the town centre on the Six Nations Territory, still welcome newcomers, who can hardly claim these specific affinities – but also from definitions of ownership, community, and society that underlie how territory is viewed in the first place. Claims to the land are also, significantly, about the birthright to these ideas and identities. The *Places to Grow Act* is simply one manifestation of a broader, deeper discourse that assumes both ownership and the rights to manage and direct the future of the disputed lands in the Haldimand Tract.

Kenneth Olwig explicates these ideas in his history of the concept of "landscape." He explains that though place is geographic it "is also a special ensemble, with a history and meaning, incarnating the experiences and aspirations of a people."[128] Thus, a "common place" landscape connects place, community, and self, both literally and figuratively. The relations between these three are then debated in an ongoing socio-political discourse.[129] For instance, the notion of "country" as both political community and geographic entity has developed over time and in deliberate ways. As Ronald Niezen points out, "nationalism and the nation-state were novelties in the nineteenth century [though] their connection with modernity was concealed by nationalist identifications with natural ties, permanent homelands, archaic cultures, and timeless bonds of common history."[130] Far from being the only such configuration of community, self, and place, this new particular concept of "country" was the result of a long historical process, through which Britain was defined as a world apart from continental Europe and America's founders defined America as a new world from Britain and Europe.[131] These "New World" discourses, ostensibly concerned with land and nature, also broach and reconfigure hidden historical agendas. Landscape, nature, and nation are equated by way of complicated notions about race, gender, belonging, and exclusion from the political body:

> *Nature* shares a common root with *nativity, native,* and *nation,* and it is also related conceptually to *kin* and *kindred* and to the Latin concept of the *genus,* from which words like *gene, genetic,* and *generate* derive. There is thus a link between this sense of nature and the etymologically primary meaning of *nation* as "an extensive aggregate of persons, so closely associated with each other by common descent, language, or history, as to form a distinct race or people usually organized as a separate political state and occupying a definite territory." Whereas *country* was seen to be constituted as a legal community united by customary law, the *nation* was an expression of the bonds of blood and territory.[132]

Olwig regards landscape – both the concept and the physical entity – as a historical document. Local custom and common law become inscribed on land through physical practice. Cartography and planning crucially assist in this make-believe process of creating "common sense" by providing methods to create "not only maps but also the illusion of perspective."[133] What, then, might Olwig have to say about how Ontario's *Places to Grow Act* that assigns human density to one area and a "green belt" to another? By asserting its right to manage the landscape and the people living on it, what is the government also claiming?

Conjure up Caledonia – that quintessential southern Ontario town – perhaps our first mental images are of its tidy main street and picturesque businesses and parks. We might next envision bulldozers and construction. Houses, which become homes and neighbourhoods, may intrude to do battle with memories of barricades and torn-up roads, human walls, flags, and fences. Wind the reel backwards several decades and we may resurrect footage of the paving of early town squares, the "pioneers," the erection of plaques commemorating town founders and forgotten "Indians," the ploughing matches, and the fall fairs. Hit reverse again to the 1800s – a new settler's farm here, a Seneca village there – perhaps there is still plenty of space, both physically and culturally. Squint carefully to the 1780s and we might glimpse

Joseph Brant as he surveys the lands of the Grand River and declares them to be a good home for his kinsmen that will assure them a sound future as sovereign Haudenosaunee people.

These images created the Grand River landscape – both cultural and visible – that we encounter today, and the disputes over land in the region are, more importantly, competing claims to the right to shape its political and corporeal future. Place creation is an interactive process between humans and their surroundings.[134] People carry out far from meaningless actions to alter their environments: erecting boundaries, building homes and defending them, raising memorials and markers, naming places, telling stories, building social networks, and enacting rituals and practices such as harvests and celebrations at the same locations and times each year. These individual and collective experiences develop social intelligibility of place so that "people can be seen to be dependent upon the concept of place for their self-identity (and social-identity), just as places are dependent on people for their identity."[135] The building of Caledonia, then, was more than the building of bridges, dams, schools, and churches. As Donald Moore, Anand Pandian, and Jake Kosek explain, contested terrains are shaped by characterizations and orderings, namings and listings, to create "geographies of belonging and exclusion," landscapes of identity: "Nature as contested terrain both grounds material struggles over environmental resources and refracts racial essences through the discursive prisms of nation, population, and gene. Race and nature reach far beyond biology and ecology, science and state, also crafting interior landscapes of sentiment and selfhood."[136]

The organization of the New World was accomplished by assigning Aboriginal peoples to the taxonomies of flora and fauna, firmly below the colonizers on the ladder of the "natural order of things" – their bodies, populations, and histories rightfully exposed to subjugation, exclusion, and erasure from both culture and landscape.[137] Powerful groups utilize nature to establish and maintain subjects, truths, identities, and differences. For instance, in labelling a particular place wilderness, it is possible to symbolically (and, later, physically) erase the (different) people who live there. In this way, struggles over resources and territory are both figurative and material. Self, community, and landscape are irretrievably interwoven: "Material practices through which places 'make sense' often have profound emotional reverberations [while] sentiments themselves work to fashion the living world of experience" through particular imaginaries of landscape and place.[138] Racialized histories are deeply implicated in these processes: "Identities are the names we give to the different ways we are positioned by, and position ourselves within, the narratives of the past."[139] Sherene Razack asserts that spaces do not evolve separately from their inhabitants. Rather, they twine material and symbolic processes: "Perceived space emerges out of spatial practices, the everyday routines and experiences that install social spaces."[140]

Stories such as Caledonia's, including events weaving race and space, identity and geography, discourse and political difference, have been told by scholars working in diverse disciplines, often with potent relevance to this particular dispute over land. Razack and Bruce Braun explore the ways in which privileged white people are able – and define themselves by their ability – to externalize risk by creating spaces purged of undesirable land uses or peoples.[141] National mythologies of innocence posit that white people came to lands that, for all practical (if not actual) purposes, were empty. Aboriginal peoples either did not count or were presumed doomed to inevitable assimilation or actual extinction. Encounters with the "wild" and visits to the Other are firmly situated in modern conversations about nature and nation, and these conversations establish racial and class orders as "common sense." The disruption of Caledonia's figurative (sometimes literal) picket fences, then, disturbed the established spaces of security and order. James Clifford notes the surprise with which indigenous people are greeted by societies accustomed to a certain order of things. When "distinct ways of life once destined to merge into 'the modern world'" invade white society's collective consciousness and demand to be heard, they are viewed as invasions.[142]

In a more extended treatise on exclusion and erasure, Braun exposes the temperate rainforest of Vancouver Island as a cultural and political space that is nevertheless presented as a blank canvas outside politics. Scientized discourses portray the forest as solely natural (and therefore not human). Early explorers separated descriptions of "nature" from those of the Native peoples who actually lived there, and environmentalists have much to gain by presenting the forest as a wilderness where noble First Peoples used to live. These ongoing colonial presentations of space continue to remove the Nuu-Chah-Nuulth people from their real and present habitations there and to exclude them from decision making. The economic and the cultural, the political and the epistemological, the technical and the ecological are not distinct domains. As Braun puts it, "the discursive and the material do not just coexist – a notion that retains their essential difference – but implode into knots of extraordinary density ... The chain saws and bulldozers of industrial forestry are not merely machines; they embody cultural and economic relations too."[143]

Braun's work has much to say about the power of "rational" discourses emphasizing management and planning – discourses that operate so powerfully at Douglas Creek Estates and in others designated by Ontario's *Places to Grow Act*. He also emphasizes how the colonial "past" still shapes the present. Such continuities may not always result from intentional plans to exclude and silence but, rather, from discursive practices that "simply reiterate other, earlier displacements that have receded from memory to become taken-for-granted."[144] In a similar vein, Cole Harris shows how the history of land theft and reserve creation in British Columbia, undertaken almost completely without any form of agreement with the First Nations living there, resulted from settler discourses positing native incivility – discourses that created a theatre for social engineering primed to eliminate undesirable (usually Aboriginal) elements.[145] The "Indian land question" raises fundamental questions about individual and group-differentiated rights in a liberal democracy such as Canada, where a "universal" socio-cultural evolution culminating in "civilization" left little room for continuing cultural difference. Policies such as an 1846 edict declaring that only Native land that was fenced or built upon could be regarded as properly owned – all other land was regarded as waste – turned the intangibles of cultural difference into concrete theft. In a conclusion that could have been written about Caledonia, he says:

> The initial ability to dispossess rested primarily on physical power and the supporting infrastructure of the state; the momentum to dispossess derived from the interest of capital in profit and of settlers in forging new livelihoods; the legitimation of and moral justification for dispossession lay in a cultural discourse that located civilization and savagery and identified the land uses associated with each; and the management of dispossession rested with a set of disciplinary technologies of which maps, numbers, law, and the geography of resettlement itself were the most important.[146]

The legitimation of the continuing dispossession of Six Nations rests securely on reanimated ideologies and visions of Canada as tolerant and progressive and on inferences about Six Nations' (in)ability to govern itself and (un)willingness to "fully develop" the land. According to this reasoning, if Brantford and Caledonia already have plans for lands under claim then Six Nations does not deserve to have those lands – because the disputes go so far back, they should be forgotten – and the *Places to Grow Act* is forward-looking, so there is no need to think about how our multicultural society was forged on the basis of unjust legislation and racist colonial policies and how it continues to rely on these logics as it develops disputed land.

"Us" and "Them" 3

Borders, of both exclusion and inclusion, serve as powerful parts of Canadian narratives even as multiculturalism is preached, and the Caledonia dispute is no different. The framing of the occupation in its local context occurred swiftly: the town was discursively positioned as a place of "normalcy" – a space of calm, rationality, and tolerance; of orderly growth and expansion according to Canadian property and industry law; and of friendly relations with its neighbours at Six Nations – a normalcy, however, that had been rudely disrupted by the protest and reclamation. These ideas, though riddled with contradictions and ironies, continue to reverberate, marking Douglas Creek Estates, as well as Caledonia itself, as spaces where Six Nations people do not belong and criminalizing their actions. The dispute has consistently been shifted away from the central topic – the land – toward a "return to normalcy" for the victimized Caledonia community.[1]

Haldimand County Council began to release official statements about the reclamation on 22 April 2006, two days after the attempted removal of the protesters and, more important, after the road blockades had been erected and the occupation had more directly impacted the Caledonia residents. Yet none of the county's releases directly mentioned the police raid: it was as though the barricades had been erected at the whim of capricious protesters. Citizens were asked to "remain calm to avoid the escalation of tension."[2] Toby Barrett, Hamilton member of provincial parliament (MPP), felt that the road barricades, which had been erected in response to the police action, were a result of the police's failure to immediately remove the protesters: "What we're seeing today is the price you pay for hesitation and prevarication ... What the government is doing now, I'm afraid, it's all too little, too late."[3]

Despite events such as the police raid of 20 April 2006, Caledonia and Canada were positioned as places of rationality standing in contrast to the protesters. Mayor Marie Trainer called on people to "think with their heads, not their emotions,"[4] a stance shared by the Secretariat of Aboriginal Affairs: "We know we can make more progress, but the solution will come easier if all parties remain calm and cool heads prevail."[5] The "challenge" that was inherent in the dispute was placed in opposition to the "positive attributes": "This is a challenging time for everyone involved, but it's also a time for the positive attributes of humanity to shine through in a meaningful way."[6] Frequent calls to "be patient and try our best to work through our differences at the negotiating table" implied that Six Nations was overly impatient – an implication that ignored, for instance, its 2004 decision to pause litigation in favour of negotiated approaches.[7]

The idea that Caledonia is a "normal" place of composure and rationality that should not have to endure disturbance was also at odds with the events of Victoria Day, 22 May 2006. To Six Nations, this date was Bread and Cheese Day, which had begun as an annual event during which the British thanked the Haudenosaunee for their military support. These celebrations were discontinued by the Crown in the late 1800s, although the Confederacy chiefs maintained the tradition until 1924, when the Elected Band Council took it over. The day is thus a reminder of the relationships of Crown alliance that Canada had gradually abandoned and of the forced imposition of a largely unwanted Elected Band Council. Despite some resulting ambivalence, Bread and Cheese Day is Six Nations' largest annual gathering, drawing home many who live away from the territory. To the rest of Canada, Victoria Day is simply a holiday.

As 22 May 2006 approached, nearly four months since the beginning of the occupation, discussions between Canada, Ontario, and Six Nations had grown more serious. The Haldimand County Council had expressed its hope that "the barricades will be lifted by the end of this week ... a very positive gesture of goodwill that would go a long way towards re-building and improving relationships between Six Nations and surrounding communities."[8] Partial access to Highway 6 had already been granted by the protesters as "a show of good faith," according to Hazel Hill and Janie Jamieson, who emphasized that "this has never been about pitting Six Nations people against Caledonia residents."[9] Protesters had also welcomed a moratorium on construction at Kanonhstaton, and they were aware of the third-party position of Henco, which had been caught in the middle, since the government had sold property "that didn't belong to them."[10]

On 22 May, protesters removed rubble from Argyle Street in preparation for opening the road to traffic. As Clyde Powless, a frequently vocal protester, said, "we'll show how peaceful we are, and how much peace we want to keep by opening a road for them and start negotiating with them."[11] However, Caledonia residents, angry about the month-long blockades and the development moratorium – which were generally and logically, from their point of view, seen as an infringement on Henco's property rights – created their own blockade and refused to move it. The confrontation escalated, with large crowds of supporters on both sides. Bringing forward a cedar branch and a club, occupation spokespersons asked Caledonians to choose – if they moved, so would the protesters. Haldimand County Councillor Lorne Boyko begged the residents to accept the peace offering: "It's in your hands. Not only are your children watching here in Caledonia but all of Canada is watching. For the future of the community we have to move back. This has to end."[12]

After Caledonia residents refused to move, protesters began digging up the road with a backhoe. Former premier David Peterson rushed to the scene. As he later said, "I jumped in my car and rode down here at excessive speeds. My greatest fear ... is that something could set off an incident here where somebody is hurt or somebody is killed, and you sustain an international stain on Caledonia."[13] By mid-afternoon, Ken Hewitt, spokesperson for the Caledonia Citizens Alliance, a group that had sprung up in opposition to the reclamation, was calling for the military: "We're in a state of emergency. The army is the only thing that will bring order back to the streets."[14] In the melee, a nearby electricity transformer was set on fire, and Mayor Marie Trainer blamed it on the protesters: "It was definitely natives."[15] She declared a state of emergency due to the power outage affecting Caledonia and Six Nations and established an emergency shelter and telephone information line to meet "the needs of the community."[16] The next day, Hewitt picked up and carried a peace branch over to the protesters' side of the barricade. Protesters removed the Argyle street barricades, and Trainer decided not to call on the army after all.[17] Press releases following the events focused on tips for disposing of spoiled food.[18] The state of emergency remained in effect until 8 June, although power was restored in two days.[19] Other than the fear of injury or death, these reactions to the standoff hit notes of distinct absurdity: fear of damaged reputation, calls for the military, and potentially spoiled food trumped concerns about tensions between protesters and town residents and the anger demonstrated on both sides during the standoff.

Depictions of these events vary, of course, depending on who is doing the talking. David Peterson commented on the importance of the barricade's removal in order to address larger claims issues: "The barrier became a symbol of disunity. The big issue is the land issue, this has to be engaged with. [Removing the barricade] is only one step, but it was a big step and it's important."[20] Premier Dalton McGuinty on 22 May denounced the "confrontation" as having "no place in our society" and as "do[ing] nothing to help resolve this situation," but he made no attempt to represent the actual sequence of events. He called for "all parties to renew their shared commitment to building a strong community," an invocation of togetherness that attempted to point toward "common ground" but did little to address realities.[21] Later, in a release from the Secretariat of Aboriginal Affairs detailing the "progress made" in the "situation," the complex events were reduced simply to "Argyle St. barricade removed and reopened to traffic."[22] Weeks later, after protesters removed the remaining barricades over the highway bypass and rail line, McGuinty praised the "good influence" exercised, promising that the removals would "go a long way to get the community's social and economic life back to normal."[23] When the barrier blocking the front entrance to the site was also removed, Ken Hewitt commented: "I guess the visual barricade has opened up but I wouldn't make a right turn down there and expect that we'd be welcome."[24]

Early emphases on the perceived dangers of the reclamation proved tenacious. The Haldimand County Council promised to ensure continued provision of emergency fire and ambulance services to the community,[25] and Deputy Mayor Tom Patterson asserted that the potential for violence would drop if the occupiers left during the negotiations: "If they were to leave, people in Caledonia would certainly feel less anxious."[26] Toby Barrett similarly equated resolution with the end of the occupation: "All involved wish – and are working – for a peaceful resolution ... The messages I'm getting are clear: everybody involved wants the situation 'fixed.'"[27] A frequent theme in conversations about the dispute was that most Ontarians were in favour of an imposed deadline on negotiations. Given that an accurate and contextual understanding of First Nations issues is not readily available to most Ontarians, this simplistic response to the Caledonia occupation is understandable, if uninformed. However, it is reminiscent of past approaches that have failed to produce fair solutions or even any solutions at all. Barrett's account of further hostilities between protesters and angry Caledonians in mid-June relied on "eyewitness accounts" from Caledonians, implying that all violence had been initiated by protesters.[28] By August, local disgust for the occupation had risen to the point that trustees of a school neighbouring the site admitted that their desire to erect a wooden fence between the two was "not so much a case of danger, it's a case of constantly viewing this."[29]

The fence-building efforts were read by the protesters as a message that said "let's do something ... plant trees, build a fence or something, so that the Caledonia people don't have to look at the Indians any more."[30]

The long history of Six Nations' dispossession was similarly ignored in Haldimand County Council's published timeline of events at Douglas Creek Estates. The same document expressed the council's willingness to "participate in programs intended to restore any broken relationships between Six Nations and Haldimand County residents resulting from the Native demonstration."[31] This framing, especially considered alongside other statements, clearly places the blame for any dysfunction in the relationship on the shoulders of Six Nations, ignoring the long history that led to the direct action: "Removal of the blockades will give everyone in the Caledonia community and Six Nations the opportunity to re-establish and further develop healthy community relationships which they have developed together over many years of living side-by-side as friends and neighbours. This is what all responsible community members want and what they deserve to have."[32]

The unspoken corollary was that any community members choosing to disrupt these apparently peaceful relationships were not "responsible" and did not "deserve" to have anything. Caledonia was also placed front and centre through a constant focus on the events' economic impact: halted development, lost business patrons, and an assumed reduction in housing values. At least some of the lost business was due to the loss of Six Nations customers alienated by resurfacing racism, even those who chose not to be directly involved with the dispute. Similarly, the attention paid to Caledonia's economic hardships overlooked the economic difficulties that Six Nations had suffered for decades as a consequence of unpaid land rents and sales as well as the mismanagement of funds that did accrue. On behalf of the Caledonia Citizens Alliance, Ken Hewitt announced that "residents of Caledonia don't support a transfer of land to the native protesters. This would cripple the economic development of the county."[33] One of Haldimand County Council's first priorities was to issue a series of press releases encouraging people to frequent businesses in Caledonia, emphasizing the "economic impacts" and "economic hardships" on the community and a need for outside expertise and funding.[34] Although the council talked of the need for "a comprehensive education program, either separately or jointly with Six Nations," this call was framed in terms of what "the land claims issue ... means to existing or potential land owners in Haldimand County."[35] Indeed, many Six Nations people owned homes in Caledonia and also paid taxes to the municipality.

The immediate construction of a "we" community and the focus on "normalcy" illuminated the ways in which Six Nations–Caledonia relations had been superficially tolerant and neighbourly. Many statements focused on the strengths of the relationship – indeed, in many ways the two communities were positively integrated socially, recreationally, and economically. According to the county's official releases, "the Six Nations and Haldimand County residents have a long tradition of cooperation and living in harmony. The County will continue to work with all groups to ensure this is maintained."[36] Mayor Trainer's early comments acknowledged that Caledonian families and friends were divided on "the issue" but predicted that when the dispute ended "we will still be living with one another. These are our friends and neighbours."[37] Deputy Mayor Patterson made a call for acceptance and friendship:

> If we could just get more of that throughout the community, instead of having a racist attitude: well, I'll give you an example. When I shopped at IGA when this was all going on, there were Natives coming in there. I'd say hi to them, hello, how are you, and try to make them feel welcome. Be neighborly. Speak out. You may not know who they are personally, but at least put out your hand and say "hi, I'm glad that we're neighbours."[38]

At the first sign of dissatisfaction from Six Nations, however, the simmering history on which these apparently amiable relationships relied – the keeping of Natives in "their place" – was exposed. Although often well intentioned, calls for the bare minimum of "tolerance" too often showed a disturbing lack of awareness of the twisted history of the settlement of the Grand River and how Six Nations people had gradually been pushed onto the "reserve" by encroaching settlers. Brian Haggith, the OPP's Haldimand commander, believed that "the communities of Six Nations and Caledonia have lived alongside each other for hundreds of years, in harmony. When this is over, as it will be, we will continue to live together in harmony."[39] Though again, he surely meant well, this statement indicates an overwhelming suppression of difference and a definition and prescription of the terms of friendship: "It's our community and the future development of this community we're all concerned with."[40]

These misconceptions were accompanied by direct complaints about the actions that Caledonia's "neighbours" were choosing to take. Already in May 2006, Haldimand Member of Parliament (MP) Diane Finley declared that the role of negotiations was to get life in Caledonia "back to normal" – a state of affairs in which Six Nations' land rights were ignored in favour of continuing development.[41] Haldimand County Councillor Buck Sloat was also soon fed up with the shenanigans, declaring: "I've had enough."[42] Nearly two years later, fellow councillor Craig Grice described how the reclamation had destroyed the foundations of the community:

> I would ask that each person remember that our number one goal is an end to the occupation. Everything else that has stemmed from the initial occupation, everything that we witness and everything that we deplore as a community is a symptom of this root. Our lack of faith and belief in our police service; our sleepless nights and feelings of desperation or abandonment; our anger at the rules of conduct, decency and tolerance which we have all lived by and hold dear to our hearts are being flouted by a few, are all very real ... This community is our home. It is where we come for sanctuary, family, and friendship. It is where our children play, learn and grow before our eyes.[43]

Although Grice was careful to avoid naming "the few" directly, his meaning was clear. There was no need for "tolerance" of those who had disrupted Caledonia's peaceful self-image or steady suburban growth. While the town was indeed now affected by the government's neglect of Six Nations, Six Nations' own long-standing "desperation and abandonment" was accepted as the norm. The "coercive harmony" at work in Caledonia, where disruption was viewed as uncivilized and peace was valorized over justice, is widespread in situations of unequalized power, as Laura Nader explains in her article on the dynamic components of power.[44]

Although all of the comments drawing lines between "us" and "them" served to racialize the dispute, some comments invoked racial logics more explicitly. In interviews on CBC television and on CBC radio, Mayor Trainer claimed that Caledonia workers were being hurt by the blockades because they did not have "monies coming in automatically every month." Many people understood this to be an allusion to welfare. As Clyde Powless exclaimed, "how do my people have money coming in automatically? I'm shocked at you and I will never want to address you again." Trainer contended that she was explaining "the frustration of the Caledonia people," such as tradespeople who were not being paid for work not done and who were paid by the hour instead of automatically receiving a salary: "They needed to know what the people of Caledonia thought. I have to stick up for my people, just like they're sticking up for themselves."[45] After a meeting during which the Haldimand County Council distanced itself from Trainer's "personal comments" and "personal views,"[46] the mayor apologized: "I apologize if I offended anyone. I had not intended to offend anyone. I made a mistake."[47] It is impossible to know the meaning that she had intended for her statement, but it certainly caused tension, even if unintentional. Later, after blaming Six Nations for the transformer fire, she made statements sympathizing with those from Six Nations who disagreed with the reclamation: "I'm not painting everybody with the same brush, for sure. A lot of Natives are not happy about this at all. They feel they are all being made to look bad and that it's damaging good relationships they have with people." Again, the council distanced itself from her comments, as there was no evidence as to who caused the fire.[48]

However, the Caledonia "we" community proved remarkably durable. For his attempts to convince protesters to dismantle their barricades after Caledonians refused to remove their own, David Peterson was called an "Indian lover" and accused of sympathizing with the Natives: "Anything the Indians want, you'll give them."[49] This sentiment was expressed, despite his publicized role of focusing "on urgent concerns, aiming to restore calm and return the community to normal conditions, paving the way for discussions on the longer term, underlying issues."[50] Racist threats also manifested themselves in an e-mail that was circulated in early June by a group promoting a "Caledonia Unites" rally, calling on residents to gather at the community centre to "restrict access to the arena to people who are not welcome in our community."[51] A scheduled youth game staged by Six Nations Minor Lacrosse Association was cancelled despite Haldimand County Council's attempts to relocate it. In a press release addressing the event, the council cited its "extensive history of positive relations with Six Nations community" and invoked its "for the sake of sport" policy, "which does not tolerate violence or racism."[52] Yet later that month, Councillor Buck Sloat announced: "I don't believe a resolution will ever be accomplished by more and more long, drawn-out negotiations with the protestors ... We are constrained in our freedom to express ourselves or act resolutely by the sensitivities of those who are politically correct or endlessly patient."[53]

Despite such statements, the Canadian embrace of a vision of deracialized multiculturalism, unity in progressive liberal thinking, and communities founded on economic growth and prosperity was evidenced in comments such as the one from MP Diane Finley early in the reclamation: "Together with our friends in Six Nations, we have established a long tradition where people from many different backgrounds can live side by side and I am confident that this will continue."[54] Premier McGuinty spoke of the need to "find a lasting solution that allows all parties to renew their shared commitment to building a strong community."[55] He did not expand on this desire, but his vision did not seem to be one that welcomed challenges to the status quo. The Ontario Provincial Police (OPP) also made calls for "tolerance and understanding while the peace process continues," although there was no specific mention of who or what needed to be "tolerated."[56] Federal and provincial ministers from the Department of Indian Affairs agreed that certain values need to be cherished by everyone: "Common to all of us who live in this wonderful country and province are the underlying and import-ant values of peace and justice. We cannot and will not be intimidated by the activities of the violent few who will sometimes seek to disrupt these cherished human values."[57] Hidden within these laudable calls for peace and unity was a quiet suppression of difference and uniqueness. The OPP's call for harmony on Canada Day in 2006 was a more transparent example of history overlooked.[58] Referring to a "planned fireworks display along the historic Grand River," police asked that everyone "come together, celebrate Canada's rich history and enjoy the company of friends and loved ones," promising that the police presence was meant to "ensure that peace is kept realizing that there is a level of tension arising from the land reclamation issue." Again, the appeal for peace was commendable, but the references to an "event that is symbolic of the goodwill that Canadians possess" presented a disconcerting vision of Canadians "tolerating" Six Nations.

In contrast, Six Nations often explicitly referred to racism and cultural genocide, viewing these issues as being closely linked to its present-day search for reparations. When the OPP brought in Aboriginal officers in the first days of the occupation, Dawn Smith said that though they were not from Six Nations they were "our people and have a better understanding of what we're going through." However, they still "carry that badge" and could be brought in to enforce the injunction.[59] In her words, there is a clear connec-tion between identity and justice. Since the officers shared the experience of difference from mainstream Canada, they could be counted on to have some understanding of the protesters' perspectives – but their voluntary affiliation with the Canadian justice system divided them from the protesters in more crucial ways. After the protesters removed the barricades, Hazel Hill stressed that "safety is the biggest concern for our people ... because of the anger and racism that was shown."[60] Six Nations' *Road to the Reclamation* radio series explained: "Non-Native reaction and the perceived 'neighbourly thing to do' would have been for Caledonia to respect the land claim and demand that their government settle with Six Nations. Rather than take the high road ... and stand with Six Nations, the choice was made to stand against the Reclamation ... Racism that for years has been undercurrent, but replaced by a certain tolerance, has been resurrected."[61]

When the *Hamilton Spectator* revealed that the RCMP had launched a special operation dubbed "Project O Caledonia" in the early days of the reclamation, the Mounties insisted that nothing should be read into the fact that many officers had special training in such areas as criminal intelligence, drug trafficking, and border and customs control. Hazel Hill saw things differently: "We're criminals, drug-smuggling, gun-toting terrorists whose mission is to destroy the government. That's the lump sum of the attitude."[62] Court injunctions and warrants were read as "act[s] of aggression" and as "attempt[s] to criminalize us and declare war against us."[63] She emphasized that "we have to stay focused on why we are here. We are a survival people. We've been here for thousands of years ... We've survived genocide practices. We've survived assimilation practices. We're not going to disappear."[64] Leroy Hill also used strong language, citing the imposition of the Elected Band Council: "In 1924, at the reckless stroke of a pen by your government, Six Nations received a death sentence as a people. Genocide was attempted on our people and we are fighting for our survival to continue as a distinct people to this day."[65]

Discontent over the failure to eject the protesters from Caledonia soon funnelled into accusations of "two-tiered justice." According to this idea, Six Nations protesters were not being punished for their misdeeds, while (white) Caledonians acting out their frustrations, often at Friday night "citizen's rallies," were arrested. Uneasy and shifting definitions of "us" and "them" were complicated further by the polarizing figure of Gary McHale, a resident of Richmond Hill, about one hour's drive from Caledonia, who continues to this day to treat the "two-tiered justice" campaign as his mission in life. Blazing into town sporting t-shirts with slogans such as "Caledonia-Ipperwash: One Law for All," McHale launched a website titled Caledonia WakeUp Call, which is loaded with vitriol directed at the "terrorists" who disregard the rule of law.[66] McHale's public call was for respect for regulation. "Native people think that they are above all laws," he complained.[67] His campaign exposed and encouraged the attitudes of those who already resented how they perceived the reclamation to be handled by government and police. Disturbing endorsements of McHale's messages, for instance, came from Mayor Trainer, who blamed OPP Commissioner Gwen Boniface for the "chaos" in Caledonia: "The native population have been feeling they can do anything, anytime, anywhere to anyone and the police will only watch."[68]

What is interesting in the context of Caledonia's self-image and perceived "normalcy," however, is that though many agreed with McHale's basic premise many also felt that, as an outsider, he had no business stirring up trouble by organizing rallies and protests in Caledonia. McHale often found himself with surprisingly little support. The outsider bent on creating disturbance prompted a backlash – Caledonia was for Caledonians, not for Six Nations or for the Gary McHales of the world. The OPP released a statement alluding to McHale's activities: "Sadly there are always some who take advantage of a fragile situation to further their personal causes or beliefs. The spreading of rumours or outsiders coming into the community to advance their own agenda by attaching it to this issue is counterproductive towards a peaceful resolution."[69] Minister David Ramsay went so far as to rebuke a local Hamilton television station for referring to allegations made on Gary McHale's website: "It is deeply regrettable and disappointing that despite being advised by the Government of Ontario that the allegations alluded to on a certain website are false, CHTV still chose to broadcast these."[70] In response to a rally planned in Caledonia for mid-October 2006, for which McHale was asking for 20,000 supporters to converge on Douglas Creek Estates, Ramsay released a statement that recognized the public's "right to engage in peaceful protest" but expressed concerns about "potential risk to public safety" and publicly distanced the government from the rally. It is unclear whether Ramsay was drawing parallels or contrasts with Six Nations protesters in his call for "peaceful protest," but his emphasis on public safety implied that any disturbance would be viewed as bad form. Despite at least some apparent sympathy for his message, Mayor Trainer, citing safety concerns, also announced that McHale would never get a permit from the county for his march.[71] The county closed the Caledonia community centre "due to the anticipated illegal rally," enforced a no-stopping zone in the proposed rally area,[72] and took pains to distance itself from the use of an altered form of the county's logo on McHale's website.[73] In addition, MP Finley issued a release declaring that the federal and provincial governments were already "fully aware and engaged" with the dispute in Caledonia: "We do have a relative peace at the present time, but as we all know it's a fragile peace and I for one won't support the efforts of those with no stake in our community" to draw attention to the reclamation.[74] Even the spokesperson for the Caledonia Citizens Alliance explained that "most people from the community are really torn. The community is concerned with the image of Caledonia, its future and its relationship with its neighbours. We don't want to see any of that be affected negatively by this protest."[75] In the end, a few hundred people showed up for the October rally. Councillor Craig Ashbaugh was "extremely proud of Caledonia for not supporting that rally which was imported into our community."[76]

McHale continued to visit Caledonia to raise money for his causes and to foment trouble. Again in December 2006, Mayor Trainer asked him to stay away: "Caledonia people really don't want him in their business. They'd like him to stay home."[77] The council echoed her sentiments: "Haldimand County does not welcome anyone into our community who has the intention of breaking the law, getting arrested or inciting violence."[78] Although the press release referred to McHale's plans, the county's rejection of "law-breakers" also resurrected the spectres of "lawless" protesters and "two-tier justice." McHale's rallies resulted in the creation of official "no-go" zones around Kanonhstaton, spaces of land tens of metres wide that served as no man's land to separate protesters from their opponents.

Protesters had mixed reactions to McHale. After the October rally, Hazel Hill felt that the potluck hosted by Six Nations on the same day had gathered a larger turnout. She was glad that some Caledonia residents who disagreed with the reclamation nonetheless resented McHale's intrusion even more, stopping by the site to complain in common with the protesters: "We gained an opportunity to invite these guys back to the site any time."[79] She also pointed out, however, that "it is unfortunate that we even have to deal with publicity hounds like Mr. McHale when we have the very real rights of Six Nations people at stake here."[80] Despite awareness of the ill will among some Caledonians, protesters often publicly welcomed Caledonia citizens' rallies for their attention-grabbing potential. According to Clyde Powless, "it brings the town closer together. I don't see no reason why it should [spark tension]. They're saying the same thing I'm saying: Wake up, government ... They're just adding to our voice, and I like it."[81]

What is remarkable about McHale and his publicity stunts is not his gripe, which was a common one, but the way in which his status as an outsider reinforced "we" sentiments in the community. His message was welcome, but Caledonia appeared to be a place in which one either fits in or definitely does not. McHale and Six Nations protesters were often both denied legitimacy and acceptance. These exclusions were further spelled out in controversies over the placement of Haudenosaunee and Canadian flags. The "flag flap," as it was christened by the media, was a powerful physical manifestation of anxieties over terms of citizenship, rights, and freedoms. The flag is meant to invoke Canadian identities of tolerance, multiculturalism, and patriotism, but its use in this situation certainly invoked negative emotions. In December 2006, a group of about thirty people, including McHale, attempted to plant Canadian flags across the street from Kanonhstaton, citing support for troops in Afghanistan. Nobody bought the line, and the police stopped them. Dana Chatwell and Dave Brown, a couple living directly next to Douglas Creek Estates, had been especially negatively affected by the presence of the protesters, given their direct proximity to the disputed site and its often rowdy, intimidating occupants. After the police stopped the flag-raisers, an understandably frustrated Chatwell declared: "I cannot believe that we cannot put up a Canadian flag in Canada in this spot right now. It's disgusting, I'm not even proud to be a Canadian."[82] Logically pointing out that the protesters had erected Haudenosaunee flags on Douglas Creek Estates, McHale declared:

"It's not illegal to put up a Canadian flag. No laws are being broken."[83] Another attempt at a flag-raising rally in January 2007 was declared by the OPP to be "irresponsible," "provocative," and "mischief-making." The police force took care to point out that "lawlessness will not be tolerated."[84] McHale and a fellow organizer were arrested and later released. A few days later, Hazel Hill held out an olive branch, though she made it clear that flying flags other than Haudenosaunee flags was a sign of respect, not subordination:

> To put an end to the Canadian flag issue, and in respect of both Canadian and American supporters who have lent their time and support to Six Nations and sent flags to Kanonhstaton, and to reflect the dual citizenship of our peoples, Kanonhstaton will be flying both Canadian and American flags along with the Haudenosaunee flag. But let us be clear about this. This is about the land. Our land. Our rights. It is unfortunate that some people see this for what they can gain while using the insecurities and fears of the Caledonia residents to promote the goals of hatred, racism and bigotry.[85]

It was not enough. Mayor Trainer called the site a "mess": "You're in the middle of a lovely town and you've got this unsightly thing in the middle of it. It doesn't help anything. The occupiers need to leave and the flags need to come down."[86] MPP Barrett complained:

> For many, the year has created a numbing acceptance of what would normally be an unacceptable state of affairs. Case in point – there are currently Warrior and Haudenosaunee flags flying above the Canadian and American flags on the main street of Caledonia. Would this breach of flag protocol have been the case a year ago? Would this be acceptable in any other town?[87]

The flag flap continued. Canadian flags flying today in Caledonia seem to be both manifestations of "we love our country" and "back off, this is our country." Thickly swaddled in rule-of-law discourses, flags are material markers of claim staking, manifesting physically what are often otherwise abstract debates over justice and citizenship. Canada's emphasis on immediate geography – Caledonia – inevitably conceals the dimension of history. Its focus on the hardships of Caledonians ignores Six Nations in the solution. The focus on "progress made in Caledonia" is a powerful frame through which we are invited to view the dispute.[88] Perhaps Mayor Trainer summarized it best: "Everyone agrees it's a land claim. It's the occupation that is a problem. We just can't go through another summer like we have. The people just can't handle that. Get the police back on the 6th Line [a road running behind the Douglas Creek Estates, unpoliced by the OPP for four years] and clear the site."[89] Overall, the discourses framing the occupation in its immediate geographic context within the town of Caledonia prioritized "normalcy," thus revealing *and reinforcing* a Caledonian space that did not welcome disruption of its continual growth and comfortable persona that claimed "tolerance" and "friendship" with its neighbours to the west. The actual dispute over land was placed in the background to Caledonia's crisis, and the injustices fought by Six Nations were buried in the rubble.

This is not to say that the occupation of Douglas Creek Estates did not affect Caledonians. Especially during the month-long period that the main street through town was blocked (following the failed OPP raid) and the weeks after that until the blockade on the highway bypass outside of town was removed, life was affected often in a very visceral way, especially for those living closest to the disputed land, such as Dana Chatwell and Dave Brown, whose house was bordered by disputed land on two sides; those living on the 6th Line (running roughly east-west along the southern side of Douglas Creek Estates); and those on Braemar Avenue and Thistlemoor Drive (two residential streets on the northern side). The protest was small when it began, but the number of protesters grew exponentially after the police's foray on 20 April 2006. Many who showed up on Douglas Creek Estates, both Native and non-Native, were not from Six Nations. It was perhaps inevitable with a congregation of people that large that there was for a period of time considerable noise and disruption. Some who chose to affiliate themselves with Smith and Jamieson's initially peaceful protest were much less peaceful. The military-style fatigues and bandannas worn by many were undoubtedly unnerving, and although allegations of "bunkers" of weapons on the land were false, there certainly were firearms on the site at times, especially on 20 April but also likely afterwards. Protesters would patrol the site on all-terrain vehicles, and for several weeks those wishing to cross the barricades, including residents who lived within them, had to produce "passports" – pieces of paper with approved licence plate numbers on them. The OPP even took Dave Brown to the police station when he refused to adhere to a seemingly arbitrary "curfew" after attending a baseball game in Toronto. Not surprisingly, he and Chatwell are, and continue to be, angry about how the land dispute affected their lives and home.

The seriousness of the situation to Caledonians is not to be trivialized. What should be considered, and is often missing in accounts of Caledonia, however, is context, which is one of the main reasons I wrote this book. While the broader picture cannot justify the serious incidents of intimidation, vandalism, violence, and often plain old rudeness used by a small minority – on both sides of the dispute – it can help to explain them. As understood by many in Caledonia, "they" disrupted "our" town and do not care about the effect of their actions on "us." From the point of view of many Six Nations, "they" stole and continue to steal "our" land and do not care about the effect of their actions on "us." And there are many people who are either caught, or choose to be, somewhere in the middle: Haudenosaunee people who own property in Caledonia; Caledonians who have family, good friends, co-workers, employers or employees from Six Nations, and vice versa; and both non-First Nations and First Nations people who simply understand that there are two sides to every story.

It is also important to remember that at the height of the tension, many people who chose to align themselves with the occupation, or thought they were doing so, were unknown to the actual protest leaders. It is obviously impossible to describe all of those present at Douglas Creek Estates at one time or another as identically motivated, informed, or even involved. People are attracted to protest movements for a variety of reasons, some of which are not necessarily sanctioned by the protest leaders. For instance, I have met several non-First Nations people who spent some time at Douglas Creek Estates, as they have at many other protest movements. More than one of these people freely admitted to having been arrested for civil disobedience in environmental protests and stated that resistance to "the law" could be justified if they felt that the law itself was unjustifiable. Some, not all, were well informed about the issues underlying the dispute over Kanonhstaton. How should we understand their involvement? Are they simply people looking for a fight? Are they career protesters who simply have it in for the police and "the law"? Would our feelings change if they were on our side in a given dispute rather than on the other side? Do we view their perspectives as more objective, or less legitimate, if they are not personally affected by the outcomes of the issues at stake?

You cannot always choose your "friends," any more than you can always choose your "opponents." This is as true of those affiliated with Six Nations as it is of Caledonia. Recall Haldimand County Council's disapproval of some of Mayor Trainer's protective reactions, for instance, and the embarrassment many in Caledonia felt after the cancellation of the lacrosse game due to racist threats to Six Nations youth. Recall Gary McHale, who was a very controversial figure; Caledonia was not the first issue that had received his intense attention. Consider that many at Six Nations condemn the use of disputed land for the sale of contraband cigarettes, while many in Caledonia and its environs purchase their smokes from those same trailers. Lines and networks demarcating (and linking) "us" and "them" are astoundingly complex and can shift gradually or in the blink of an eye. These intricate issues call not for simplification but for willingness to consider new ideas and different ways of viewing the same set of events.

Intolerant Tolerance

Juanita Sundberg explicitly calls on us to take race seriously "as a critical variable in organizing inequality." She notes that "processes of racialization are rarely incidental to the distribution of natural resources, predominant visions of appropriate land use," and other elements of decision making.[90] The story of Caledonia and Six Nations is a modern-day continuation of the ways that, as Sundberg explains, indigenous, mixed-race, and non-male persons have historically been deemed unqualified for citizenship and sidelined from a supposedly liberal society of universal rights. Meanwhile, European conceptions of orderly development have rejected indigenous agriculture and environmental management as "irrational" and "unproductive," and legal systems continue today to be structured around white privilege and priorities.[91]

The processes that tie together territory, land, society, and identity are global. In Canada, the United States, Australia, and New Zealand, however, a particular brand of colonialism has inscribed British concepts of law and title on indigenous lands.[92] This uniqueness only emphasizes the non-neutrality of colonialism's trajectories. If imperialism were a given, and if indigenous peoples and lands were simply vacant canvases awaiting civilization's benevolent hand, surely these processes would have functioned uniformly across time and space. Edward Said explains how European occupation was justified through a belief in the fundamental distinction between "us" and "Others." He points out the heart of it all: "Underlying social space are territories, land, geographical domains, the actual geographical underpinnings of the imperial, and also the cultural context. To think about distant places, to colonize them, to populate or depopulate them: all of this occurs on, about, or because of land. The actual geographical possession of land is what empire in the final analysis is all about."[93]

Canada's creation myth – peace, order, and good government – is plaited throughout the discourses employed in the conflict along the Grand River. This myth and its sidekicks – economic development and multicultural tolerance – are so entrenched in the public consciousness that only shorthand references are required for us to hear them, with crucial repercussions for the perceived legitimacy of the struggles of Aboriginal peoples in Canada and for the national landscape that has been shaped by these ideas. In many ways, this country is built on racialized foundations of colonialism that oppose Canada with Aboriginality, on exclusive liberal conceptions of individual rights, and on the primacy of capitalist visions of economic development.

The Canadian cultural imaginary works through simultaneous denial of, and opposition to, the nations that played fundamental roles in the shaping of this nation.

Societal discourses designate for a given time and place what can and cannot be said.[94] Certain expressions and ideas are conserved across space and time; others are revised, reactivated, or incorporated into new texts and contexts. As noted earlier, the conversations that constitute the dispute in Caledonia reiterate national beliefs and self-portraits and, in so doing, provide powerful evidence of the (possibly unconscious) strategies that work to exclude from legitimacy and recognition Six Nations' identities, priorities, and rights to shape space and society. The blatant colonialism of years past has been appropriated by the paradigm of economic development; public identities have shifted from declarations of difference to avowals of sameness in multiculturality; and racism hides in the language of law and rights. As Howard Winant explains, "the successes of anti-racist and anti-colonial movements in recent decades are being transformed into new patterns of racial inequality and injustice. The 'new world racial system,' in sharp contrast to the old structures of explicit colonialism and state-sponsored segregation, now presents itself as 'beyond race,' 'color-blind,' multicultural, and post-racial."[95]

Teun van Dijk points out that individuals' statements are part of the (often elite and powerful) institutions they represent. In fact, statements such as those made by representatives for Canada in the Caledonia dispute, when taken on their own, are typically not intended to be racist nor do they appear as such. It is when they are considered in the aggregate or along with policies and actions that structures of discrimination become visible.[96] Since elites often view themselves as moral leaders and attempt to dissociate themselves from racism as they define it, they typically respond to challenges from minority or protest groups such as Six Nations with denial and marginalization, quickly forgetting "the norms of tolerance and the values of equality that they supposedly espoused" and claiming that "political correctness" has gone too far.[97] We heard just such a claim about political correctness from MPP Toby Barrett in his not-surprising frustration over the slow pace of negotiations. There are many more examples.

The difference between *asserting* that one is "against racism" and consistently *supporting* anti-racist actions, then, is crucial. For instance, although organizers of a public meeting held in a town near Ipperwash during that protest in 1995 were anxious to affirm that the group was not anti-Native, one attendee observed that "if the organizers had said 'Let's get the Indians' the place would have emptied in a minute."[98] Homegrown anti-Native movements often arise during conflicts over land, and politicians' use of terms such as "one law for all" and "all Ontarians are equal," which we heard in Caledonia, are undoubtedly influenced by public sentiment, lending support to the suggestion that in Canada "Indians have rights as long as they do not try to exercise them."[99] Public experts, academics, and the media all influence politicians and administrators – who still, however, "set the terms and boundaries of public debate and opinion formation."[100] Their discursive moves, set amid "loud claims about freedom, democracy, tolerance, hospitality, and 'long traditions,'" are significant.[101]

In Caledonia, there is evidence of discursive tactics working to create exclusionary "us" and "them" spaces in circuitous ways. For example, disclaimers such as "we respect our neighbours at Six Nations, *but* ..." are often followed by negative statements. Apparent altruism is at work in claims that it would be better for Six Nations if it could resolve its internal governance issues – "for their own good," not for ours. Quasi-objective numbers are used strategically. When Canadian representatives complain about taxpayers' money being offered as compensation for land claims, figures are generally not quantified as percentages of budgets or seen in comparison to the damages paid to other (white) parties filing grievances against the government. The terms encountered in public conversations about multiculturality and First Nations' cultural difference pose diversity as a "problem" that must be solved or managed, usually without "their" participation.[102] A public discourse of homogeneity is masked by the dominant rhetoric of tolerance and good intentions. Such rhetoric assumes that (individually) tolerant behaviours are the antidote to racism.

It is more difficult to combat hegemonic and institutionalized racism when attention is steered from the political and societal toward the personal. Michael Clyne explains that the ability of "race talk" to hide within discussions of "cultural difference" and egalitarianism reminds us that racial hierarchy lives on in virtually every setting, be it explicitly or indirectly. Blatant racism is easy to identify – covert racist discourse pretends to objectivity, pragmatism, and acceptance of a shared liberal framework, and it can "have the effect of confusing the uncommitted into accepting a racist position as a rational and broad-minded one."[103] Even the speakers themselves are typically unaware of the race-based claims they are making, as was evident in Caledonia. What makes (racialized) Eurocentric identities particularly shifty, as James (Sakéj) Youngblood Henderson explains, is that they do not make bare assertions about privileged norms vis-à-vis other cultures, instead couching their ideas in claims of universality and generality. "Because colonizers consider themselves to be the ideal model for humanity and carriers of superior culture and intelligence," he says, they "believe that they have the power to interpret differences, and this belief shaped the institutional and imaginative assumptions of colonization and modernism."[104]

Six Nations' definitions of what constitutes a "normal" state of affairs regularly took second spot to Canadian conceptions of order, (Canadian) law, progress, and multiculturalism marked by "tolerance" for one's "neighbours." When Diane Finley promised to get Caledonia "back to normal," she was staking a discursive claim to the right to define what is acceptable, besides marking a space where "we" belong and where "they" do not. As Audrey Kobayashi and Linda Peake argue, these racialized realities are so pervasive that no interrogation of organized society can take place without noting white privilege and acknowledging powerful ideologies of "normalcy" and "ordinariness" marked by moral superiority, safety, and corresponding deviations by others.[105] In Canada and elsewhere, racism still manifests itself physically in the form of stratified access to lands and resources, health care, longevity, literacy, and income. It succeeds in this way despite a growing tendency for white society to operate as if oppression has been largely rectified – as exemplified by Caledonia, where there are constant references to the rich history of the Grand River and healthy relationships with Six Nations and where past and present injustices are ignored. "This new, officially *post-racial* politics," says Winant, "may be more effective in containing the challenges posed by movements for racial justice ... than any intransigent, overtly racist backlash could possibly have been."[106] Canada officially denounces racism, but it has shifted from open domination through segregation and colonialism to hegemony that functions by appeasing moderates through apparent reforms.

The consequences of racism can be identified more easily than its distanced perpetrators. The ways in which Canada was defined and structured in opposition to indigeneity were easier to identify in the past, but important continuities persist. The popular concept of social evolution, for instance – that human development moves along a scale from barbarism to civilization – found remarkable stability in Ontario school textbook descriptions of Natives as late as 1980.[107] Young Canadians have been raised on deeply racialized notions since before Confederation. These ideas may be contributing to the ongoing criminalization of Aboriginal people by the highly discretionary authority of the police and the courts.[108] Socio-economic class (which is highly correlated with race) and strategies whereby Aboriginal people deliberately position themselves in opposition to Canadian law likely play parts in this process as well. The "victims" of crimes for which Aboriginal people are charged are often notional communities, as in cases of public disturbance, for instance. In addition, and with dismaying consistency over centuries, media representations of conflicts between European and Aboriginal people in Canada have been constructed in terms of "us" and "them."[109] The reporting from Caledonia merely followed the same course. "We" – the white audience to whom the dominant intragroup discourse about the minority "them" is directed – are governed by reason, follow the law, make rational decisions, and offer thoughtful insights into problems. "They," on the other hand, are dominated by emotion, are prone to "cry" and "confront," cost "us" money by causing trouble, are more susceptible to corruption, and pose threats to "our" economic development.

The mere existence of this intragroup discussion is a marker of differential access to the media's power – a power that, like the powers of the law, the criminal courts, and the education system, has long been controlled mainly by white Canadians. Media coverage helps sustain the public's ignorance about official policy regarding Aboriginal people as well as amnesia regarding the links between Canada's colonial history and the starkly unequal relations between Aboriginal and non-Aboriginal people today.[110] Active biological racism has subsided into a sanitized ethnocentrism that preaches equality of opportunity and cultural pluralism. White Canada's ability to shift discourse away from Six Nations' concerns such as land rights and sovereignty toward limited issues such as financial compensation and to abstract the dispute "issue" from its historical and political contexts has had a colossal impact on today's public debates.

However, First Nations people are not simply positioned at the bottom of the social evolutionary ladder in the Canadian nation-building project. More than that, according to Daniel Francis, there was a time when everyone assumed that Aboriginal people "were disappearing from the face of the earth, victims of disease, starvation, alcohol and the remorseless ebb and flow of civilizations."[111] What reason is there, then, to interact with them as people (as opposed to essentialized sages or warriors)? This attitude manifests itself today in a "get with the program" discourse that demands that Six Nations cease calling for recognition of rights – Canada is going to march on, with or without you. We would feel better about ourselves if you hopped on the economic bandwagon, but if you don't want to, at least don't get in the way.

Venerated Canadian artists such as Paul Kane and Emily Carr assumed the task of documenting these species vanishing "into silent nothingness." Indeed, their artistic success depended on romanticized images of supposedly destroyed Aboriginal cultures.[112] Denial of enduring Aboriginal cultures and nations officially persisted until the failure of the 1969 White Paper (unofficially, it continues). In the discussions leading to the drafting of the White Paper, Prime Minister Pierre Trudeau commented: "In terms of *realpolitik*, French and English are equal in Canada because each of these linguistic groups has the power to break the country. And this power cannot yet be claimed by the Iroquois, the Eskimos, or the Ukrainians."[113] Trudeau was to be proved wrong in his assumptions about the strength of Aboriginal opposition, but he was prescient in pointing out the connection between protest and recognition, both of which were evidenced in Caledonia. Francis explains that even his own perceptions of First Nations people continue to conflict. What leaps to his mind first is a man sitting at a roadblock, holding a rifle, and only afterwards does he recall Elijah Harper calmly twitching an eagle feather in the Manitoba legislature in dissent with the Meech Lake Accord, "bringing the process of constitutional change in the country to an abrupt halt. The warrior versus the wise elder; it turns out that the images of Indians we are offered today are not much different from what they have always been."[114] The ambivalence in Canada's history – defining our civilization and development in opposition to Aboriginal barbarism, yet revering Aboriginal people for their unique relationship with nature – did not prepare us well for a relationship predicated on equal partnership rooted in real appreciation and comprehension of difference, nor does this ambiguity help us come to terms with ourselves as North Americans.[115]

Jennifer Reid tackles the Canadian imaginary through an analysis of Louis Riel's influence on the modern Canadian state.[116] She argues that the different ways in which the myths of Riel have been mobilized by various peoples in Canada point to "the profound inadequacy of the concepts of *nationalism* and the *nation* in the Canadian situation."[117] Various characterizations of Riel as hero, martyr, traitor, embodiment of resistance against the federal government, and forerunner to populist politics have been deployed by a variety of agendas, forcing us to recognize the plurality and dichotomies at the heart of Canada – French/English, east/west, Aboriginal/non-Aboriginal – as well as the impossibility of a national narrative based on unity. Positing Canada as a nation-state instead of a confederation based on hybridity works to conceal the tangled relationships of colonialism, as well as the violence – physical, structural, and symbolic – implicated in the creation of the country. Despite Canada's professed foundations of peace, order, and good government, its history is riddled with sub-nationalisms, ethnic oppression, separatism, and uprisings. Reid says that our creation story, instead of defining the Canadian state according to ethnic or ideological uniformities, should explicitly acknowledge civil unrest, avoid the pretence that Canada was founded on multiculturalism, and acknowledge that some of Canada's constituent parts are indeed different.

Agreeing with Reid, Erin Manning calls attention to the systems of governance that exclude those who renounce, or do not comprehend, the nation's semantics. Qualified (presumably, white immigrant) bodies accept Canadian sovereignty in its linguistic, cultural, and political personifications as well as in its claims to liberty, harmony, and equality. Manning points to "a violent discourse of national exclusion that is masked in the myth of Canadians as a harmless, open, and generous people. For despite that the discourse of generosity and benevolence prevails within the Canadian national imagination, the categories of 'us' and 'them' remain standard practices."[118]

At various points in history, the cracks in Canada's carefully constructed identity have become more apparent. Maria de La Salette Correia shows how the land dispute crisis at Oka in 1990 proved to be a "microcosm of the questioning of western master-narratives, the blurring of lines *between* cultures and the divisions *within* cultures that are hallmarks of the post modern age."[119] I believe we may extend this claim to Caledonia. First Nations' decolonization movements work against Canadian master narratives about the tolerance inherent in peace, order, and good government – indeed, the orderly development of British Canada *required* standardization and homogeneity. The Mohawk protesters at Oka were well aware that the Haudenosaunee Confederacy possesses one of the oldest and least hierarchical constitutions in the world, and they demonstrated a clear awareness of this,[120] commenting, for instance, that "if the Mohawks hadn't taken a stand ... they would have been just 'wooden-cigar-store Indians.'"[121] Carefully crafting postmodern identities and strategies, the Mohawk warrior "borrowed what he wanted from the image and arsenal of the international soldier, he challenged a province possessed of a national identity to accept his own national identity, he called himself Lasagna or Spudwrench or Noriega, and he spoke of the Longhouse and the Great Law of Peace. In other words, he demonstrated an amazing ability to understand and articulate within and between cultures."[122]

Oka mirrors Caledonia in many ways. The government of Quebec sent in the police, and Quebeckers rejected the racist label, even as many burned effigies, hurled rocks, and roared *maudit sauvages* (though in both places there were supporters of the protesters as well). Meanwhile, the prime minister went on vacation, and the federal government, still recovering from the Meech Lake fiasco, played hot potato with Quebec over jurisdictional responsibility. "On the other side," says Correia, "the Mohawk rejected the characterization of the conflict as one of Law and Order and refused to get involved in a language war; instead, they spoke of nationhood, of the Great Law of Peace and the Covenant Chain and the inherent right to self-determination."[123] Perhaps one of the best-known images of the Oka dispute, she explains, is a photograph depicting a Canadian military private and a warrior staring each other down. As it happened, the warrior was not

Mohawk or even Iroquois, but Ojibway. The private – an icon of law and order – was a cocaine user later arrested for a hit-and-run accident and discharged from the military. Correia's deconstruction of the complex identities mobilized in this struggle highlights both the clarities and the confusions inherent in Canadian identities structured in opposition to Aboriginality and in alliance with claims to the "rule of law."

As the Royal Commission on Aboriginal Peoples explains in its report, the "normal" relationships that have developed between Aboriginal and non-Aboriginal people over the past four hundred years have been based on false premises – Canada was not unoccupied, and its inhabitants were not wild, untutored, and ignorant: "A country cannot be built on a living lie."[124] Notwithstanding Canadian roles in articulating and ratifying international human rights standards, the historical process by which Canada was formed involved a renunciation of the rights of its first peoples to self-determination. The law directing the division of authority relating to Canada's First Nations declares without question the state's legislative power over them. Federal jurisdiction is derived from section 91(24) of the *Constitution Act, 1867*, which the judiciary has interpreted as authorizing Parliament to single out Native people and treat them differently from non-Native people under some laws and the same under others.[125] And provincial laws applying to land ownership and hunting and fishing rights discriminate against First Nations' cultural and economic practices and laws while appearing impartial. Western liberalism's emphasis on individual rights and rationalism originated in the social contract's purpose, which was to ensure security for (property) rights as humanity left the state of nature, but these rights have been denied First Nations in crucial ways, and, as a consequence, Canada has been shaped in ways that exclude Aboriginal priorities, practices, and histories.[126] In Caledonia, a discursive emphasis on the rights of the property owner carried enormous weight with the public and leaders alike – again, whites were claiming the right to shape society according to their legal system's conceptions of possession and justice.

Michael Lee Ross suggests that nothing less than Canada's "national soul" is at stake in the inconsistency between its congratulatory self-image and the attacks it has made on First Nations' lands and rights. Canadians often claim a history relatively free of conflict with First Nations, which suggests that "how Canadians look upon their historical and current relationship with First Nations peoples and how they envision their future relationship are integral parts of their national self-image."[127] John Borrows argues that the legitimacy of Canadian claims to sovereignty can and should be challenged if Canada is to abide by its cherished principles as "a free and democratic society."[128] Fundamental constitutional principles belie Canada's claim to underlying title, and the democratic principles of consultation and consent, which have been followed in the cases of all other governments entering Confederation, were ignored when the First Nations were yanked into the Dominion's federal structures.[129]

Current attempts to negotiate the swirling waters of Canadian identity and relationship with Aboriginal peoples are confounded by Canadians' uncomfortable peripheral awareness of the injustice lying at the core of their nation's history.[130] As Asha Varadharajan puts it, "the contradiction between the ironic self-deprecation with which Canada represents itself on the outside and the demonstrable power differentials in the materiality of its existence on the inside only serves to cloud the issue further." This fantasy of harmonious diversity[131] rules out possibilities for dissidence and genuine difference.[132] Varadharajan calls for a truly multicultural space that acknowledges and embraces controversy over meanings, identities, and values in order to properly recognize the importance and complexity of struggles for self-determination and equity. If a discursive space according to Varadharajan's vision had been provided for in the negotiations over Kanonhstaton, rather than one delineated by Canadian versions of history and relationship, we might have seen a different outcome.

The discomfort in this nether-region of "tolerance" of Aboriginal peoples is potently conveyed by Kristina Fagan, who explores a widespread tendency in Canadian society to separate Aboriginal culture from Aboriginal politics. She tells how her non-Native students reacted enthusiastically to oral narratives emphasizing the importance of homelands to Aboriginal people, but negatively to a more overtly political piece arguing that First Nations should not be considered citizens of Canada. Both texts are deeply political expressions of Aboriginal nationality, but the students viewed only the first narratives as noteworthy and acceptable cultural artifacts. I can attest to this inclination in my own early hypothesis that the dispute in Caledonia was about clashing "cultures" and "values." I understood the term "culture" in a way that ignored its shifting and deeply political implications. While many Canadians are enthusiastic about Aboriginal culture, the idea of continuing title to land is profoundly disturbing to spatial imaginaries such as those along the Grand River. Although Aboriginal self-representers are regularly accused of using "ideological filters" in their portrayals of Aboriginal identity, Theresa McCarthy argues that the dominant culture also ideologically interprets, represents, distorts, and dismisses certain issues and realities.[133] She quotes Sherene Razack on "the perils of essentialism," which mean that an emphasis on cultural diversity can descend, "in a multicultural spiral, to a superficial reading of differences that makes power relations invisible and keeps dominant cultural norms in place," making it difficult to deconstruct "the Canadian nationalist ideology of tolerance."[134]

Racialized Economies

Canadian imaginaries of peace, order, and good government have shaped more than the delusional identities of deracialized tolerance. Orderly society also calls for Canadian economic space to be shaped by "progressive" development, the engine of national society. The historical prioritization of squatters' rights over those of Six Nations was rooted in British colonial economic expansion and the rejection of Aboriginal ways of managing the land. Landscape and society along the Grand River have been deeply structured by the resulting demands. The requirements of trade mandated the building of highways, dams, mills, and towns through the acquisition of Six Nations' land, which pushed the Haudenosaunee onto a "reserve" while the land around them was built up and developed. Today, any suggestion that development in the Haldimand Tract area should be halted until Six Nations' land grievances are resolved is met with disbelief and anger. Canadian representatives in the Caledonia dispute are energized by anxiety about economic and business interests. Both themes surface often in their narratives about Douglas Creek Estates.

In economist Ozay Mehmet's interrogation of Eurocentric profit-driven economies, he argues that development theories rest on strong nationalistic premises that substitute assumptions for the realities of race, gender, and environment.[135] Economics, he says, is not a description of reality but a value-laden discourse like any other. Western capitalism, a culture-specific by-product of the Protestant work ethic and rationalist post-Newtonian Europe, takes for granted the paradigm of "positive" rather than welfare or normative economics and prioritizes economic growth in the form of capital accumulation. Western empiricism portrays human progress in terms of a deterministic replication of Western stages, evaluating everything according to European norms and relegating non-European economies to the domain of failure or – perhaps more generously – to that of potential transformation.[136] Arturo Escobar similarly argues that in the history of cultures, the economy is peculiarly treated as a neutral production system even though it "is not only, or even principally, a material entity. It is above all a cultural production, a way of producing human subjects and social orders of a certain kind."[137] Power and control are critical. The "economy" and development policies demand that populations be regulated with the movements of capital. Social classes are enforced, and "man" is restructured as a normalized subject – as *homo oeconomicus* in a disciplinary society.[138]

Prioritizations of "normal development" are so evident along the Grand River that they hardly require explication. Canadian economic imperatives have meant that landscapes were progressively shaped for settler priorities and progress, whether people were already there or not.[139] The land was charted in a new way – while the Haudenosaunee defined social relationships by the land, the colonizers mapped resources.[140] The Royal Proclamation was viewed as an impediment to settlement, development, and Native assimilation. Aboriginal territory was redesignated as Crown land and Aboriginal nations as "bands," which served to suppress Aboriginal autonomy in favour of Canadian sovereignty. Ironically, when Six Nations asserts its sovereignty today by similar means – that is, by *exercising* it, not just by stating it – their efforts are rejected.

Canadian societal discourses masked motives of economic expansion behind prevailing settler ideologies of social Darwinism and deeply embedded notions of progress. These views justified the relegation of Native people to the category of physical impediments to white settlement by highlighting their savagery, cultural inadequacy, and moral inferiority.[141] The constitutional principles on which Canada was founded ostensibly recognized the supremacy of God and the rule of law even while masking the economic and political goals directing Canada. In this way, the collective rights and responsibilities esteemed by Aboriginal societies were papered over in favour of European concepts of individual entitlements. The entire project of cultural-economic hegemony, then, is hidden by the rhetoric of "rights." At the same time, native law and cultural forces are left out of the debate.[142] Meanwhile, the resort to neo-liberal discourses tying citizenship to land through economic "logics" continues apace. David Rossiter and Patricia Wood conclude that the 2002 public referendum over the BC treaty process was not merely about the allotment of lands and resources. By focusing on First Nations' participation in market economies and by erasing the historical and geographic realities of Native-newcomer encounters, the referendum became a contest over the very terms of Aboriginal citizenship.[143]

Sidney Harring weaves together racialized colonial and Canadian imaginaries and economic policies as they apply to Six Nations. He casts it as a story of a legal and physical landscape shaped by hypocrisy and deceit. The reasoning the colonizers relied on when dispossessing Native people of their land – a reasoning on which Canada still relies for its legitimacy – included rationalizations such as the "weight of history," which provides "a legal basis for government actions done in violation of law – so long as they were done long ago."[144] The language of liberal benevolence excused structural violence by distinguishing it (for reasons that were generally specious) from the sometimes more physical American frontier brutality. The land

and commercial priorities of British law and order demanded an approach of "punishing violators and providing a framework for organizing land and resources so that development could go forward."[145] Years later, the reverberations of these policies, and the legal disorder associated with them, continue to be felt. Six Nations' constant assertions of sovereignty and land rights were set in opposition to the settlers and squatters whose (racialized) political and economic power "influenced the government to refuse to enforce its own land laws protecting Six Nations against settler interests."[146] Despite identifying with Britain's love for law and order, the colonial regime ignored its own directives. Harring concludes that the dispossession of Six Nations from most of their territory was underpinned partly by racism and ethnocentrism, which were

> forces at work in the expansion of the British empire and the formation of colonial settler states. On the simplest level, settlers believed that they could make productive use of lands that Indians wasted. But that may cast their dispossession of Indians in too neutral a light. The idea that Six Nations' laziness and chicanery in land deals were responsible for the squatters is rooted in mythology and in misrepresentation of the actions of the two thousand Indians living there. Most basic to this was the idea that the Indians were "improvident," relying on government annuities for survival because they had an aversion to labour and this encouraged their natural indolence and improvidence.[147]

These payments, made in lieu of surrendered land, amounted to only about four British pounds per resident of the Six Nations Reserve in 1844 – hardly adequate to sustain profligacy. We can hear the echoes of this discourse in Mayor Trainer's assertions that Caledonians cannot simply sit by and wait for cheques to arrive, as Six Nations protesters apparently can. Racism was further embedded in early colonial policies linking land and political body, exemplified by the disqualification of John (son of Joseph) Brant's election to the newly created Haldimand County riding in 1832, on the grounds that most of his votes had been cast by unenfranchised non-landowners. The franchise was thereby denied to those without property (a clear example of the prioritization of capitalist prerogatives). Moreover, the policy was doubly exclusionary to those from Six Nations, since their land was ostensibly not properly "owned" but, rather, "held in trust" by the government. Canada's legitimacy and self-image as a country, after all, depended on its assertion of sovereignty over Native people and lands. And even though Six Nations had authority under the common law as landholders to remove squatters – trespassers – by force, "such action in the context of a hostile legal system might have constituted assault and been punished under colonial law."[148] Again, the racism inherent in the legal system prevented assertion of land rights and sovereignty – the British and Canadian authorities, who had both the muscle and the legal mandate to eject the squatters, did not do so. Instead, as Harring charges, "by the 1820s Canadian authorities were permitting squatter occupation of the Grand River lands as one element of a strategy to force the Six Nations to cede their lands to the Crown, in turn promoting a policy of forced assimilation."[149]

In short, the discursive strategies in Caledonia emphasizing law, universal "normalcy," jurisdiction over, and differentiation from, Six Nations, and raceless "multiculturalism" are clearly connected to overarching Canadian cultural imaginaries, and they also equally clearly accept as the status quo a situation where the rights and interests of Six Nations consistently play second fiddle to those of everyone else. Harring's scrutiny of Six Nations' land rights case provides a clear illustration of many aspects of Canadian identity: "legally" premised in opposition to Aboriginal peoples; weaving land, law, economic priorities, and politics tightly together to shape the land and the nation; justifying its (in)actions with discursive moves emphasizing individual rights; and claiming that the relative lack of corporeal violence provides proof that Canada is a peaceful state characterized by law, order, and good governance. Government representatives in the conflict over land in Caledonia rely on these same Canadian narratives for legitimacy and justification. The police action at Douglas Creek Estates makes sense in light of the discursive strategies that classify the protesters as different and un-acceptable. The *Places to Grow Act* is permitted to erase Six Nations from the map and ignore its priorities because the economy comes first and be-cause Six Nations' own visions for economy and development do not count in the first place.[150]

Caledonia connects the dots between discourses and physical landscapes. When the rubber hits the road in struggles over landscape, identities heavily weighted by race, place, and history come to the fore. As Donald Moore, Anand Pandian, and Jake Kosek point out, symbolic and material struggles occur together, proving false the supposed distinction between symbolic recognition and resource allocation: "Race, nature, and difference simultan-eously shape both the very terrain that produces political subjects and the claims that these subjects make to rights, resources, and their redistribu-tion."[151] As we saw in Chapter 1, discourse analysis uncovers the "sayable," exposing the boundaries around what can and cannot be expressed. These rules are profoundly implicated in relations of power and suppression that we see at work in Caledonia and in Canadian–First Nations relationships more generally. Words and customs are part of the contested histories, economies, legalities, and identities, represented and rearticulated in this dispute over land: the marking of spaces of "normalcy" and legitimacy by excluding others who do not belong; the reinforcement of relationships predicated on assumptions of superiority and sovereignty rather than equality; the law's role in categorizing certain actions as "acceptable" or "unacceptable"; and contradictory notions of justice, legitimate history, and truth.

A History of Sovereignty   4

The dispute in Caledonia appears to be about land, but, in fact, it is about much more than just this one issue. As I have suggested in the preceding three chapters and will argue expressly here, it is also about identity, authority, power, and sovereignty. These notions may evoke images of First Nations people physically claiming sovereignty over their traditional territory, and those images would be accurate. But how have they come to be in a position where they must stake these claims to land and to autonomy? And how do histories, and declarations of "truth," work out on the ground in Caledonia? Embedded in claims to autonomy are crucial prerequisite claims to a recognition of one's own version of truth and identity. And this is where things break down. When First Nations' histories and truths are discarded in favour of Canadian versions – often on the basis of "legal" premises crafted by the colonial settlers – it is impossible for a real discussion to take place. James Clifford describes the case of the Mashpee Indians in New England, who in order to have their land claim accepted for litigation had to first prove the continuity of their "Indianness." As Clifford explains, "in the course of their peculiar litigation certain underlying structures governing the recognition of identity and difference became visible. Looked at one way, they were Indian; seen another way, they were not. Powerful *ways of looking* thus became inescapably problematic [and the trial became an] experiment in translation, part of a long historical conflict and negotiation of 'Indian' and 'American' identities."[1] In Caledonia, Canada is asserting its sovereignty over Six Nations each time it refuses to acknowledge other possibilities for "reality," "facts," and legitimacy. Throughout the dispute at Caledonia, Six Nations representatives have referred casually but crucially to the history of the Haudenosaunee people and the treaty alliances reached with the new-comers. Meanwhile, Canadian representatives refer nonchalantly to jurisdiction, governance, and "understanding." Land, sovereignty, and identity are inextricably knotted in this geographical space, and attempts to negotiate over the future of the land, while ignoring the competing histories of sovereignty that are implicated in the dispute, are doomed.

The Haudenosaunee Confederacy, often known as the League of the Iroquois, formed many centuries ago when five fiercely warring nations – the Mohawk, Oneida, Onondaga, Cayuga, and Seneca – symbolically buried their weapons under the roots of a great white pine, the Tree of Peace.[2] The Peacemaker, a messenger born on the north shore of Lake Ontario, brought the Great Law of Peace,[3] which focused on collective peace and righteousness, to these First People from the Creator.[4] He delivered the Great Law of Peace with the assistance of the first Mohawk Confederacy chiefs, providing a governance structure that continues to this day.[5] The first person to receive this law, Tsikonhsaseh, secured for women the right to select the members of the Confederacy Council, comprising representatives from each of the fifty clan families of the united five nations. International consensus was sought for major decisions in a league-wide forum, and if consensus could not be achieved nations or groups were permitted to act autonomously, enabling independence within the alliance and peace through diplomacy.[6] The Confederacy nations conceptualized their alliance as a longhouse arranged from west to east, reflecting original national geographic locations in the territory – the Onondaga served as the central keepers of the fire and the Seneca and Mohawk as the eastern and western doorkeepers.[7] The Haudenosaunee clan and its nation structures and naming schemes also knot land and identity together. The word *otara* in Mohawk means land, clay, earth, and clan, and an individual who is asked to which nation he or she belongs replies literally in terms of territory: "I am made of *this* earth." The Seneca, for instance, are the "Great Hill People," while the Mohawk are the "People of the Flint."[8]

As a societal model based on balance and consensus, the Great Law of Peace has inspired extensive study both within and outside the Haudenosaunee. Although a number of accounts have resulted, coherent visions have emerged of the Haudenosaunee relationship to the land and its tightly configured jurisprudence. The law addresses, among other domains, the boundaries of, and travel within, the unified national territories; the links between territory and national identities; the kinship systems of interdependence between clans and nations; the processes for replacing deceased leaders through powerful condolence ceremonies; and the collective responsibilities and rights of all individuals. Several wampum belts and strings set down certain internal treaty principles of the Great Law of Peace – for instance, the Dish with One Spoon specifies that, though national distinctions persist, each nation is to share resources and land responsibly, taking only what is needed and not more than can be sustained by nature.[9] A scholar wrote in the 1800s: "The regard of Englishmen for their Magna Charta and Bill of Rights, and that of Americans for their national Constitution, seem weak in comparison with the intense gratitude and reverence of the Five Nations for the 'Great Peace.'" He described the Haudenosaunee as a linguistically, culturally, and religiously advanced people "imbued with the strongest possible sense of personal independence, and resulting from that, a passion for political freedom."[10]

The Haudenosaunee, who adopted the Tuscarora as "little brothers" and the sixth nation of the Confederacy in the 1700s, were a powerful political and military force to be reckoned (or allied) with, both by other First Nations and by the newcomers who arrived later. Faced with increasing European presence, the Confederacy at first seemed stronger than ever, incorporating various European technologies and successfully controlling the Great Lakes fur-trading routes.[11] Their traditional lands comprised an enormous area from the Hudson River in the east to Lake Erie in the northwest and including the northern part of Pennsylvania in the south,[12] and it expanded in the seventeenth century as refugees from other First Nations sought to join the Confederacy and were accorded representation in compliance with the Great Law of Peace.[13]

Yet, today, the largest population of Haudenosaunee, Six Nations, lives on a patch of land referred to as Indian Reserve 40, which comprises about 22,000 hectares along the Grand River between Brantford and Caledonia. In total, there are eighteen Haudenosaunee communities throughout Ontario, Quebec, Wisconsin, Oklahoma, and upstate New York, each of which includes varying compositions of the various six nations of the Confederacy as well as members of other dependent nations. How did the famed League of the Iroquois come to be so physically fractured, its territory so reduced?

This next part of Haudenosaunee history will sound eerily similar to the stories of other First Nations on Turtle Island, for it touches on the crucial issues of territory, cultural history, and sovereignty. Euro-American interrogations of indigenous land title began at Contact and were rooted in the shifting nature of the relationship between the newcomers and Turtle Island's original people.[14] Europeans, often unable to convince the occupants to cede all of the territory they desired, developed a framework that permitted them to take it without consent – the "legal" concept of *terra nullius*, denoting empty and therefore unpossessed land. This framework indexed Aboriginal peoples as the most primitive members of the human race. The Lockean notion that "in the beginning, all the world was America" neatly encapsulates this racist view of societal "evolution" and "development." In this "state of nature," as it was perceived by the colonizing Europeans, there was no nationhood nor were there territorial jurisdictions, property rights, or legitimate governments, and all encounters were dealt with according to the law of nature.[15] The term sovereignty itself, in fact, comprises a contested spatial imaginary: colonizers' notions focused on a common power held over a group of men – a "Commonwealth" – for defence and security, attained through either force or voluntary agreement.[16] (It is unclear whether this definition implied inclusion of those individuals, such as many First Peoples, who neither had been conquered nor had agreed to join the Commonwealth, and who did not believe themselves to have entered it but were assumed by others to have done so.)

However, prior to the invention of *terra nullius*, treaty alliances with Native peoples were often considered necessary in order to avoid unnecessary colonial wars.[17] The powerful Haudenosaunee Confederacy was constantly sought as a friend and ally, first by the Dutch and later by the French and English. When the Dutch at the Fort Orange trading post proposed a trading treaty in the 1600s, the Haudenosaunee insisted on an arrangement similar to the intergovernmental alliances of the Confederacy. This alliance led to the creation of the Two Row Wampum in 1613.[18] A well-known symbol of co-operation and autonomy, the belt embodying the relationship recognizes simultaneous interaction and independence between the Haudenosaunee and the first European settlers. It is made up of two parallel rows of purple beads, representing the Haudenosaunee and European governments respectively, separated by three rows of white beads symbolizing peace, trust, and respect. Themes of separation and integration consistently recur in Crown–First Nations relations.[19] The Two Row Wampum principles were later borrowed by the British in their relations with other First Nations.[20]

The 1664 Fort Albany Treaty conveyed the relationship from the Dutch to the British, who sought to develop trading privileges, military alliances, and brotherly connections with the Haudenosaunee. The mutual desire was to keep the separate vessels of the Haudenosaunee and the British as peaceful neighbours and allies as they travelled down the river together, despite their different world views and histories. The treaty stipulated separate criminal jurisdictions, and recognition of each party's inherent sovereignty was affirmed at a further council in 1677. These ideas developed into a treaty relationship embodied by a silver Covenant Chain linking both the British ship and the Haudenosaunee canoe to the "Great Mountain" for the rest of time. The chain was meant to be "polished" by having regular council gatherings to reaffirm the alliance and responsibilities, and it also provided for the addition of parties on both sides of the chain.[21] The concepts inherent in the Two Row Wampum and the Covenant Chain were intended to serve as guides for all time, and they have been invoked time and again by Six Nations as central themes in the current dispute over land.[22]

In the 1701 Nanfan Treaty or Beaver Hunting Grounds Treaty, the Haudenosaunee called on the Covenant Chain relationship in asking their British allies to protect their northern and western hunting grounds against the encroachments of other European settlers.[23] At this time, the British still depended heavily on the Haudenosaunee for assistance in a possible war against the French and for dominance in the fur trade. However, at the 1744 Treaty of Lancaster signed between the Haudenosaunee and the British colonies, an Onondaga Confederacy chief demonstrated prescient comprehension of the already troubled relationship:

> Long before one hundred years our Ancestors came out of this very ground, and their children have remained here ever since ... You came out of the ground in a country that lies beyond the Seas; there you may have a just Claim, but here you must allow us to be your elder Brethren, and the lands to belong to us before you knew anything of them. It is true, that above one hundred years ago the Dutch came here in a ship ... During all this time the newcomers, the Dutch, acknowledged our right to the lands ... About two years after the arrival of the English, an English governor came to Albany, and finding what great friendship subsisted between us and the Dutch, he approved it mightily, and desired to make as strong a league, and to be upon as good terms with us as the Dutch were ... Indeed we have had some small differences with the English, and during these misunderstandings, some of their young men would, by way of reproach, be every now and then telling us that we should have perished if they had not come into the country and furnished us with strouds [blankets] and hatchets and guns, and other things necessary for the support of life. But we always gave them to understand that they were mistaken, that we lived before they came amongst us, and as well, or better, if we may believe what our forefathers have told us. We had then room enough, and plenty of deer, which was easily caught ... We are now straitened, and sometimes in want of deer, and liable to many other inconveniences since the English came among us, and particularly from that pen-and-ink work that is going on at that table.[24]

The British called for Haudenosaunee support in their war against the French in 1755, assistance that was crucial to the British victory. However, the 1763 Peace of Paris at the close of the Seven Years War saw the Haudenosaunee's land "given up" by the French to the British.[25] Tensions rose when the British upheld falsely obtained patents to land and fortified – instead of dismantling, as promised – French-built forts in Haudenosaunee territory.[26] In response to complaints from various First Nations, who were threatening to band together against British colonists, the King of England issued the Royal Proclamation of 1763, which recognized indigenous peoples as "Nations" with whom treaties must be negotiated. It technically enshrined the inalienable rights of First Nations to their lands: "And whereas it is just and reasonable, and essential to Our Interest and the Security of Our Colonies, that the several Nations or Tribes of Indians, with whom We are connected, and who live under our Protection, should not be molested or disturbed in the Possession of such Parts of our Dominions and Territories as, not having been ceded to, or purchased by Us, are reserved to them, or any of them, as their Hunting Grounds."[27]

The Royal Proclamation also declared that owing to "great Frauds and abuses ... committed in purchasing Lands of the Indians, to the great Prejudice of our Interests, and to the great Dissatisfaction of the said Indians," henceforth only the Crown would be permitted to purchase lands in the "Indian Territory," through formal and public councils that woud include representatives of the Native peoples whose lands were involved. The Crown could sell or grant the lands to others.[28] Some view the Royal Proclamation as a sort of Magna Carta for the Natives in which the Crown declared the land to be in possession of the peoples occupying it, while others view it as a document of only short-term importance – that is, a measure designed to prevent Native wars.[29] Canada's Royal Commission on Aboriginal Peoples asserted in 1996 that the Royal Proclamation continues to give consequence to a legal and political trust-like relationship in Canada.[30]

In practical terms, however, the Royal Proclamation had limited effect. Dispossession continued with the 1768 Treaty of Fort Stanwix, which included a line marking the division between Native lands remaining under the Royal Proclamation and those transferred to the American colonies lying southeast of the line. Entering the treaty was another step taken by the Haudenosaunee to stop the tide of incoming settlers, hoping that establishing an even clearer line would prevent settlers from stepping over it, though the Covenant Chain had already been tarnished by incursions permitted by the British on Haudenosaunee lands.[31] The British, for their part, viewed the treaty as a cession of land. This marked a change in territorial alliance, since previously, the British and Haudenosaunee had agreed to share hunting grounds.[32] Clearly this system was not working. Indeed, tides of settlers continued to settle in Haudenosaunee territory after this treaty as well.[33]

The Haudenosaunee continued to declare autonomy and treated the relationship with the Crown as one of alliance,[34] despite British court rulings that Indians were subjects of the British Crown and that there could not be a sovereign state within a sovereign state.[35] However, the reciprocity relationships of the Two Row Wampum and the Covenant Chain, which were entered into with mutual expectations of benefits such as military assistance and the exchange of goods, gradually deteriorated as the Upper Canadian government determined that the Six Nations people were no longer the economic and military assets they had been in early settler days.[36] Today, thanks to legislative decisions made in the Canada of former years, and to ideas that have arisen as a result, all aspects of Haudenosaunee sovereignty are threatened, including "the degree to which Haudenosaunee people *believe* in the right to define their own future, the degree to which Haudenosaunee people have the *ability* to carry out those beliefs, and the degree to which the sovereign actions of the Haudenosaunee nations are *recognized* both within the nation and by the outside world."[37]

In 1867, the sole reference to Aboriginal peoples in Canada's Constitution was in section 91(24), which authorized Parliament to enact laws in relation to "Indians, and lands reserved for the Indians." Without this unique constitutional status designating federal power over Indians, Patrick Macklem explains, the provinces would be empowered to enact laws relating to Indians and Indian lands. The fact that the government held authority in the first place was not questioned.[38] Notably, Parliament permits itself to treat Native people differently from non-Native people under section 91(24), but it must treat them in the same ways under laws passed pursuant to other heads of federal power.[39] However, the Royal Commission on Aboriginal Peoples points out that "the terms of the Canadian federation are found not only in formal constitutional documents governing relations between the federal and provincial governments but also in treaties and other instruments [such as the Two Row Wampum and Covenant Chain] establishing the basic links between Aboriginal peoples and the Crown."[40]

Early case law reflected the interweaving of indigenous land and sovereignty. For instance, *St. Catherine's Milling and Lumber Co. v. The Queen* in 1889 indirectly addressed Aboriginal land title in determining whether Ojibway land "surrendered" to the Queen had become the property of the provincial or federal government.[41] The Privy Council sourced the Ojibway's "prior possession of their lands" in the Royal Proclamation, dependent on the sovereignty and protection of the British Crown.[42] This decision recognized First Nations' title to unceded lands but neglected the opportunity to clearly set out the rights of Natives in Canada.[43] In short, the court ruled that the Crown had proprietary ownership of land even before treaties had been signed, leaving Native title a mere "burden" on Crown title.[44] The racism inherent in the court's declarations regarding Native title without representation of First Nations themselves is astonishing.[45]

The 1884 *Indian Advancement Act* sought to replace traditional governments with elected band councils and designated Canadian Indian Affairs officials as council superintendants.[46] The Confederacy denounced this act as well as the provisions that made it illegal to raise money for the purpose of advancing legal claims against Canada.[47] Although the Confederacy Council was willing to work with the Department of Indian Affairs and/or the governor general as representatives of the Crown, according to the treaty relationship, Six Nations asserted independence through delegations, petitions, and claims and by continuing to govern its own affairs as much as possible. For instance, a letter sent to the governor general in 1890 in protest of that year's version of the *Indian Act* recalled the treaty relationship and the existence of the Haudenosaunee's own laws and customs. The Confederacy reacted to the First World War by voting to donate $1,500 toward a patriotic fund and by offering to enlist its young men, but when Ottawa refused to recognize Six Nations' standing as an ally, the council reaffirmed allegiance to Great Britain and decided to officially support recruitment only if requested by the king.[48] In a later declaration of autonomy, the council authorized its Speaker, Deskaheh (Levi General), to alert the International Court of Justice of the Haudenosaunee's plight. He travelled to London in this effort, giving speeches with messages such as this one in August 1923: "We would not have consented to take Canada's franchises if she had asked us politely to do so ... We are very willing to remain allies of the British against days of danger, as we have been for 250 years ... but we wish no one-sided alliance, nor will we ever be subjects of another people, even of the British if we can help it."[49]

Deskaheh later travelled to Geneva to address the League of Nations with a similar message. His petition, titled "The Red Man's Appeal to Justice," described the increasing presence of the RCMP on the reserve as an increasing attempt to undermine and destroy Six Nations' governing body and to establish Canadian authority in its place. Seeking international recognition for Haudenosaunee claims to the right of self-government, Deskaheh and Six Nations were prepared to accept the associated obligations of membership in the League of Nations. Despite expressed support from countries including Estonia, the Netherlands, Ireland, Panama, Japan, and Persia, the issue was removed from the agenda thanks to Great Britain's interwar influence and assertion that this was a matter internal to the British Empire and to Canada. Due to the sympathy garnered for his plea, however, Deskaheh was able to deliver his address during a meeting of friendship convened by the mayor of Geneva at city hall. However, his efforts ultimately failed, and Six Nations was unable to continue its efforts after his death several years later.[50]

This pattern was repeated at other international meetings, including the one in San Francisco where the UN Charter was drafted.[51] Six Nations' military importance decreased as settler populations grew and the policies of assimilation were increasingly promoted. By the 1870s, for instance, Canadian government officials had abandoned all attempts to interact with the Confederacy Council, according to anything resembling Haudeno-saunee protocol.[52] Following repeated assertions by the Confederacy Council of its responsibility to govern Six Nations people and lands, make laws, and appoint leaders, and due to the fact that Six Nations had never yielded its sovereignty either voluntarily or in war, the Indian superintendant in Brantford advocated that the unruly council be deposed.[53] In October 1924, an official from the Department of Indian Affairs read an order-in-council that voided the authority of the Confederacy Council and called for elections of a new band council. The RCMP seized the wampum strings and records and locked the Confederacy Council house. Control was later handed over to an Elected Band Council consisting of thirteen positions, voted in with the support of only twenty-seven people.[54] Although a minority in the community had petitioned for an elected council, the Department of Indian Affairs' main goal was to establish firm control.[55] Considering also that the community's desires were rarely taken into account in other issues, it is unlikely that the prompting of a political minority in Six Nations was the main reason for the change. The Department of Indian Affairs believed that it knew what was best for Native people, so it formulated and implemented policies without consultation. Six Nations responded by contesting specific federal regulations and by denying the authority of the department itself.[56]

Six Nations' persistent claims to sovereignty exceeded those of many other Native peoples and were advanced with force and resourcefulness by the Confederacy Council both in Canada and abroad. This publicity reflected poorly on the Department of Indian Affairs and on Canada as a whole and led to harsh responses, including a permanent police presence at the Grand River, the use of informers, and the intimidation of sympathetic international governments by the British diplomatic corps.[57] A 1959 attempt to retake the council house and officially reinstate the Confederacy Council was crushed by the RCMP. As Susan Hill explains, "while the Government of Canada could not tell Six Nations people who their leaders were, they could decide who *they* were going to deal with – and who they would allow to access the trust funds of Six Nations."[58] Both councils still exist – the Confederacy Council, though driven underground for years, continued to hold meetings in the Onondaga longhouse – assemblies not recognized by the Canadian government.[59]

Despite various laws and *Indian Acts* passed over the years, it gradually became clear that Aboriginal peoples such as Six Nations, living within the geographical area that slowly crystallized as "Canada" all around them, simply were not adopting the ways of the newcomers as completely as the colonial administration had hoped. A final attempt at "integration" was made in the 1969 federal White Paper. According to Dale Turner, the White Paper sought to "legislate Indians into extinction." Instead, ironically, it catalyzed a new intensity in Aboriginal activism, culminating in the recognition of "existing Aboriginal rights" in the *Constitution Act, 1982*.[60] The defeat of the White Paper indicated a formal overthrow of a long-standing paradigm of assimilation: "If the old policy was to be pursued, it would have to be indirectly, by subterfuge."[61] Constitutional thought gradually began to turn toward the notion of a permanent Aboriginal presence in Canada and what that would mean for relations between societies.

These conversations have played crucial roles in the shaping of Canadian law, geography, and politics, and they reverberate powerfully in Caledonia. The federal government quickly presented the reclamation as an illegal action, a policing matter regarding property title that did not require consideration of the historical, geographical, and cultural contexts in which it occurred and that belonged under provincial jurisdiction. By emphasizing geographic and legislative jurisdictional boundaries, Canada was erasing the history of the nation-to-nation relationship with the Haudenosaunee that it had assumed from the British Crown at the creation of Canada, as well as Six Nations' right to have its land grievances addressed. This continuation of colonial relationships has naturalized spatialized power relations by assuming the rights to land and its management, while also rendering these histories of power invisible. The jurisdictional battle siphoned government representatives' energy away from the question of the land for several months. From Six Nations' perspective, the question of land rights was intimately woven with assertions of sovereignty, and the reclamation could only legitimately be addressed by Canada in right of the Crown, with whom the original treaties had been made.

Although all of the parties, except for the federal government itself, called regularly for the federal government to "deal with" the Caledonia occupation, their reasons differed, though all were rooted in assumptions of sovereignty. To the provincial and municipal governments, it was a matter of jurisdiction. Since the federal government had controlled the Department of Indian Affairs since Confederation, the occupation and Six Nations were their problems. Though they were correct according to Canadian legislative distribution, this enduring colonial attitude obscures both the injustices done to Six Nations and its unique status in Canada. As Mayor Marie Trainer concisely summarized, "they're wards of the Crown."[62] Minister of Indian Affairs Jim Prentice agreed with this general sentiment but still managed to sidestep responsibility, maintaining that the Constitution had delegated policing, property and civil rights, and the administration of justice to the provinces: "What's missing here is the justification for the province to say this is a federal obligation to pay for this. While the federal government has responsibility for Indians, that doesn't override provincial law."[63]

Ontario Provincial Police (OPP) Commissioner Julian Fantino made a direct call: "It has to be a federal response here. These are federal issues that go back to treaties."[64] However, according to Prentice's spokesperson, the dispute had "nothing to do with the federal government. This isn't a lands claim matter. The actual root of the problem is not a land claim. For the time being, it's a protest."[65] Member of Parliament (MP) Diane Finley agreed: "While the federal government always has an interest in aboriginal issues, land development and policing are under provincial jurisdiction."[66] The lack of interest in "Aboriginal issues" in all this discussion was palpable, though Prentice did promise that "like all Canadians" he would "continue to watch the situation as it unfolds."[67] Prime Minister Stephen Harper was dismissive: "Look, I have a lot of sympathy for a lot of people who have done nothing wrong, have been severely inconvenienced ... It really is a provincial land use matter and a provincial law enforcement issue."[68]

These comments frame the dispute as an inconvenience, a dispute between private parties, and a criminal action. Harper does not mention having any "sympathy" for First Nations whose land claims have gone unaddressed for decades. The initial response from the federal Department of Indian and Northern Affairs, in fact, nearly a month after the reclamation had begun, consisted merely of appointing a "fact finder" to undertake a "fact-finding initiative related to the ongoing situation involving members of Six Nations of the Grand River near Caledonia, Ontario."[69] Confederacy Chief and spokesperson Leroy Hill pointed out the inadequacy of this proposal: "The federal government's runner is a positive first step but the federal government needs to take further steps and send a delegate with a stronger mandate."[70] In early April, the fact finder, Michael Coyle, explained that the federal and provincial governments' dispute over who was legally responsible for Six Nations' land claims would make settlement very difficult.[71]

Writing to Six Nations' Confederacy Council later that month, Prentice continued to avoid federal responsibility:

As mentioned in my April 13th letter to the Haudenosaunee Six Nations Confederacy, I have taken note of your concerns. The issues that you raise in your letter are important ones. I have addressed the areas which fall under federal jurisdiction ... I fully subscribe to the view that traditional beliefs, values, and practices of Six Nations need to be better understood by governments and local interests. I also believe that a community/public education campaign on the history of Six Nations land interests will be beneficial ... We are prepared to fund processes to support these two objectives, as well as processes to address internal Six Nations governance issues.[72]

This letter attempts to trivialize Six Nations' land rights by indexing them as "traditional values." Furthermore, the paternalism in the offer to assist Six Nations with its internal governance implies that the problems are entirely the fault of Six Nations, resulting from an inability to govern itself.

The jurisdictional battle between the federal and provincial governments is one clear example of political differences in Canada. There are also discernable differences between the Liberal and Conservative parties approaches to relations with Aboriginal nations. Public statements indicate that the Liberal provincial government is at least somewhat inclined toward recognizing grievances. For instance, Brant County Liberal MP Lloyd St. Amand made public efforts at contextualization: "I know enough about the background issues of land claims generally to say the level of impatience and frustration is understandable and, frankly, justifiable. This and other land claims should have been dealt with well before now. Unfortunately, the manifestation of that frustration [the occupation] is getting the lion's share of the public attention."[73] Conservative representatives for Haldimand County – Member of Provincial Parliament Toby Barrett and MP Finley – as well as Conservative Minister Jim Prentice are more brusque. Echoing Harper's earlier brush-off, Barrett decries "putting political sensitivities before the law": "I oppose negotiating until the rule of law is restored."[74]

Political differences at Six Nations are also alive and well and are publicly acknowledged as such. The conflict between the Elected Band Council and the Confederacy Council, for instance, is well known and publicized. In the early days of the reclamation, however, the Elected Band Council sent a letter to Prentice and Ontario Minister Responsible for Aboriginal Affairs David Ramsay requesting that the Department of Indian and Northern Affairs recognize the lead of the Haudenosaunee Confederacy Council in this matter and placing itself in a supporting role.[75] In practical terms, this request meant that Chiefs Allen MacNaughton and Leroy Hill, who had stepped up as Confederacy spokespersons, would become the official representatives for

Six Nations in the negotiations. However, Elected Band Chief David General continued to have a voice at the discussions, and opinions varied as to the level of support for the respective councils.

For many, though not all, at Six Nations, support for the Confederacy Council or the Elected Band Council goes back to the issue of sovereignty. Initial spokespersons for the reclamation and the on-the-ground protesters – especially Janie Jamieson and Hazel Hill – are avid Confederacy Council supporters who view the Elected Band Council as colluding with the *Indian Act* and policies of assimilation.[76] Hill has attributed any "internal governance issues" to the legacy of the imposed elected system, which she referred to as attempted cultural genocide.[77] She believes that most Six Nations people support the Confederacy Council, but she also acknowledges division on the issue. She argues that the people of Six Nations made a clear choice for the Confederacy Council during the police raid on 20 April 2006, when "we took back our land from another forced invasion initiated by the Crown, and we put the Confederacy Council in the lead to deal with our lands and our treaties."[78] David General, the elected band chief at the time, periodically objected to the inclusion of many of Six Nations' perspectives in negotiations.[79] He was replaced as the elected band chief in November 2007. His successor, Bill Montour, at least initially favoured a relationship between the Confederacy and the Elected Band Councils according to which the Confederacy Council would be responsible for eight points of jurisdiction: the Great Law of Peace and the Haudenosaunee Constitution, lands, treaties, international relations, citizenship and membership, the installation of Confederacy Council chiefs, the preservation of the ceremonies, and justice and law. The Elected Band Council would address "administrative aspect[s] of community life," he said, but he did not intend to sit at the negotiating table as a spokesperson.[80]

Canadian representatives often construct Haudenosaunee political conflict differently, blaming negotiation failures on "internal governance issues" at Six Nations. Indeed, the imposed political structure has caused confusion and dissent both within and outside of Six Nations. Narratives presented by the Department of Justice also imply that the current composition of Haudenosaunee people at the Grand River reserve is somehow inauthentic because some who eventually followed Brant to the Grand River settlement had chosen to remain neutral instead of fighting for the British and because his followers also included a number of non-Aboriginal Loyalists.[81] Governments play key roles in the categorization of indigenous people and in the tying of identities to land and resource rights in racialized ways, fixing boundaries "not only by processes of political mobilization but [also] by the places of recognition that others provide."[82] Neither "side" in this dispute over land expresses uniform opinions or views. Yet as Six Nations academic Theresa McCarthy explains, racist undertones often emerge when "characteristics of diversity in general are coded differently in reference to Aboriginal peoples ... Mainstream representations of difference reflect 'good citizenship' in Ottawa, while these are interpreted as 'disunity' in Aboriginal contexts."[83] As Oren Lyons has put it, "no one, for example, seems to seriously argue that the United States ceased to exist during or because of the Civil War."[84] Although ongoing colonial efforts to assimilate Aboriginal people have been far from a success, cultural fragmentation has occurred, resulting in a sometimes uncomfortable mixture of Aboriginality and Eurocentrism.[85] McCarthy, citing a caller to a Six Nations' radio show, points out that discord in challenging circumstances is unsurprising:

> The reservation ... is no different than any group ... Whatever fears, or loves, or likes, or ... little flocking togethers of birds-of-a-feather, or whatever it is that MAKES people split into groups – those same things cause splits within the reservation. Maybe Indians are THE most splittable people. Our land has been split. Our tribes have been split. Our culture split. Our beliefs split. Our laws split. Our thoughts, hopes, and decisions, then, have a nice long history of forks in the road. Some of the non-Indian roads have brought gladness and some have brought a crushing of hope. So there's lots of distrust.[86]

I do not wish to paraphrase McCarthy's concise insights on the subject of "legal" arrangements for First Nations' governance:

> When Aboriginal diversity confounds homogenous assumptions entrenched in legislation, i.e, the Indian Act, mainstream interpretations tend to emphasize "disunity," intrinsic weakness, and inadequacy. It is rarely understood that the criteria for "membership" and for leadership in Aboriginal communities are legislatively imposed and far from equitable. Nevertheless the mainstream political strategy often accelerates public disdain and resentment, reaffirming the authority and superiority of dominant ideologies and political systems. This "playing up of differences" creates and cyclically reinforces the impression that Native peoples are incompetent and incapable of self-determination.[87]

Respect for diversity is a crucial part of Haudenosaunee culture, as was demonstrated even in the formation of the Haudenosaunee Confederacy and its governance structures, which allowed for autonomy within interdependence. However, structures such as the Elected Band Council imposed in 1924 included no provisions that would foster political parties – for instance, they left reserve communities with the sole option of overthrow in cases of intractable differences. And, as McCarthy explains, because the federal government only recognized the Elected Band Council (until the reclamation, at least), the stakes are high.

McCarthy, a Haudenosaunee academic who grew up in Caledonia, turns the lens onto her childhood community, describing several "factions" that have aligned themselves at various points along the spectrum from approval to disgust of Six Nations and the occupation at Douglas Creek Estates (often treated as one and the same). She points out that no one would ever ask whether the existence of conflicting groups points to alarming cultural disunity in Caledonia or Canada or calls the future of either into question. Yet such factions are likely to be validated by "mitigating factors, like fear, ignorance, confusion, and ironically frustration and inconvenience" and even used to "excuse some Caledonians' racist outbursts, as well as other expressions of aggressive and violent behaviour."[88] At the same time, the existence of "external stressors" is not used to explain political dissidence within the Haudenosaunee. Instead, it is implied that they are "victims of their own making" – part of a trend toward associating Iroquois factionalism with "primitive politics and underdeveloped 'weak states.'"[89] In 2008, federal negotiator Ron Doering published an explanation as to why negotiations in Caledonia had failed to produce resolution. In it, he implicitly blamed the delays on divisions at Six Nations. However, McCarthy says, though settlement and intercommunity healing remain distant, Six Nations is focusing not only on outsider confirmation and recognition but also on the internal significance of the land reclamation to its national identity. The conflict once again proves to be more than a dispute over the right to shape geographies – its significance for political relationships within Six Nations *and* within Canada – as well as between the two – is colossal.

At any rate, leaving aside arguments that Six Nations' political tensions had caused problems, federal representatives' initial abstraction from the dispute significantly delayed progress in negotiations. MP Finley's "Caledonia update" of 11 July 2006 (still "current" on her website in spring 2007) indicated her detachment: "Thank you to everyone who has contacted my office regarding Caledonia this week," she wrote. "Discussions at the negotiating table are progressing well, and all parties are encouraged by the co-operative manner in which the discussions are being carried out. I have every reason to believe these talks will continue in a productive fashion and I will continue to update you as soon as new information becomes available."[90]

At one point, relations between federal and provincial governments on the issue deteriorated so badly that Prentice cancelled a scheduled Ottawa meeting with Ramsay, in response to Premier Dalton McGuinty's attempted shaming of the federal government the day before.[91] Ramsay issued a press release expressing his disappointment at "another example of the federal government failing to live up to its obligations to the people of Ontario."[92] He pointed out the federal government's "too slow" pace of settling land claims, and he foregrounded the occupation by referring to the Caledonia "situation." His characterization of "the people of Ontario" was unlikely to include the deviant Six Nations along with the long-suffering Caledonians. Chief Allen MacNaughton pointed out that the public squabble between the provincial and federal governments was causing still further delays in the Haudenosaunee's two-hundred-year wait for justice.[93] Mayor Trainer agreed that Canada's behaviour was childish, but, even so, her account cast Caledonians as the victims: "We're in the middle. We're the ones suffering. I'd like them to stop acting like children. I wish they would quit holding Caledonia residents as hostages. It's pretty frustrating."[94] Eventually, the federal government agreed to take a leadership role in the negotiations.[95]

To Six Nations, the federal disregard flew in the face of the nation-to-nation relationship that it was insisting on – the Canadian government, in right of the British Crown, was responsible for taking up the other end of the Covenant Chain. The slap in the face was even more painful since Six Nations felt that the broken promises and the abandonment of this relationship had caused the need for the reclamation in the first place. As Dawn Smith explained, "I'm not surprised. I am disappointed the Canadian government has failed our people again. This is a federal matter. It has no business in a provincial court. They have no jurisdiction. They need a history lesson."[96] Chief Leroy Hill recalled Six Nations' continual assertions of legal and cultural sovereignty over the years:

> We are not British subjects, nor Canadian. We have a birthright to live freely under our own laws and customs. This is also guaranteed by treaty with your Crown. We have never abandoned this birthright nor do we intend to. The British knew this and respected this, as did the Canadian Government in my Grandfather's time as a chief. For peace, mutual respect and friendship to be maintained between us, Canadians need to realize that it is an international crime to deny a nation of its right to home-rule. This is not something new; we have always adhered to this and shall continue to ... In the 1920s we sent one of our Chiefs (on our own passport) named Deskaheh to look overseas.[97]

Six Nations representatives constantly frame the relationship with Canada in terms of alliance and point out that much of Canada was, in fact, built on Native lands and monies. As Hazel Hill exclaims, "the TRUTH is, Six Nation's Territory is not part of Canada. CANADA IS PART OF SIX NATIONS TERRITORY!!!!"[98] And in the words of Leroy Hill, "the issue of sovereignty and dollars go hand in hand ... Six Nations believed our allies (Canada) when they said they would be responsible trustees of our monies ... In between the 1800s and early 1900s, Six Nations went from being in a sound financial and independent state to being dependent on Canada." He describes how Six Nations' money was taken without authorization to invest in projects such as the Bank of Montreal, McGill University, the University of Toronto (King's College), the Law Society of Upper Canada, the Montreal Turnpike, and the Welland Canal.[99] At the gates of Douglas Creek Estates, signs depict Six Nations soldiers fighting in various Canadian wars.[100] As MacNaughton explains, "our people paid a heavy price in these wars. We need to understand why events in Caledonia happened because it's a long history. It seems to me that when we were no longer militarily useful, we were marginalized."[101] Over and over, Six Nations people emphasize the need for Canada to uphold its end of the treaty relationship and point out the urgency of the task in light of continuing appropriation of disputed land.[102]

Shortly after the April 2006 OPP raid, in a powerful moment of history repeating itself, Six Nations Clan Mother Doreen Silversmith visited the United Nations in Geneva to emphasize Six Nations' grievances and sovereignty. The escalation of these attempts at international diplomacy and recognition signals again the importance of the reclamation in tying land to sovereignty. Her statement, delivered on 1 May 2006, requested international support for, and mediation at, the negotiations from the "friends and allies" of a sovereign Six Nations.[103] It also linked long-standing government policies to the need for the reclamation, calling for "businesslike" practices from an entity that, founded on *native land* as it was, had no right to call itself a nation-state.

MacNaughton asserted the Confederacy Council's support for the reclamation, but he also took pains to explain that negotiations would only be productive if attention was actually paid to what had caused the protest in the first place: not only the development of yet another piece of disputed land but also a long-standing dismissal of Six Nations' land rights and autonomy in general, which was at the root of the protest.[104] He had addressed Canada early on: "The Confederacy Council is not an interest group or a splinter group. We are calling on Canada to open talks with the Confederacy Council."[105] Canada's acceptance of the Confederacy Council's lead role could be read as tacit acknowledgment of Six Nations' autonomy, since the Confederacy Council continuously demanded nation-to-nation negotiations. However, initial statements regarding "the need to recognize the

Confederacy" were vague.[106] A representative for the Ministry of Indian and Northern Affairs later indicated that the decision to acknowledge the authority of the Confederacy Council was linked to the pressure of the occupation: "It's a volatile situation and we're being flexible by dealing with the hereditary council."[107] In a pre-raid letter, Prentice linked the potential for success in the negotiations to the withdrawal of the protesters: "I understand that, as of last night, the lead responsibility for causing this to happen now lies with the Confederacy."[108]

The negotiation framework that was eventually agreed upon recommitted the parties to "the relationship long ago established between the Haudenosaunee/Six Nations and the Crown. This relationship shall be guided by the principles of Respect, Peace, and Friendship, as per the Silver Covenant Chain and the Two Row Wampum."[109] However, the quarrel between Canada and Ontario re-emerged from time to time in calls from Ontario for federal compensation.[110] The jurisdictional battle over the reclamation effort marked Douglas Creek Estates as part of Canadian space to which the Haudenosaunee had no real rights, which, in turn, contoured the dispute in terms of Canadian versions of history and relationship with First Nations. While differences of opinion within Canadian government circles were treated as normal and acceptable, political differences within Six Nations were consistently indexed as a marker of disunity and as a significant impediment to resolution, further erasing Haudenosaunee legal and political legitimacy. Conversations at and about Caledonia clearly demonstrate how Canadian nation-building projects and identities have been reinforced by – indeed, predicated on – these deletions of First Nations' cultural and political rights – deletions that began in colonial relationships of old and persist in colonial relationships of today. If Six Nations is to be recognized as a nation rather than as a relic minority, Canada will need to manage land with consideration of Six Nations' priorities as well.

The Caledonia story gives lie to the term "post-colonialism." As Marie Battiste explains, "indigenous thinkers use the term 'postcolonial' to describe a symbolic strategy for shaping a desirable future, not an existing reality. The term is an aspirational practice, goal, or idea."[111] Colonial power past and present operates through discursive patterns as well as official juridical and political channels.[112] The story of self-interested settlers and remote governments is as true today as it was in the past. Difficulties managing the frontiers of development and settlement continue, as does differential access to the law. Technologies of governance both then and now include military might, capital's interest in access to land, the privileging of Western priorities, and the management of bodies and land by counting, designating, and mapping.[113] And colonialism's monologue joins it all together, telling a tale that is so different from the one related by First Nations that it is literally hard to believe they are discussing the same events.

Given that the Canadian imaginary is dogged by contradiction and circumscribed in opposition to perceived and/or actual Aboriginal identities, as we have seen in the previous chapter, the stories that are told by and about Canada and Six Nations will necessarily clash, providing artillery for this battle for legitimacy and sovereignty. Access to legitimated discursive space, however, is held principally by mainstream Canada, as the recognized and accepted authority to dictate the parameters of histories and negotiations. In so far as one's identity largely prescribes the history with which one identifies, identity and history are, in the end, the same thing – so how can a single "truth" be decided?

Perhaps at this juncture, I can only describe how "truth" generally has been decided. However, just as the current ideas of "nation" must be constantly renegotiated and just as the right to own and manage the land itself is disputed, so the prerogative to control spaces of accepted truth and history does not go uncontested. Six Nations negotiators at Caledonia assert that their ways of seeing and understanding history are just as valid as those of mainstream Canadians: they contest Canadian versions of the treaty relationship between the Haudenosaunee and the Crown; demand recognition of their own systems of law; and call for acknowledgment of their visions for justice, compensation, and ways of managing the land.

As we saw in the previous chapter with Correia's study of the incongruities at Oka, Aboriginal people's rights to define their identity and history are being deliberately challenged on all fronts. Rewritings of old, familiar stories are ongoing. For instance, Captain James Cook's account of his 1778 arrival in Nootka Sound on the west coast of Turtle Island highlights peace, order, and mutual understanding for future trading, yet ethnographers, sailors, and Native peoples describe fear, miscommunication, and violence. Cook was clearly impacted by his self-image as a representative of European civilization and agendas in non-European space. These "common sense" accounts, says Daniel Clayton, "raise questions about how and why certain representations are taken to be factual and true, while others get buried, ignored, or dismissed."[114]

Similarly, scholars scrutinizing Canadian–First Nations treaties have noted that while Canada holds fast to agreements in which vast swathes of land were apparently surrendered in exchange for tiny reserves (such as the purported general surrender along the Grand River that the government alleges Six Nations agreed to in 1841), the terms of those treaties are hotly contested. Aboriginal people viewed treaties as opportunities to shape independent economic futures by securing rights to traditional livelihoods and to the management of lands and resources. Yet Canada used the treaty process to exercise power through the *Indian Act* and the Department of Indian Affairs.[115] Interpretation problems resulted from linguistic differences as well as from discrepancies between oral and written testimonies. Often, only brief summaries of provisions were listed in the written treaty, and, as a result, contemporary Native understandings regularly do not correspond to "official" versions.[116] Since treaties had little to do with the actual areas of traditional lands and a lot to do with the political and legal control of settlement,[117] this discrepancy is not particularly surprising. Perhaps most important, Canadian law does not view treaties as international agreements between sovereign peoples, despite assertions to the contrary by nations such as the Haudenosaunee. This position is rationalized either by the argument that Aboriginal peoples (then and/or now) were not civilized and/or organized enough to qualify as sovereign or that they had "lost" their sovereignty through some process "such as the good providence of being 'discovered.'"[118]

Written texts of treaties represent only the government of Canada's understandings. Equally, as Sharon Venne explains, when elders talk about history they are referring only to the jurisdiction and political rights of "our own people" and to the desire to have places to live without interference by settlers. Reserve lands were (and are not) seen as lands given to the First Nations by the Crown or the government, and treaties were often viewed as sharing and loan agreements rather than as sales.[119] Hypocrisy is rife in refusals to acknowledge oral history and Aboriginal perspectives: "In the Eurocentric academic community, history is validated if two separate sources confirm the same information. The information passed on from the Elders has been validated over and over again."[120] Geographic accounts of pre-colonial, colonial, and post-colonial land rights rely overwhelmingly on European knowledge frameworks, leaving little room for Aboriginal views except in reactive response.[121] Dale Turner echoes the call for incorporation of Aboriginal perspectives: "The Canadian governments have been able to impose their interpretation of the treaties on Aboriginal peoples at least since the time of confederation."[122] As we have seen in the negotiations over Douglas Creek Estates, these processes continue to occur through daily discursive practices of categorization and dismissal.

Linda Tuhiwai Smith mounts another expansive critique of the ways in which history, sovereignty, and land have been claimed by the colonizers.[123] Among others, she flags these ideas as problematic: that a universal history exists; that facts are innocent and speak for themselves (that is, historians simply find them and put them together); and that history is about progress from primitivism to civilization and rationality. She notes that indigenous attempts to reclaim land, language, knowledge and sovereignty have usually involved contested accounts of the past by colonizers and colonized. These have occurred in the courts, before various commissions, tribunals and official enquiries, in the media, in Parliament, in bars and on talkback radio. In these situations contested histories do not exist in the same cultural framework as they do when tribal or clan histories, for example, are being debated within the indigenous community itself. They are not simply struggles over "facts" and "truth"; the rules by which these struggles take place are never clear (other than that we as the indigenous community know they are going to be stacked against us); and we are not the final arbiters of what really counts as the truth.[124]

She also warns against the commonly held indigenous belief (expressed by many Six Nations) that once the "truth" is revealed it will prove that past events were wrong or illegal, forcing the courts and the government to make reparations:

We believe that history is also about justice, that understanding history will enlighten our decisions about the future. *Wrong.* History is also about power. In fact, history is mostly about power. It is the story of the powerful and how they became powerful, and then how they use their power to keep them in positions in which they can continue to dominate others. It is because of this relationship with power that we have been excluded, marginalized, and "Othered." In this sense history is not important for indigenous peoples because a thousand accounts of the "truth" will not alter the "fact" that indigenous peoples are still marginal and do not possess the power to transform history into justice.[125]

Her mistrust of "facts" and the "truth" reverberates in the words of Jake Thomas. During a public recitation of the Great Law of Peace at Six Nations, he explained: "I don't believe in books. Maybe some, but not all. I don't want to get carried away either in the books, cause I know it's not true. Cause it is only one man that wrote that."[126] Haudenosaunee academic Deborah Jean Doxtator clarifies similar issues, pointing out the incompatibility between Native and European-based ideas of history. Despite attempts to "integrate" Native perspectives and voices, the history of Canada continues to be grounded in European deeds and actions.[127] Native people, she says, are viewed as having "myth" but not history; their knowledge systems are seen as tainted with normative and spiritual elements. Indeed, Haudenosaunee knowledge prioritizes neither the partition of "past" from "present" (it views change as accumulative), nor the separation of what Westerners view as different forms of knowledge. Furthermore, European-based histories are equally informed by cultural myths, and although there is some recognition that perspectives on the past change over time, European history still relies on the assigning of people to groups, the carving of time into blocks, and the separation of "myth" from "historical observation."[128] Denigration of indigenous record keeping manifested itself in, for instance, the failure by seventeenth-century record keepers to recognize that wampum belts and pictographs comprised substantial recording systems with complicated histories. Oral histories continue to be largely misrecognized today, as Western historians try to distill from them information that fits more closely with what they consider knowledge. In the process, they distort what these narratives actually say.[129]

The combination of faith in Canadian prerogatives and a refusal to acknowledge indigenous perspectives has profound implications for negotiations of various kinds between Aboriginal nations and Canadian governments. Of course, the motives of Aboriginal and non-Aboriginal parties in disputes over land and political recognition are vastly different. As Michael Coyle wrote in a report for the Ipperwash Inquiry:

> In a situation where one party is a defendant, has access to much greater financial and legal resources than the other party, and views the costs of not settling as largely intangible, there will be a reduced motivation to settle the claim quickly. (There will also be little incentive for that party to submit to third-party views on disputes over the law.) This will be true at the institutional level regardless of the goodwill and dedication of the individuals involved. Indeed, in its submission on land claims to the Indian Commission of Ontario, the province acknowledged that the prospect of deferring settlements creates a disincentive for governments to settle land claims in a timely manner.[130]

Although First Nations often turn to legal strategies in lodging claims – their assertions have bases in both Canadian and Aboriginal law – these can merely reaffirm the logic of non-Aboriginal treaty visions. Dale Turner makes an impassioned plea for indigenous intellectuals to engage the political and legal discourses of the state as "word warriors" and indigenous philosophers in order to convince the dominant culture of the legitimacy of their assertions of sovereignty, rights, and nationhood.[131] He believes that it is crucial to articulate and stand up for uniquely indigenous ways of knowing, seeing the world, and reforming Aboriginal–mainstream relations. Since it is predominantly non-Aboriginal judges and politicians who have the ultimate power to protect and enforce Aboriginal land rights and autonomy, he feels that rights must be justified in ways that these people can recognize and understand.

Turner explicates the task of overcoming competing histories and dictated terms of negotiations, but other Aboriginal philosophers see things differently. Tom Deer, a Six Nations knowledge holder, responds to the spectre of conflict over representational ownership and competition over knowledge with these candid words: "It's ok that we aren't really interested in the same questions anyways."[132] In my view, this statement effortlessly recontextualizes the rivalry over stories by relocating the importance of "historical knowledge" in epistemology rather than in ontology – that is, because indigenous and Canadian "ways of knowing" are fundamentally different, the "facts" themselves should not even really compete on the same playing field. But because Canada is always the home team in "legal" disputes, Aboriginal perspectives are discarded before the game even starts.

Legitimating History

The contests outlined in the preceding paragraphs have played crucial roles in the clash along the Grand. The rights to describe history and to have one's "truth" accepted are immeasurably critical to this dispute over land. In seeking control over the land, both Canada and Six Nations have staked claims to more than physical territory at Caledonia, though statements from Six Nations explaining the centrality of land to identity, sovereignty, and culture express this much more explicitly than do the Canadian claims to territory and managerial rights. These statements amount to central precepts for many, if not all, of the original peoples of Turtle Island, who view Aboriginal title as something given by the Creator and as dependent on a continuing connection to the land – as something deeply linked to identity, spirituality, and self-determination. Land negotiations are more than disputes over papers signifying "ownership"; they are located firmly in the context of relationships with other people. To them, Aboriginal land title does not require definition or justification by the Canadian legal or constitutional system because its source is external to these systems. As we heard from Hazel Hill, many Aboriginal people argue that the legitimacy of the Canadian state is called into question by colonial rationalizations that fail to recognize Aboriginal title.[133]

Indeed, the failures of the Canadian courts to protect First Nations' lands and sacred sites are often viewed as attacks on the people themselves – attacks that put Canada's "national soul" at stake, for "peoples, like persons, may bleed to death from one large or a thousand small cuts."[134] When negotiating treaties in the past, and when processing claims today, First Nations have always focused on retaining land rights in the face of settler and government incursions, so essential are those rights to their national and economic future.[135] Opposition from Aboriginal groups tends to be galvanized by plans for resource and land development. The struggles at Oka, Gustafsen Lake, Ipperwash, and (I would argue) Caledonia have all been "sacredized" in the sense that they have been intended to address not only the ownership of land but also the responsibilities that Aboriginal peoples assume toward it.[136] Although Western development frameworks are more likely to protect land on the basis of cultural importance if it physically manifests significance in the form of archaeological remains,[137] the commonly understood concept of sacredness can provide a discursive bridge between cultures.[138] This connection may have provided extra motivation for Six Nations representatives at Douglas Creek Estates to make frequent mention of the spiritual significance of land.

To many Aboriginal peoples such as the Haudenosaunee, opportunities to reorder relationships and gain recognition and security as independent nations are at stake in disputes over land.[139] A profound sense of identity is bound to the land. As Bonita Lawrence explains, identity dictated by colonial powers, and the resulting regulation and encroachment, have continuing implications for Aboriginal communities that are trying to set boundaries between their small remaining territories and the surrounding settler communities.[140] Regulatory systems such as the *Indian Act* and the *Places to Grow Act* are more than "a set of policies to be repealed, or even a genocidal scheme in which we can simply choose not to believe."[141] Rather, the *Indian Act* is "a classificatory system produc[ing] ways of thinking – a grammar – that embeds itself in every attempt to change it."[142] Euro-Canadian participation in Aboriginal affairs has often been interpreted as assistance in a relationship of dependence by Euro-Canadians and as interference with sovereign nations by Aboriginal peoples. Mary Becker concludes that by acting *for* rather than *with* the Haudenosaunee, the government of Canada before and after Confederation opened the door to protest.[143] Theresa McCarthy notes the same idea in her recent research at Six Nations Territory: "Regardless of awareness or citation of colonial implications – what was consistently expressed to me ... is a sense that the people want to retain autonomy, responsibility and ownership over the resolution of these issues in their community. What seemed to be most clear is their wish to do so without state sanctioned paternalism or interference."[144]

As part of the effort to define political identity and shape political space, Haudenosaunee philosophers Oren Lyons and John Mohawk have inverted the relational lens, pointing to the influence of native Turtle Islanders on the development of the democratic tradition in Western culture.[145] Explaining that "history is still being written in the passions of the times and written by the 'winners,'"[146] Lyons emphasizes that most people see only the tip of North America's "iceberg" of history, ignoring the mass of pre-Contact Native culture to be found beneath. Nor do many realize that colonists who ended up in Native society (fleeing indentured servitude, captured in raids, or rescued from the forest) rarely returned to white society when given the opportunity. Lyons hypothesizes that they preferred Indian egalitarianism and participatory democracy to the hierarchical societies of colonial America. Still, indigenous people today struggle to gain the respect as equal, self-determined societies that would be gained through recognition of "the fundamental right of peoples and their societies to be different."[147]

Canadian historian and philosopher James Tully cites two pivotal elements of Haudenosaunee culture in his appeal for mutual political recognition and respect.[148] He points to the Peacemaker of the Haudenosaunee Confederacy as an early practitioner of the conventions of mutual recognition, continuity, and consent in forming diverse governments, and he views the Two Row Wampum as a symbol of co-operation and autonomy with broad significance for the potential for interaction and independence between First Nations and settler societies. He joins Aboriginal thinkers such as John Borrows and Dale Turner in calling for a reinstatement of the Two Row Wampum's principles of peace and friendship through separation and integration.[149] As cited so often in conversations about Kanonhstaton, the Haudenosaunee have long asserted that they are allies, not subjects, of the British Crown and its successor state, though these declarations have been ignored by Canada and the United Nations.[150] As Tully puts it, Aboriginal demands at the United Nations for recognition as "nations" with "the right of self-determination," for example, essentially consist of arguments that "the prevailing criteria and reference of these terms ought to be revised to include them, rather than to exclude them, as they have done for the last five hundred years."[151]

Aboriginal struggles for recognition of distinct identities and for the land on which to maintain their societies take many forms, including the now much-recognized strategy of physical occupation. Linda Tuhiwai Smith, who focuses on decolonizing knowledge and research, has much to say about less tangible but no less important strategies for regaining control over identity. She calls for a renaming of colonized indigenous space since the act of naming lays powerful claims to place and land as well as to the legitimacy of certain ways of seeing and representing the world.[152] When the colonizers brought the land under their control by claiming it, mapping it, draining its swamps, and diverting its waterways, then "giving back" reservations to the peoples who once possessed all of it, they also christened it – a move that Smith says "was probably as powerful ideologically as changing the land."[153] Six Nations protesters who began referring to Douglas Creek Estates as Kanonhstaton were more than trying to halt development: they were seeking to shape space by naming it, thereby claiming land and sovereignty for future generations. "We won't actually meet that seventh generation," Lyons says, "but our collective actions will determine the kind of life they have and whether or not they can be all we hope they can be."[154]

Mohawk intellectual Taiaiake Alfred views Native nationalism as consisting of a stable and persistent core along with peripheral elements adapted as needed.[155] For example, it utilizes certain concepts, such as state-like nationalism, in order to challenge Euro-American institutional hegemony more effectively. He views the relationship between Native people and settlers as having four overlapping phases: an initial phase of co-operation; a co-optive period during which institutional regimes usurped indigenous control; a confrontation stage of ideological, intellectual, political, and military challenges to colonialism; and, finally, if the state had failed to change its ways, crisis and a reorientation of the Native–newcomer relationship.[156] He sees latent nationalism changing to "revival nationalism" as the co-optive aspects of Native–settler relationships become more obvious and as significant events catalyze change. For Six Nations, I suggest, the land reclamation is just such an event. Alfred describes his Mohawk community, Kahnawake, and other Iroquois communities such as Six Nations, as having asserted nationalism especially strongly because the Iroquois cultural complex and the Confederacy offered particularly sound alternatives to the Canadian state.[157]

Projecting Identity

The prism of cultural difference refracts struggles over rights, joining "the politics of recognition and the politics of redistribution."[158] Six Nations must also contend with identities that are not of its own making. Indeed, public representatives fight for legitimate discursive space in territorial contests everywhere. Terre Satterfield's study of a conflict over the fate of Oregon's forests, carried out very publicly between "loggers" and "environmentalists," uncovered many knots within and between projected identities. In a description that could apply equally to Caledonia, she explains:

> Amidst the struggle to maintain a voice in decisions about an already depleted land base, some activists from both groups are visionary, some are vindictive, some are prejudicial, some are none of these. Moreover, Oregon's loggers and environmentalists are ingenious beings. They invent, elaborate, and portray effectively their respective group identities in relation to key topics and practices in American society. They draw from and

play off the popular ideologies of democracy, science, cultural authenticity, and the normative rules for emotional comportment. Their varying discourses and behaviours are acutely sensitive to the power of these enduring cultural discourses and yet also fully attuned to harnessing them in order to promote their own versions of the cultural world of human-environment relations.[159]

Individuals and groups not only orient themselves to one another but also articulate their discursive positions with respect to ongoing societal conversations and broader identities. Satterfield discusses the links between identity formation and collective action, pointing out that "new social movements often come into being because a group's identity is regarded as threatened."[160] This is certainly true in the case of Six Nations, and many of the themes exhibited in the Oregon conflict bear striking resemblance to those in Caledonia. For instance, the ways in which emotion played into the debate(s) often marginalized those seen as "emotionally out of control, thus justifying the 'discounting' of their concerns."[161] The effects of legitimated power on perception mean that activists are often dismissed as irrational, while government representatives with equally strong views are respected. Although excessive emotion is generally viewed with distaste in North America, passion – just a hair's breadth away – is often positively perceived. It is difficult to say, then, whether Hazel Hill's passionate – or excessively emotional, depending on who is asked – updates from the site are "good" or "bad" for the reclaimers' cause in Caledonia. (It could also be asked whether she is particularly concerned about this question, and my impression is that she is not.) Satterfield observed that the environmentalists in Oregon were less concerned with restraining their anger – an approach made permissible by their social position as educated, middle-class activists vis-à-vis relatively stigmatized loggers. In this scenario, I hear echoes of Caledonian discourses. Though it was viewed as entirely acceptable and excusable for Caledonia residents to indulge in highly emotional, even racist rants about the effects of the protest on their town, Six Nations protesters expressing strong feelings about their desire for justice and the settlement of their long outstanding claims were viewed with distaste. Satterfield explains that "in responding emotionally to an event, here and elsewhere, people are staking a claim as to how things are, and they act to reassert that reality or socio-moral position."[162] At Caledonia, we hear federal negotiator Ron Doering fearing openly that the dispute will never be resolved, while Six Nations representatives talk of settler societies' fear of the truth. Both sides utilize moral shock language ("Can you believe what they did?") to kindle indignation and claim moral territory.[163] And archetypal themes of "individual freedom" and "economic liberty" are accessed in complex ways with regard to the "rule of law" and property rights by both Canada and Six Nations over the terrain of Douglas Creek Estates.[164]

Haudenosaunee protesters must also contend with the legacy of "noble savage" discourses, which often hold Aboriginal people to impossible and reductionist yardsticks of authenticity, requiring, for instance, that they place everything second to land, ignoring other necessities such as food, shelter, and jobs to the extent that these interfere with their ideals. Meanwhile, Satterfield says, Aboriginal activists have "wisely, strategically, and sometimes ironically exploited for their benefit Western assumptions about noble non-Western peoples."[165] Lyons' heartfelt appeals for consideration of the current environmental crisis and the future of the unborn generations, then, are likely to be met at least with recognition, if not approval.[166] To Alfred, however, the essentialist portrayal of a conflict between "unbroken tradition and continuity with the past" and "conscious manipulation of traditions and cultural inventions in the emergence of nationalist ideologies" is a false one. "Ideologies/peoples/nations/cultures ... of course change – and they do not."[167] This does not mean, however, that indigenous activists' concern for the environment, and sometimes seeming unwillingness to compromise, as in Caledonia, should be met with cynicism. For instance, Rodney Bobiwash cites a walkout of indigenous people from the UN Working Group on Indigenous People, accompanied by a statement emphasizing that partnerships must recognize indigenous decision-making processes, world views, and assertions of land rights as equally valid.[168] Indigenous peoples have for centuries had to adapt to processes laid down by colonial governments, he explains. The demand for recognition of indigenous ways of making decisions should not be cynically dismissed as a power ploy. Instead, it should be recognized as crucial to moving away from the disempowerment that has led to confrontation in Canada and in many other countries.[169] Aboriginal protesters such as those working to assert Six Nations' land rights are at the same time working to frame demands for territory and autonomy in recognizable terms. For instance, when they frame injustices in terms of the denial of rights rather than focusing exclusively on political economy or identity politics, Aboriginal activists are utilizing a well-known "master frame" and gaining commonality with protesters from other movements. That said, William Carroll and Robert Ratner note that "the fulcrum of contemporary Aboriginal politics is the conjoint struggle for land claims and self-government."[170]

It is a history of sovereignty: the land at Caledonia is a pivot on which Canada and Six Nations have been articulating differing views of their relationship both past and present, beginning with the history of treaties between the Haudenosaunee and settlers and continuing with present-day jurisdictional issues. Six Nations' version of the story focuses on continuing sovereignty, legitimate political diversity, and the vital link between territory and national identity. Canada's account assumes authority over Six Nations and other "Indian bands," portrays internal political disagreement within Canada and Six Nations as being somehow different, and attempts to separate the issues of relationship and territory. Confounding, yet central, to all of this is the distance between each party's vision of what constitutes "truth" and how legitimacy is determined in the first place. The negotiations that began in 2006 and that five years later are still dragging on will go nowhere without real acknowledgment of what is at stake.

In Search of Justice   5

Negotiations had begun in earnest about six weeks after the start of the occupation, two weeks after the Ontario Provincial Police's (OPP) raid. Promisingly, the parties involved – the federal, provincial, and Six Nations governments – signed a negotiating framework committing them to dialogue according to honourable relationships established previously between the Haudenosaunee and the Crown.[1] However, it was soon painfully clear that discussions could not possibly be limited to the question of Kanonhstaton's "ownership." Canada and Six Nations had fundamentally differing ideas about what a just resolution of this dispute might look like and, perhaps more important, how it might be reached. In what follows, I argue that Canadian conceptions of justice have been presented as more rational and legitimate than those of Six Nations. Racialized naturalizations of justice are perhaps most evident in the different ways that the Canadian government has treated the parties directly involved: Caledonia, Henco, and Six Nations. More broadly, however, the Haudenosaunee were once again being placed in a discursive space that reduced fundamentally different ways of being to "cultural concerns." They were being tolerated with polite detachment rather than fully engaged with, and they were often viewed as impediments to negotiations, which focused on documented "evidence" constituting "facts." For its part, Six Nations argued that the records kept by the Crown were not necessarily complete and accurate. Furthermore, they added, the relationships and historical contexts that surrounded the events would have to be taken into account. In their view, moral and just resolution would have to address the injustices directly, which meant that settlement would need to consist primarily of the return of land.

From the start, attitudes toward negotiations differed. The Confederacy Council supported the reclamation and the negotiating process because, as Leroy Hill put it, "there is prosperity all around us ... yet we are running out of land for ourselves." The council believed that the federal government had the power to end the dispute in short order by taking the protesters and the negotiations seriously.[2] Many at Six Nations viewed the reclamation as a necessary protest after years of frustration. Provincial Minister Responsible for Aboriginal Affairs David Ramsay, meanwhile, asserted that "it's just unfortunate that a small group of people got impatient" and claimed that exploratory talks had been progressing under Dalton McGuinty's Liberal government.[3] The federal government likewise maintained that "progress" was under way with the Elected Band Council on some of Six Nations' more straightforward claims.[4] Former premier David Peterson, who had been involved as a kind of peacemaker, hoping to help reduce increasing tensions in Caledonia, explained:

> I can't guarantee timelines, can't guarantee success, [and] can't guarantee what the resolution will be. But we'll muck around and hopefully we can find something ... Everyone feels aggrieved, everyone feels their side is the victim and being taken advantage of. The genius here is to find common ground ... The reality is, this has been going on for 200 years, so we have to find something that everybody wins with, and I can't guarantee anything.[5]

Peterson sounded well intentioned, and his acknowledgment of the long-standing grievances was crucial, but this conception of success failed to recognize that justice may call for something other than a win-win-win scenario. Those at the negotiating table are supposed to talk and listen, learn from one another, and work together to address problems with a give-and-take approach. From such a process, outcomes cannot be predetermined. Peterson's claim of "no guarantees" served as a reminder that the status quo of unaddressed claims favoured Canada and not Six Nations. The government had chosen to enter negotiations, but it had the power to choose otherwise – as it had on 20 April 2006. Calls for "a solution that reflects the interests of the community of Caledonia, Six Nations, and the affected developer and builders" placed the three stakeholders on an even playing field, with their interests to be considered equally.[6]

The Confederacy Council had early on been designated the official representative for Six Nations in the negotiations. Ontario designated Jane Stewart, a politician originally hailing from Brantford, as its official representative; the federal government chose Barbara McDougall, an experienced lawyer and politician, with lawyer and administrator Ronald Doering assisting.[7] McDougall was mandated to develop a work plan "to address and resolve outstanding issues related to land claims and governance."[8] According to Ramsay, "this is more of an accounting of the land. Were they properly credited for the land as it was disposed of?"[9] This construction of the negotiations as a question of accounting ignores the possibility that Six Nations may not have surrendered the land at all, notwithstanding Canadian national narratives and official geographies. And the early appointment of a "fact finder" by the Department of Indian and Northern Affairs spoke volumes about its approach to the dispute. Both federal and local officials emphasized the need for authoritative "evidence": "We have to come to grips on the history part – what the claims are. Records are pretty spotty when you go back that far."[10]

The Confederacy Council negotiators expressed hopeful (or diplomatic) feelings that "there are some apparent concessions here. Governments are taking some accountability and are coming to the table in good faith ... We are going to keep up diplomacy, in adherence to the Great Law."[11] However, there was also considerable cynicism. According to Six Nations academic and historian Rick Hill, "it could be solved quickly if you looked at it creatively. But it's hard to have faith in a process when the people who say 'Trust us' are the ones who have deceived us over the years."[12] Spokesperson Hazel Hill emphasized the necessity of forcing Canada to the table:

> Hopefully, it will be the last time our people have to go through anything like this. The message to Canada is that it must now deal with the issue of our land and the trust that they have never been accountable for, it must honour our treaties, accept responsibility for its own abuses against our people, deal with the theft of our land and resources, and begin righting the wrongs in an acceptable time frame. The lands claim process designed by the government through the department of Indian affairs is a scam. The whole process is designed not to protect our interest in the land, but to continue to sell land that they deem "surplus crown land" (meaning any land that belongs to our people that they want or can use/sell) and no where in that process is it ever intended to return land, they only want to get out the cheque book and usually that is AFTER development. This is no longer acceptable and must be stopped![13]

Indeed, Premier McGuinty conflated advancement in the early negotiations with the "obvious progress" of the removal of the visible barricades that had been erected on Highway 6 and around the contested land.[14] A conciliatory gesture came in mid-May, when the Ontario government confirmed the imposition of an immediate moratorium halting any development on the Douglas Creek lands for a period of time to be agreed upon by the representatives of the Confederacy, Canada, and Ontario. However, the letter to Six Nations with the announcement also carried a warning: "In order for talks on Douglas Creek Estates and the long-term land grievance to proceed, we must see continued progress on removal of the barricades on the transportation corridors."[15] And a joint statement from Conservative Minister Jim Prentice and Ontario Minister Responsible for Aboriginal Affairs David Ramsay blamed the "tensions" in the community on the blockades that had been erected by Six Nations rather than on the unresolved land claims that had led to the protest, and he implied that the government's full attention would not be directed toward the table until Caledonia was safeguarded:

> There has been a commitment throughout that these talks will accelerate further as peace returns to the community ... We are asking that these blockades be removed as a matter of urgency in order that the source of tensions in the communities be eliminated. This will mean that all involved can focus their resources and efforts to the task of resolving the outstanding issues at the table.[16]

By all appearances, the path toward justice was winding and poorly marked. The slow pace of "progress," as defined earlier, was regularly lamented in the first months of the negotiations. Failing to acknowledge the decades that Six Nations had been waiting for its claims to be addressed, Haldimand Member of Provincial Parliament (MPP) Toby Barrett complained that "this snail's pace fails to reflect the urgency felt by all sides." He called for "a Premier who will act like a true CEO – one that will get the job done, rather than procrastinating for months."[17] By October, despite often lauding the importance of negotiation over litigation, Doering sounded distinctly threatening: "The alternative to reconciliation is to use some type of force. For my part, I'd rather negotiate than use some type of force."[18]

The issue of the ownership of Douglas Creek Estates had been relegated in July to one of four "side tables" reporting to the main negotiating table. (The other tables were "Public Education and Awareness," "Consultation," and "Archaeology and Appearance.")[19] However, beginning in the autumn of 2006, the parties began to trade narratives on the history of Kanonhstaton. These accounts were deeply revelatory of differing approaches to "facts" and "justice" and to land and landownership. In Six Nations' summary of its twenty-eight outstanding land claims, published by its Lands and Resources Department, the "Hamilton-Port Dover Plank Road Claim," which encompasses Kanonhstaton land, alleged that Six Nations had only intended to lease the lands used to construct the Plank Road and the lots on either side of the road, not to sell them, and that in any case it had been deprived of rent, mineral royalties, and compensation for the lands.[20] The Crown defence responded that the "Six Nations submitted these lands for sale in 1841 and affirmed its decision to sell in 1843 and 1844."[21]

It gets more complicated at this point because this alleged 1841 surrender was the subject of another unsettled Six Nations' claim, the "1841 Purported General Surrender Claim."[22] Six Nations' allegations in this claim were more detailed, listing documents noting official recognition of a squatter problem; the Upper Canadian government's attempts to convince Six Nations to sell certain parcels of its lands rather than lease them; and Lieutenant Governor Samuel Jarvis's conclusion that a small deputation of Six Nations people had agreed to his proposal to sell all of the remaining lands in 1841. The claim also described the petitions that immediately followed the purported surrender. Documents and delegations asserted that Jarvis had intimidated the group into signing the documents, that proper and usual procedures for surrender had not been followed, and that, in any case, the signatories had not been chiefs. Finally, Six Nations' claim narrative pointed out that Jarvis had been dismissed just a few years later as chief superintendant of Indian Affairs for embezzling Indian funds, and it contended that the 1841 surrender could not be valid since clear surrender documentation and maps were both lacking.[23] According to Six Nations, justice would have to take into account the context of the purported 1841 surrender – a context that included repeated affirmations of Six Nations' desire to lease, rather than sell, land, its cultural valuing of land (and, it follows, the contradictions inherent in the idea of selling it), and the underhanded tactics of a dishonest government official. This narrative was replicated in other documents, including an account of the Plank Road claim published on Six Nations' website.[24]

The Crown, however, focused on "facts" backed up by documents that, though not official documents of surrender, appeared to make clear Six Nations' knowledge of the terms of the land surrender. In September 2006, federal negotiator Ron Doering conceded in writing that federal negotiators did not possess a specific order-in-council or maps concerning these decisions, nor did it possess evidence of money entering Six Nations' trust accounts for the supposed sale of the land.[25] However, Canada called in turn for Six Nations representatives to produce evidence that the lands had not been surrendered: "If they don't convince us we're wrong, the federal government will stand by its position."[26] The Crown also presented a document outlining the Department of Justice's official position on the history of the surrender of the Plank Road Lands (including the Douglas Creek Estates) at a meeting on 3 November 2006.[27] Ignoring the long pre-war relationship between the Crown and the Haudenosaunee, the document emphasized the Simcoe Patent's restriction on Six Nations' power to alienate land unilaterally and invitations to certain white settlers to take up land, as well as the Crown's efforts to prevent land sales and leases and its official actions against squatters.[28] In 1840, the document related, Samuel Jarvis had recommended "a compact and homogenous reserve, with the rest of the land sold, and the proceeds deposited in Six Nations' trust account."[29] This proposal was accordingly made to the Confederacy in January 1841, and "on the 18th of January, two weeks after Jarvis' initial proposal for a comprehensive surrender, the [Confederacy] Council assented to the proposal."[30] Subsequent inquiries concluded that the surrender was valid, and the boundaries for the new reserve were eventually confirmed by the chiefs on 24 December 1844. The decisions were recorded by David Thorburn, a commissioner appointed to settle the final reserve. The Crown also cited an 1846 petition related to the reserve's western boundary as evidence that the chiefs "understood and agreed to the surrender of the Plank Road Lands, including what is now the Douglas Creek Estates."[31] By foregrounding the sales and leases of Six Nations' land undertaken mainly by Joseph Brant, holding Six Nations partly responsible for the squatter problem, and detailing the difficulties of Six Nations chiefs in determining the boundaries of the reserve, the narrative presented Six Nations as cognizant of its decisions but incoherent in its governing practices.

In response to the Department of Justice's report, Six Nations presented its account of the events surrounding the purported general surrender of lands. Hazel Hill recalled it as "an excellent day and opportunity to not only put our position on the table, but also to put OUR records and documentation of history on the table, our Wampum." Two Confederacy chiefs spent the morning giving an oral presentation explaining the history of the Haudenosaunee from the Creation story to the coming of the Europeans and up to the present, using several historic wampum to illustrate and contextualize the relationships with the Crown as they understood them.[32] Moving from discussions of Six Nations governance and the sharing of land through the Dish with One Spoon concept, negotiators explained their understanding of the Plank Road agreement, according to which the lands were "to be leased only to ploughs depth."[33] Historians pointed out that when the RCMP had taken over the council house in 1924, records were stolen and never returned and that since most of these documents were drafted in English, they may not have accurately represented the Six Nations' understanding of agreements in the first place. Furthermore, their understanding of the term "surrender" was not that the land was given up but, rather, that it authorized the Crown's peacekeepers to look after the squatters. Hazel Hill asserted: "It was never said we'd given up our land. It is forbidden for Chiefs to think that way, we have to help our people preserve for the future."[34] And as Leroy Hill indicated, "for every conclusion they have, we can find published documentation to the contrary." For instance, Six Nations cites as evidence notices of eviction given to settlers along Plank Road who lacked the Confederacy Council's permission to settle there.

Perhaps most significant, according to Rick Hill, was the fact that "just because it is written doesn't make it true." He argued that written records are incomplete if they do not take into account oral records, and he suggested that legal trickery had occurred. As the federal government later described Hill's presentation, "the central challenge he posited was for the parties to acknowledge their differing interpretations of the historical *facts* and to find creative ways to accommodate those differences."[35] This point is crucial since, to the Crown, a document stands as fact, while, to Six Nations, it is a piece of paper according to one perspective.

And so the battle to claim "truth" and define justice continued. Phil Monture, the principal land claims researcher representing Six Nations at the negotiations, tabled a response document asserting that procedures established by the Crown regarding the alienation of Native territory had not been followed in the case of the Plank Road lands.[36] He described the Crown's obligation to protect Six Nations from squatters, and he cited an 1843 statement from the Executive Council of Upper Canada "assur[ing] Six Nations that the Government had no wish to take any portion of their lands against their free wishes." Monture concluded that there had been no legal surrender document for the Plank Road lands; that the Crown deliberately induced the sale of Six Nations lands against their constant protests; that these failures constituted breaches of the Crown's fiduciary duty to protect Six Nations' lands against trespass; and that Six Nations did not authorize the building of the Plank Road and was never compensated for its construction.[37] Monture further pointed out that nineteen years had passed before Canada responded to the Plank Road claim "and only then as a result of the February 2006 Douglas Creek Land Reclamation."[38] The document clearly argued that the circumstances surrounding the purported 1841 surrender of land were just as essential in the search for justice as the documentation, or lack thereof, regarding the alleged surrender.

The federal government retorted with the "Federal Legal Response to Haudenosaunee/Six Nations' Presentation of November 14, 2006," tabled on 25 January 2007, which explained:

Although the presentations dealt with a broad range of matters, this paper offers only the *legal views* of the Government as to how the issue of the surrender of the Plank Road Lands would *most likely be addressed in a Canadian Court of Law* ... the paper *does not* presume to speak to how the various events between 1841 and 1844 might be interpreted under the *Great Law of Peace,* as we have no expertise in matters other than Canadian law.[39]

The document explained that, while the elders' presentations were "instruct-ive" about Six Nations' views on the nature of its special relationships to the Crown and to the land, Canada's legal response relies "on the written evidence which we believe indicates strongly that Six Nations leaders intended to surrender the Plank Road Lands for sale," based on a sequence of events and documents taken together, rather than on one "surrender document,"[40] and that it believes the Crown would be found by the courts to have satisfied its fiduciary and other duties.[41]

Eventually, both sides conceded that a stalemate had occurred over the rights to Kanonhstaton and over what kinds of "facts," "evidence," history, and context must be taken into account to reach a conclusion reflecting justice. According to Hazel Hill,

> the Crown is still insisting that they have a valid surrender. We know it wasn't. They were reminded by our delegates that it was Canada that was making a "claim" to our lands, and that if they wanted to offer proof of their claim, Canada could go ahead and gather up that proof and evidence ... The Crown believes their position as stated by their department of justice hasn't changed. We know ours hasn't changed. We also know that we are not sitting at the table according to "Canadian law" so their department of justice opinion means nothing.[42]

Fair Compensation

Negotiations continued regarding other claims. Divergent ideas about justice surfaced in debates over what would constitute fair compensation, with Canada focusing on financial payments and Six Nations insistent on the return of land. From the start, discussions of the monetary costs of the reclamation occupied a prominent place in public discussion about this dispute. Canada's approach appeared to depend on who was demanding justice. The developers and Caledonians who experienced difficulties as a result of the occupation were awarded monetary damages in short order.

Since the early days of the occupation, local leaders had been complaining about the utility costs incurred at Kanonhstaton, the costs of purchasing the land from Henco, and Ontario's expensive contestation of Judge David Marshall's injunctions at the Ontario Court of Appeal that allowed the protest to continue.[43] Premier McGuinty played the money card when pressuring Ottawa: "I want to put the feds on notice. We've been caught up in this for a long time. More importantly, the people of Caledonia have been caught up in this for a long time. Now it's costing Ontario taxpayers all kinds of money."[44] In a similarly worded press release, Ramsay grumbled: "Ontario families – particularly those in the Caledonia area – find themselves caught in a dispute between the federal government and Six Nations. Ontario taxpayers have paid, and continue to pay, a hefty price for the ongoing occupation in Caledonia."[45] Silenced by all of this talk of money was the demand that Ottawa address land claims more quickly. Looking at the "Six Nations (Caledonia) Negotiations Costs to Date," the costs of the occupation were listed at $46.26 million, which comprised about $20 million to buy Kanonhstaton from Henco, $2 million to assist businesses, and $21.6 million to defray the costs of policing.[46] The title of this Internet update placed blame for the occupation entirely at Six Nations' door but did not answer these pertinent questions: How much money had the failed OPP raid and its aftermath cost? What about the extra security needed for Gary McHale's rallies?

Hazel Hill recontextualized the demands for justice through money by referring to Six Nations' own grievances, calling for utility bills to be sent to "#1 Reclamation Drive" or, "better yet, send them to the Queen, she's holding all of our trust monies."[47] Leroy Hill pointed out that rather than having taxpayers' dollars used to defray reclamation costs, Six Nations would much prefer receiving the money owed to them, accompanied by a sincere apology from the prime minister or governor general.[48]

The government's characterization of the dispute as an economic burden on Caledonia's economy diverted attention from the root causes of the protest and implicitly blamed protesters for the problems: "We certainly know that the developer and the contractors that are there to build that subdivision have been financially hurt. We want to work with them and find out what that financial pain is and see if there's anything we can do to help them through this."[49] "Progress" in the negotiations was often related to funding assistance for Henco and Caledonia businesses, not to Six Nations' issues.[50] Haldimand County press releases focused largely on monetary assistance for "affected businesses"[51] and for the builders.[52] In May, a few months after the protest began, the county announced $500,000 in funding assistance to "local businesses which are at risk of closure due to the Douglas

Creek Estates blockades."[53] Just a few days later, these funds were being disbursed from a local Business Emergency Relief Office.[54] The attention immediately showered on Caledonia did not go unnoticed. Janie Jamieson believed that Judge Marshall's injunctions against the protesters were intended to protect business interests. She referred to the lives risked by attempted enforcement on 20 April: "Their main focus, the agreements that have been made, have been with the businesses of Caledonia that have received money. It's been with Henco Industries – they've received money. And it's all about really making sure that the corporation does not suffer ... It doesn't matter that lives may be at stake because of it."[55]

When Ontario bought Douglas Creek Estates from Henco in June 2006, the press announcement of the purchase did not list the cost of the land. However, the same release announced an additional $1 million in business assistance as well as "emergency assistance ... to residents directly impacted by the situation in Caledonia."[56] The Ontario Ministry of Economic Development stated: "Our plan is to continue to work to get businesses, which are the engines of the local economy, back on their feet as quickly as we can."[57] Although Ramsay highlighted the potential of the purchase agreement to "cool the temperature in the community and around the table so that we can get some long-term decision-making at that negotiating table done,"[58] Jamieson was not appeased:

> That title and jurisdiction isn't placed back with Six Nations, is it? And that's what the issue is. They haven't begun to resolve anything with us, but as far as corporate Canada – they've done everything to appease them. Of course they would pay several million dollars to appease the developers and the business people. They would spend that money before they would even begin to resolve the land issue, which is the meat of the story anyway.[59]

Meanwhile, Haldimand County Council connected the economic difficulties with the failure of the police raid:

> For well over a year, Caledonia, and recently other communities in the County have become the lightning rods for First Nations frustrations over land claim inaction by the Federal Government. The result is a climate where the many development opportunities in Haldimand County are not being realized because of fear of occupations or demonstrations – occupations that the Ontario Provincial Police cannot or will not intervene in, other than to keep the peace. This is grievously affecting

the County's economy and if allowed to continue much longer, will result in permanent damage because of lost opportunities ... We cannot stand on the sidelines and watch this municipality's economy fail. We can no longer tolerate a situation that inhibits any future planning to realize this County's potential.[60]

The Ontario Secretariat of Aboriginal Affairs declared that "a land claim can create a chill in economic development," necessitating settlements in order to bring about certainty.[61] Mayor Marie Trainer said that Ottawa and Toronto "have really lost focus about what this whole thing is about. They're forgetting about the [Caledonians] who are suffering every day – their nerves are shot, they're on tranquilizers, they're on heart medication. It's not a good thing."[62] MPP Barrett lamented the "shroud of uncertainty" created around Haldimand County construction and farming "due to the threat of illegal land seizures" and asserted that some area property values had dropped 20 percent.[63]

In June 2007, fed-up Haldimand County officials called for a face-to-face meeting with Prime Minister Stephen Harper. Citing the "millions and millions" that developers had invested in projects, Mayor Trainer understandably demanded: "Why should they be held hostage for the rest of Canada? It's not fair."[64] Six Nations' interests were submerged again when Member of Parliament Diane Finley took the initiative to ask Caledonians for opinions as to what should be done with the Douglas Creek Estates' land when negotiations concluded, asserting that the land would still be owned by Ontario. "I have heard lots of talk of a swimming pool and a park," she said.[65] Canadian statements consistently equated "progress" with "justice" for everyone except Six Nations. Hazel Hill's remarks on the subject were numerous:

> If I suggest that while the province of Ontario was quick to pay Henco over 15 million, put millions of dollars into the town of Caledonia for its trauma and hardships, perhaps it should put some of those millions into Six Nations since we do own the land, have never been paid any lease monies on any of the lands and their bill right now exceeds hundreds of billions of dollars, and they got the nerve to whine about a couple of hundred bucks for utility bills. Send the bills, but make sure you're ready to cut a cheque for at least a hundred million to start covering the damn rent you owe![66]
>
> I heard the most ridiculous statement yesterday, that developers and 3rd parties who have been stopped from proceeding in their development plans actually believe we need to compensate them for their losses!!!!! All

my brain could comprehend when I heard that statement is that once again history repeats itself and I thought of how the crown was compensating the squatters for improvements on our lands in the 1800's (with our lease monies), totally ignoring the fact that Six Nations hold title to those lands ... Only one thing I got to say to those developers and third parties ... It is the Crown who duped you, and it is the Crown who will answer to you ... Look how quickly they took care of the Henning brothers.[67]

On 30 May 2007, the gauntlet was laid down with the federal government's offer of compensation of $125 million for four of Six Nations' claims (which all dealt with lands other than those of Douglas Creek Estates), totalling about 38,000 acres.[68] The relative size of the offer must be contemplated in light of the foregoing conversations about compensation and justice and the millions spent on policing the occupation, as well as Six Nations' assertions of priorities to acquire land, not money. In the early months of the protest, on the suggestion of Six Nations negotiators, Ontario had agreed to delay development of 7,300 acres of publicly owned land for a two-year negotiating period.[69] This early recognition of Six Nations' need for land was replaced by an offer of money. Excerpts from a December 2006 Confederacy Council press release clearly state Six Nations' negotiating stance: "Resolution to outstanding Six Nations land rights will not be resolved simply by throwing money at Six Nations."[70] The same release states that while Canada had placed the onus on Ontario because it had no land to return, and Ontario was standing by its land registry system, Six Nations felt that "that land was stolen from us and we are looking for fair equitable compensation for the loss of that land. Whether it was swindled or stolen it amounts to the fact that the underlying title is ours. Promises were broken and land has to be returned." To Six Nations, receiving money to buy back lands they believed they already owned would not constitute justice. When this first offer was tabled, Confederacy Chief Allen MacNaughton reiterated these statements yet again: "It being in an initial offer, we realize initial offers are never accepted anyway. I guess it's a starting point to talk about things and I guess the only positive is it's obviously a recognition they owe us something."[71]

Jim Prentice rationalized that "the ability I have under the policy is to advance money. And the money, of course, can be used to secure land, and that land can be converted to reserve status."[72] Officially, the Confederacy neither accepted nor rejected the offer.[73] Unofficially, representatives were less equivocal. As Leroy Hill stated, "on the issue of land, our mandate is clear. Land is what we need. Land is what we are after and land is what we are going to get."[74] MacNaughton restated Six Nations' reasons for grievance and hopes for solutions:

We made our position clear right from the start and for the whole year that it is not about money. We need the land back, we have concerns about the environment, encroaching development on our doorstep, not just here but all up and down the Haldimand Tract. It's about historic agreements that have never been addressed. Our priority is to get the land back and to discuss land usage and development along the tract. They came to us with a monetary offer and tried to put a spin on it saying we are asking for money. No! What we are asking for is an accounting of sales and leases over the past 200 years. We made these sales and leases for the sake of our people's upkeep and perpetual maintenance. We have been asking since the 1920s. At that time the response was an imposed elective system of government. Now we're asking for accountability again and they come up with $125 m ... To compensate us for four claims? That $125 million wouldn't buy you two blocks of Moulton Township. They won't break that down.[75]

The Confederacy's answer to the offer prompted a mid-June letter of reply from Ron Doering, who explained that Canada simply did not own any significant land in the area to return. He sidestepped the notion of "extinguishment" of rights to land, instead focusing on "the need to achieve certainty and finality [to] ensur[e] that, from the conclusion of an agreement forward, the legal status of the lands is clear and all persons can rely on that status in the conduct of their affairs."[76] The letter explained that the offer considered the specifics of each of the four claims as well as "actuarial and risk principles" and the consideration of "intangible values, like, for instance, the desire to settle a matter sooner rather than later." Since many of these factors could not be assigned specific dollar values, he clarified, money was being offered as a package deal.

The protesters did not buy it. In August 2007, a demonstration was staged in front of Toronto's Osgoode Hall Law School to point out how Six Nations' stolen funds had been used to build the law school: "They are offering us money that was made from the lands they stole from us."[77] Hazel Hill cited moral and spiritual grounds for justice, referring to Canada's violations of agreements with the Haudenosaunee as well as violations against Creation.[78] The status quo situation – unresolved claims – does favour Canada, at least in the short term, and the costs are downloaded to Six Nations and Caledonia or other places caught in the middle. As Barbara McDougall put it in February 2007, "peaceful negotiations – that's the way to go. If it takes a long time, it takes a long time."[79] The offer of monetary compensation is evidence that the federal government is trying to address the unresolved land claims. That said, Six Nations' wait of many decades stands in stark contrast to Henco's much faster compensation. The Henning brothers maintain that they still lost significant money on the deal – and this may well be the case – but their losses were at least addressed relatively quickly. Federal avowals that no land is available to offer Six Nations are probably truthful (they may also reflect an unwillingness to lose face by acceding to the protesters). Even so, Six Nations has been repeating its calls for land rather than money since the negotiations started. To Canadians, this may seem a silly distinction – and even among Six Nations, some advocate simply using the money to buy land – but it remains that the Confederacy Council is, first, calling for land and, second, calling for compensation for the loss of land use. In this case, the government's willingness to shell out $46 million in the first year of the occupation alone is telling when placed next to $125 million to settle four long-standing claims.

The Right to Justice

The conversations in Caledonia regarding justice and compensation are multi-layered. The discourses at work include debates about the slippery nature of "facts"; about the veracity of reports and documentation;[80] about the disparities between the attention and compensation paid to Caledonians and the compensation offered to the Haudenosaunee; and about the appropriateness of monetary settlements. Underpinning all of these issues are the profound differences in the ways that Canada and Six Nations view themselves and their history of relationship. Both are asserting that they have come to the negotiating table only under their own legitimate laws. Canada has based its conclusions about the legality of the surrender on British law passed down to Canada.[81] Six Nations maintains just as strongly that its own interpretation of the events is based on the Great Law of Peace and the Silver Covenant Chain relationship established between the Haudenosaunee and the settlers.[82]

Stances on appropriate justice and settlement are summarized in the Conservative government's statement regarding its refusal to ratify the September 2007 UN *Declaration of Rights of Indigenous Peoples*.[83] The government explained that the declaration failed to

> recognize Canada's need to balance indigenous rights to lands and resources with the rights of others ... Since taking office in 2006, Canada's New Government has acted on many fronts to improve quality of life and promote a prosperous future for all Aboriginal peoples. This agenda

is practical, focuses on real results, and has led to tangible progress in a range of areas including land claims, education, housing, child and family services, safe drinking water and the extension of human rights protection to First Nations on reserve ... Canada's position has remained consistent and principled. We have stated publicly that we have significant concerns with the wording of provisions of the Declaration such as those on: lands, territories and resources; free, prior and informed consent when used as a veto; self-government without recognition of the importance of negotiations; intellectual property; military issues; and the need to achieve an appropriate balance between the rights and obligations of indigenous peoples, member States and third parties. For instance, in Article 26, the document states, "Indigenous peoples have the right to the lands, territories, and resources which they have traditionally owned, occupied or otherwise used or acquired." This could be used by Aboriginal groups to challenge and re-open historic and present day treaties and to support claims that have already been dealt with.[84]

The statement implies that unless the rights of "others" are safeguarded, indigenous rights will smother them. By pairing the words "consistent" and "principled," the statement implies that refusing to see a new point of view is comparable to doing the right thing. The opposition proposed between the government's "tangible" and "practical" goals and the declaration insinuates that the declaration would ignore priorities such as drinking water and education. When it invokes the possibility that greedy First Nations might reopen settled land claims, the statement is ignoring the majority of claims, which sit unaddressed in a growing backlog. More significantly, the statement speaks to a forward-looking identity focused on "real" progress rather than to "old" grievances. Although the government has since quietly ratified the declaration in November 2010, the decision does not appear to reflect any serious recognition of unique Aboriginal rights: "The Government of Canada today formally endorsed the United Nations Declaration on the Rights of Indigenous Peoples in a manner fully consistent with Canada's Constitution and laws."[85]

In December 2007, newly appointed Ontario Minister of Aboriginal Affairs Michael Bryant declared: "I don't think people care about the constitutional responsibilities. I think they care about getting solutions and government stepping up to the plate. This government is stepping up to the plate."[86] Six Nations' "internal governance issues" are a favoured theme. As Mayor Trainer put it, "they can talk all they want, but who do you make the deal with? Six Nations have no one to blame but themselves."[87] Six Nations' determination to make development decisions resulted in the founding of the Haudenosaunee Development Institute (HDI) in the fall of 2007, a means of tangibly asserting that Six Nations people were free to exercise their sovereignty over land. As Hazel Hill put it, "as far as I'm concerned, the land is already ours, given to us by the Creator. It really doesn't matter how the Crown registers it on their side of the wampum, that's up to them. All we need to do is start using it."[88] The statement released with the Haudenosaunee Development Protocol explained that the HDI was meant to address the growing numbers of developers approaching the Confederacy Council to discuss building on disputed land. The protocol required developers to approach the HDI directly to ask permission to develop on disputed lands: "The [HDI might] grant permission for development in or on the areas described" if its environmental standards were met, if the proponent agreed to enter contracts deemed necessary by the HDI, and if the development was "in accordance with any Regulations or policies developed pursuant to this Protocol."[89] The HDI required copies of project plans and provided for possible levying of fees for permission to proceed.[90]

Chief MacNaughton described the HDI as a "positive tool" that lays out the consultation processes for developers caught in a void "being created by the Crown's, in right of Canada and Ontario's, failure to resolve Six Nations' land rights." He called for the municipalities to work with the HDI "in accordance with the laws of Canada, in right of the Crown, which requires them to fully consult with the Haudenosaunee of the Six Nations prior to the issuance of permits for any development on our unceded territory,"[91] and compared the HDI to Canada's ministries.[92] As lawyer and protocol drafter Aaron Detlor explained, "if you do not have a permit and you proceed, it's our position that you are doing so in an unlawful manner."[93] A letter was sent to Haldimand County Council announcing that unless the HDI was consulted, "all development will come to an utter and complete stop."[94] To Hazel Hill, the HDI was a "positive" step, taken because Ontario "continued to advise the developers that it was business as usual on unceded lands and continued using the Grand River Notification Act that requires them only to notify the [Elected Band Council] that a development is being considered."[95] Referencing court decisions ordering consultation and accommodation, Hill asserted, "WE DO NOT NEED ANYONE'S PERMISSION TO MAKE AND ASSERT LAWS UPON OUR LANDS. We are at liberty to enter into agreements with whomever we so desire to protect the interests of our future generations, and we fully intend to continue doing so."[96]

Brantford MPP Dave Levac interpreted the HDI as an attention-grabbing move to try to get the federal government to recognize and deal with claims, pointing out that the HDI was not based in Ontario law or land registries.[97] Mayor Trainer asserted that the HDI was infringing on "everybody's rights" and called for the government to "take a stand."[98] In late October, Ontario stated: "Any attempt by the Haudenosaunee/Six Nations to extract conces- sions or payments from private landowners as a condition for allowing de- velopment to continue on private property has no basis in Ontario's land use planning system.[99] The Confederacy Council's response reiterated calls for recognition of the Two Row Wampum and Covenant Chain relationships, noting Ontario's lack of authority to dictate Haudenosaunee governance structures: "If land was stolen, as we know it was, provincial support for a registry system that authorizes that theft is institutional racism directed at the destruction of the Haudenosaunee." The HDI was intended to "determine that development, if it is going to proceed, does so in a manner consistent with Confederacy law which places a priority on the protection of the en- vironment."[100] MacNaughton repeated Six Nations' pledge that it would never deprive third parties of their lands: "It is unacceptable that Ontario should continue to deprive our people of our lands and land rights. The Confederacy has no issue with how Canada or Ontario in right of the Crown administers its planning and development decisions along the Grand River, as long as it has had prior approval by the Confederacy."[101]

Once again, a stalemate resulted that favoured the status quo. Bryant insisted that "in our view, consultation does not mean a veto over develop- ment,"[102] and he stood by Ontario's title system: "I would encourage [Ontarians] not to participate in anything that sets itself outside of the existing process for development in the province of Ontario ... as to what- ever dealings we're going to have with the, so called, Institute, I just can't really say right now."[103] The HDI did receive some recognition from develop- ers "trying to work with the Haudenosaunee," as Hazel Hill described it. Others, Hill said, did not understand that "attending one confederacy council meeting, or having one meeting with the HDI isn't construed as consultation and doesn't mean a hill of beans as far as accommodation." However, development that was "in accordance with who we are, and what our law requires us to do, and that in simple terms is consistent with pro- tecting the environment and the future," might be allowed to continue, she said.[104] From their comments in the media, it appears that the developers talking to the HDI are motivated partly by a genuine desire for open com- munication and understanding and partly out of fear of work stoppages by Six Nations protesters. The mixture undoubtedly varies from time to time – as business owners, builders must consider their bottom line.

On 12 December 2007, Canada tabled a second offer of financial com- pensation, offering $26 million to compensate for the flooding of Six Nations' lands when the Welland Canal connecting Lake Erie and Lake Ontario was built. Ron Doering felt that "we've done everything we can" and spoke of his hope that settlement on an "easy" claim might "tone down the direct action," although negotiators had "agreed to disagree" on the Plank Road claim.[105] The second offer sounded oddly familiar, asserting Canada's faith in negotiation over litigation and its commitment to "resolving the complex issues along the Grand River in Southern Ontario."[106] Both in this press release and on the Department of Indian Affairs' website, Canada implied that Six Nations preferred litigation and that its earlier lawsuit for "historical" grievances was petty and unrealistic.[107] It once again removed the historical and political context from the "issues," while statements that Canada "remains committed" masked the effort it took Six Nations to get the government to the negotiating table in the first place. Doering's speaking notes related to the offer were peppered with familiar discursive moves emphasizing "a few basic facts" and the usual terms of "certainty."[108] To the media, he described "a very fair and generous offer."[109] He continued: "We are serious about the negotiations. They can use the money to acquire other land on a willing-seller, willing-buyer basis,"[110] and explained: "You can buy a lot of land for $26 million."[111] MacNaughton agreed that the offer was something that the Confederacy could consider,[112] but warned once again that Canada should not consider the negotiations to be restricted simply to financial compensation[113] and made skeptical comments about perceived attempts to extinguish Aboriginal title.[114] Leroy Hill cautioned: "I don't think the problem is the people who are at the table. It's the orders they've been given."[115] Whether this perception that Canada is not serious about negotiations today is accurate or not, there is certainly a long history of inaction and duplicity. Building trust and moving forward will take time.

The two sides' negotiation policies were so tightly intertwined that it was impossible – indeed, neither illuminative nor desirable – to separate strategies from deeply rooted principles. For example, Canada's contention that financial settlement was reasonable because the money could be used to buy land could be viewed cynically as a strategy to avoid raising public ire by "giving" land to Six Nations. MacNaughton recognized, for instance, that one likely hindrance was the occupation itself: "Come hell or high water, they don't want to give that land back. They don't want to be seen to be giving in to protesters."[116] However, Canada's stance could equally be viewed simply as a manifestation of a genuine cultural tendency to value goods in practical monetary terms. Likewise, Six Nations' propensity to invoke spiritual and moral considerations in discussions of justice could be skeptically seen as a calculated and disingenuous strategy to play "the culture card" to force Canada to tiptoe in fear of failing to be politically correct. Alternatively, both stances could simply be taken at face value. Dissecting parties' motives into convictions and tactics might be an interesting exercise, but such an analysis would inevitably obscure the power relations that have discarded Six Nations' conceptions of history and justice in favour of Canadian notions. These ideas are presented as universal values and norms in a discursive national space that excludes (yet again) Six Nations from legitimacy, from the government's list of priorities, and from the index of actors possessing the right to shape spaces and places for themselves.

Andrew Woolford's study of the British Columbia treaty process has much to say that is relevant to the negotiations of the Grand River Territory, for it spells out a multiplicity of visions of "justice" and "certainty" elucidated by the parties involved.[117] As we have seen, to the Canadian government, certainty requires that conflicts between Aboriginal and Crown title be resolved to achieve clarity of landownership and jurisdiction. Non-Aboriginal governments, Woolford explains, also focus predominantly on "creating future relationships," thereby doing symbolic violence on First Nations by ignoring colonial realities and by using power to define the negotiating context, prioritizing economic interests over a serious reckoning with the past. The government's statement regarding the UN *Declaration of Rights of Indigenous Peoples* unquestionably demonstrates this posturing. "Certainty" discourses also legitimate the socio-economic logics of mainstream Canada, axiomatically linking them with (economic) well-being. However, as Woolford points out, certainty depends on the perception by all parties that justice has been achieved. Some First Nations or members of First Nations may indeed perceive government priorities as being in line with their own, while others may provide counter-definitions, speaking of compensation in terms of morality and justice, as fair recompense for harm done and as a necessary element of public acknowledgment. Temporal objectives are another source of tension. Is a treaty intended to repair the past or to shape a new future? For Six Nations, just futures lie clearly through acknowledgments of past wrongs. Conversely, Canadian parties often express the belief that discussions of "history" long past simply bog negotiations down.

My aim in this book has been to unpack some of the baggage that ideas of "truth," "facts," and "justice" carry with them. Quite frankly, these concepts are relative to each culture. I share the unease of James Clifford, who refers to culture as a "serious fiction" and who struggles to go beyond relativist and pluralistic depictions of culture, searching for "a concept that can preserve culture's differentiating functions while conceiving of collective identity as a hybrid, often discontinuous inventive process." Yet I also identify strongly with his conclusion that "culture is a deeply compromised idea I cannot yet do without."[118] It seems that Canada's definitions of history, evidence, and legality have been privileged throughout this dispute, while Six Nations' efforts to demonstrate the nuances of past and present relationships, events, and historical contexts have been relegated to the dustbin of "cultural concerns," despite being inherently neither less nor more "cultural" ways of viewing the world than those of Canada. Yet even if one chooses to accept Canada's colonially asserted right to demarcate the boundaries of justice, the baldly obvious differences between Canada's treatment of its Native and non-Native wronged remain. Notwithstanding the very severe difficulties, financial and otherwise, that Don and John Henning experienced as a result of the occupation of Douglas Creek Estates (and that other developers have experienced in Brantford since then), it remains that Henco's grievances were addressed within a few short months, while Six Nations' claims have been ignored for decades. To focus mainly on Caledonia's very real difficulties during the reclamation, while ignoring Six Nations' enormous economic losses over the centuries, is equally unfair, as is the unapologetic proffering of British law as justification for all of this debacle when the Haudenosaunee neither asked nor wanted to be colonial citizens in the first place. In short, Canada's own "rule of law" has been applied differentially, economically, and along apparently racially justified lines in Caledonia.

A final topic to which I have paid only passing attention in this chapter is equally, if not more, problematic: the notion of the "extinguishment" of rights, which seems automatically included in government priorities when it comes to dealing with all issues Aboriginal.[119] Michael Asch and Norman Zlotkin posit that federal insistence on extinguishment clauses originates in the belief that Canada holds underlying ownership and jurisdiction to the land. Although Canadian courts have acknowledged difficulties in accommodating Aboriginal understandings of Aboriginal rights and title, the idea that these are "undefined" and require judicial interpretation to make them clear is a product of underlying assumptions about the relationship of Aboriginal rights and title to the Canadian constitutional framework.[120] It is to this topic – the very ability of our Constitution to accommodate Aboriginal rights and sovereignty – that I turn in the next chapter.

Constitutional Territory 6

One point in particular – a point demonstrated by both Canada and Six Nations in Caledonia as well as by various Aboriginal and other academics and writers, and one on which I hope I have not already hammered with excessive force – is crucial. Land and territoriality are closely linked in that land is a tangible expression of nationhood and identity. The acknowledgment of First Nations' land rights, then, is vital to the shaping of a stronger and fairer society in Canada. And though the government often asserts otherwise, the Canadian land claims process has proven largely ineffective both quantitatively, in terms of percentages of claims addressed, and qualitatively, in terms of satisfaction with the claims that have actually been settled. First Nations have been demanding justice for decades using whatever means seems necessary – through politely and strongly worded letters, through "legal" and "illegal" channels, and through negotiations, arbitration, protest, and delegation. First Nations peoples are simply calling for what most (white) Canadians assume from the government: adherence to its own law.

As legal scholar Bruce Clark suggested nearly two decades ago, existing constitutional law recognizing Aboriginal and treaty rights must be honoured in order to close the gap between discursive principle and practice.[1] Alternatively, he says, "a constitutional amendment deleting existing aboriginal rights would make the constitutional principle conform to the existing practice of ignoring that existing right."[2] As we have seen, the Canadian landscape is fraught with frauds and denials of various kinds. Although huge tracts of land were ostensibly given up, these surrenders occurred when the Crown was acting as fiduciary trustee, mandated to deal honestly with First

Nations instead of leading them to underestimate their own bargaining positions. Due to the illegitimacy of many of these "surrenders," huge swathes of territory may still rightfully belong to Aboriginal peoples. Note also that in many cases no surrender was actually made or (as in the case of the purported 1841 surrender) bribery and duress were possibly at work: "As contracts, each treaty conveyed or released only what the conveying or releasing parties, the natives, intended. And as a matter of law it is difficult to argue that the natives intended to relinquish something that their trustee's representatives tricked them into believing they did not have."[3] Oh, the power of words to shape the world. Clark writes neither out of sentiment nor out of a sense of social justice, he says, "but because due observances of the rule of law require it."[4]

Other scholars follow him in pointing out that Aboriginal title is mandated under Canadian law. Patrick Macklem concludes that whether one prefers law or government action to recognize Aboriginal title, it remains that proprietary power in Canada is unlawfully distributed.[5] There is some debate as to whether the government or the courts are best suited to reshape Canadian space according to this imperative. In its report, the Royal Commission on Aboriginal Peoples emphasizes treaty relationships, calling for government action to recognize Aboriginal rights to greater lands and resources, legitimated by nation-to-nation negotiation. The same report views the courtroom as less able to deal with the wide range of issues implicated in Aboriginal title, which is "a relatively abstract articulation of the ideal of mutual coexistence."[6] Others argue that the courts, referencing property law, should explicitly recognize unjust distributions of land title (which are based on the "legal" justification of underlying Crown title in Canada, as detailed in Chapter 1) and reallocate it accordingly. The law has consistently dispossessed Aboriginal peoples because the legal encumbrance of Aboriginal title on the Crown's underlying ownership has never significantly curbed the exercise of either Crown proprietary power or Crown legislative authority.[7] The relative bargaining power of the parties is a function of the distribution of property rights brought about by legal choice in a long succession of decisions. But this distribution need not have been, and was not, decided once for all time. Shifts in allocation are possible today with each court ruling on the nature and scope of Aboriginal, Crown, or third-party title as well as with each legislative decision made by Parliament or the provincial legislatures relating to property rights and/or Aboriginal people. Macklem explains: "Indeed, legal framing of disputes between Aboriginal people and the Crown – what makes a political dispute a legal dispute – signals the distributive function of the legal system."[8] Thus, to view the law as "too blunt an instrument" to address the intricacies of Aboriginal lands and resources is to ignore its long history of defining rights and establishing relative powers. Law's implication in distributive justice requires it to intervene by allocating proprietary power in ways that oblige the government to act.[9] No matter the source of the proposed solutions, it is clear that discursive strategies have justified Aboriginal dispossession in the past and continue the trend today by structuring society through the "rule of law" according to Canadian conceptions of property rights.

Canada's existing federal claims processes, purportedly designed to rectify these spatialized injustices so deeply sedimented into society, are inadequate. Since they are grounded in policy statements with questionable legal status rather than in binding legislation, they can be changed on a whim. Since Aboriginal people do not have a recognized statutory right to participate in claims processes, they can be left out in the cold with no legal redress.[10] Furthermore, the current system has the federal government playing both defendant and judge of claims against itself in a blatant conflict of interest. The federal focus on the extinguishment of Aboriginal title as a precondition for negotiations causes difficulties, and blurred jurisdictional boundaries are also problematic with the provinces often refusing to participate.[11] As Chief Justice Antonio Lamer explained in the 1997 case *Delgamuukw v. British Columbia*, which addressed Gitxan and Wet'suwet'en land title in British Columbia, detaching federal jurisdiction over Natives from provincial jurisdiction over their lands had disastrous consequences: "The government vested with primary constitutional responsibility for securing the welfare of Canada's Aboriginal peoples would find itself unable to safeguard one of the most central of native interests – their interest in their lands."[12] The federal government stands as the Crown's representative in relationships with Aboriginal peoples and can enact mechanisms for claims resolutions and offer financial settlements, but the provinces, holding "jurisdiction" over First Nations' lands, must also be involved in the solutions.

When new agreements are forged, their success, like that of the old treaties, will depend not only on the words they contain but also on the daily practices that interpret and implement them (or not). As I have detailed throughout this book, Aboriginal negotiators of treaties of old thought they had obtained what they intended. Problems developed later, in the Crown's unilateral interpretations. Although modern agreements are much more technically complex and codified, the real test will again lie in whether they are actually allowed to do their work of reshaping Canadian–First Nations landscapes and relationships.[13] There is also doubt as to whether Aboriginal rights, which pose a fundamental challenge to the government's reliance on large-scale, corporate resource consumption as a primary economic driver, will ever in fact transform business-as-usual scenarios or whether these rights will remain largely rhetorical.[14] However, the continual sidelining of land claims has economic implications for Canadians as well. As long as First Nations lack sufficient land bases on which to safeguard some measure of economic and governmental independence, federal spending on top-down programs will be increasingly less effective.[15]

When development threatens to infringe on the rights of Aboriginal resource users, section 35(1) compels a consultative process, which was further explicated in the 1990 case of *R. v. Sparrow*.[16] A government, be it provincial or federal, that wishes to hamper Aboriginal or treaty rights must prove that it has a valid legislative objective and that it is acting in a manner consistent with the honour of the Crown by consulting with the Aboriginal nations involved.[17] The duty to "consult and accommodate" that figured so prominently in statements made by Six Nations protesters and negotiators also arises from the glacial pace of land claims settlements. While negotiations drag on, land that may well turn out to belong to First Nations continues to be sold to, and developed by, third parties. Ironically, as Aboriginal land rights are slowly recognized, cumulative environmental impacts and the resulting environmental regulations necessitated by resource harvesting undertaken by settler societies may mean that it will be difficult for Aboriginal peoples to benefit economically from their resources.[18] Although Supreme Court of Canada rulings such as *Delgamuukw* in 1997 and *Haida Nation v. British Columbia* in 2004 clearly state that consultation and accommodation are required, parameters and guidelines have been left largely undefined, as the judges prefer to rely on the "Honour of the Crown" and good faith negotiations.[19] Obvious questions about judicial activism and legitimacy also arise, given that judges in Canada are appointed, not elected. Successive rulings have tended to push Aboriginal policy toward more progressive interpretations of the Constitution more quickly than would have elected governments, motivated by different concerns than the judiciary (for example, the desire to be re-elected and for budgets to be passed). In many cases, such as in Caledonia and Brantford, constitutional obligations have been disregarded in favour of a "wait and see" approach favouring the status quo.

A research report generated for the Ipperwash Inquiry pointed out the vacuum of policy in Ontario addressing consultation and accommodation as well as the lack of recognition of the historical context for Aboriginal claims and the fact that Aboriginal rights are also enshrined in British law (for example, the Royal Proclamation of 1763) and Canadian law and Constitution.[20] Further complicating Canadian notions of "rule of law" is the fact that almost all of the claims outstanding against the Ontario government involve contraventions of basic legal norms – through fraud, theft, breach of formal agreement, or other offences – that Canadians take for granted.

As noted earlier and demonstrated at Kanonhstaton, "jurisdictional" battles between provincial and federal governments often impede resolution in land claims. The Ipperwash report also urged that land claims processes strengthen relationships between First Nations and the Crown; that they be perceived by all parties as fair, preferably by operating outside of elected government; and that they protect the interests of the general public.[21] The report concludes that the title of the federal specific claims policy, "Outstanding Business," is only too suggestive of the present approach to First Nations' land and treaty rights, which assumes that the responsibilities of the government can be satisfactorily ascertained through discretionary "claims" processes.[22]

But how is Canadian society to be reshaped on foundations of recognition? Suggestions for justice for First Nations vary from the wide-ranging Ipperwash recommendations to more detailed and sophisticated compensation models.[23] Standard methods of economic valuation are often ill suited to addressing diverse values such as spiritual significance and loss of opportunity for cultural practices and ways of managing land. Furthermore, distrust of accepting financial recompense for land and resources is common among Aboriginal communities such as Six Nations, which emphasize that they seek land bases for the future, not what are often perceived as short-term economic gains. Yet, as David Natcher explains, the duty to consult is often unlawfully delegated by the government to resource developers proposing to work within traditional Aboriginal lands since industry stands to gain the most from development.[24] In turn, developers, buttressed by governments' discourses supporting economic development and "forward thinking," often believe development to be rightful and inevitable. The result is conflicts such as the one at Douglas Creek Estates. Everyone stands to gain from good relationships between industry and First Nations' communities, but it is illogical to expect companies to place Aboriginal interests ahead of their own in cases of conflict. As we have seen along the Grand River, the unwillingness of all levels of government to enforce meaningful consultation with Six Nations regarding development on claimed lands has meant that developers are caught in the middle. The reality is that they are simply looking out for their own interests and are following their country's laws in continuing to build. It is Canada's responsibility to act with First Nations on a nation-to-nation basis. By passing consultation to industry, Canada is failing in its constitutional responsibilities to recognize and protect Aboriginal rights. Until it takes an active approach to land use disputes through fair accommodation processes, the dissatisfaction of First Nations can be expected to intensify.[25] This alternative is socially (and, one could argue, economically and environmentally) unsustainable, and it will result in continuing conflict between Canada's laws and self-image and its on-the-ground actions as well as in persistent calls for justice from Aboriginal peoples in the form of protests, occupations, and lawsuits. Though reshaping Canadian landscapes and dialogues will require considerable time, energy, and resources, political will for other daunting projects such as reducing deficits has been mustered by the public. At the same time, the social and economic costs of not resolving outstanding land grievances will be high.[26] Canadian society's claims to justice and the "rule of law" are at stake.

Landscapes of Relationships

So the task must be accomplished, but how can it be done, given the seemingly intractable differences in perspective? The analysis presented in this book argues that what we say about the world – the claims we stake and the truths we make – are more than just words; they shape both legal and physical landscapes. In Caledonia, groups of people are making competing claims to the land, to the rights to the land, to legitimacy, to sovereignty, to ways of seeing the world, to particular visions of justice, to what "normal" citizenship and society are supposed to look like. Since it is more than a competition over the land itself, this dispute is bigger and broader than it looks at first. And because Canada relies on logics that erase the past and that situate the conflict in Canadian conceptions of reality, law, and "normalcy," they continually suppress Six Nations' ideas and deny their right to shape their future.

A November 2007 newspaper article focusing on Ontario Provincial Police (OPP) Commissioner Julian Fantino is especially revelatory regarding what lies at the heart of the dispute that began in Caledonia. Fantino realized the significance of Caledonia to Canada as a nation: "I thought that Caledonia was a stand-alone, isolated issue. It's not. It's linked to everything else that's going on in this country ... I know that people were watching every move we made."[27] Several responses to Fantino's careful approach, reported in the same article, were equally telling. Gary McHale, many Caledonia locals, and others viewed the OPP's strategy in Caledonia, led first by Gwen Boniface and then by Julian Fantino, as manifestations of two-tiered justice. Reclamation spokesperson Hazel Hill expressed appreciation for the way "he just came to introduce himself. It was very friendly." She added that Fantino seemed to understand the importance of respect, an indicator of healthy intergovernmental relationships. Janie Jamieson, on the other hand, was mistrustful of Canadian law enforcement and still mindful of the 20 April 2006 raid on Kanonhstaton: "I don't work with any of the police forces. They haven't acted honourably. They haven't acted honestly. And they sure as hell haven't looked out for our safety."[28] Finally, Aaron Detlor, lawyer for the

Haudenosaunee Development Institute, believed that "the role of the police in Caledonia right now is to make sure they keep the peace where possible and be observers. And I don't think that there's two-tiered justice whatsoever. But we do have two legal systems: Haudenosaunee and Canadian."[29]

Neither side has agreed to fall under the other's laws, so, clearly, the terms of negotiation must be readdressed. Based on the analysis in the previous chapters, and supported by arguments put forward from both sides of this dispute, I argue that a fundamental reordering of the relationship between Six Nations and Canada (and between other First Nations and Canada, as desired by those other nations) is imperative. The Canadian government must take the lead since the business-as-usual scenario – forcing Six Nations to assert its rights against third-party developers – only breeds further mistrust, racism, and fear and since Canada largely holds the reins of power. Since the country's brief terms of leadership favour prolonging the status quo in contentious issues and because the government continues to act as though claims can be "settled" without addressing underlying questions of autonomy and nationhood, it appears that this country is not ready to change course. As outlined earlier, elites are able to influence public conversations to a remarkable degree – not only have governments been crossing First Nations out of both past and future landscapes but so also have academics and educators.[30]

We might propose a different story. How might the dispute in Caledonia have turned out if local leaders had immediately voiced support for Six Nations' efforts? Recognition of Henco's very real difficulty and immediate monetary losses would not have been precluded by such a stance, and at the outset, the protest was confined to the work site at Douglas Creek Estates and minimally disruptive. Instead of focusing on an end to the occupation and alienating Six Nations with accusations and complaints, leaders could have voiced their knowledge of Six Nations' outstanding grievances, potentially setting the tone for co-operation and strengthening relationships all along the Grand River. Instead, though government representatives at all levels have acknowledged the reality of Six Nations' long wait for justice in one way or another, the focus has always been on ending the occupation, on the economic losses suffered by Caledonia and other affected towns, and on the illegality of the activists' actions. This focus sends the unmistakable message to Six Nations and to the public that Native claims to justice only matter insofar as they affect the white settler societies around them. Thus, the need to make their grievances matter to society provides clear motivation, whether fully justified or not, for further and more extreme protest. When Ontario sent its police in on 20 April 2006, the protesters viewed it as a call to war – not a matter of law enforcement – and it was only after this police action that the barricades went up.

The Canadian government holds the balance of the power to define the trajectory of negotiations. As the representative of the dominant society, it is also the party that will have to work hardest to recognize First Nations' distinct visions of land, law, and society. By way of comparison, it is much easier for Canadians to grasp our cultural uniqueness from Americans than it is for them to recognize ours. They are more likely to view us as append-ages, when they think about us at all, owing to their lack of exposure to Canadian culture. While I believe the distinctions between the cultures of First Nations and Canadians are far deeper and broader, the analogy holds. It is hardly necessary for the people of Six Nations to learn about the ways that people in Brantford and Caledonia view themselves or their society in terms of property law or economic development. What Six Nations protest-ers and leaders are demanding in the ongoing protests, work stoppages, and land grievance negotiations along the Grand River is nothing less than recognition of their status as a distinct nation. This does not necessarily imply that they believe all ties to Canada will or should be cut. It does, however, have substantial implications for how the relationship between Six Nations and Canada will have to be restored if we are to remain allies and friends in an intermingled society.

Often, First Nations whose claims have been settled still feel as though underlying grievances have not been addressed.[31] A new approach to claims processes, then, might involve genuine apologies from the government as well as assurances that the same mistakes will not be repeated. Although many in Canada feel that what is done is done and that First Nations should move on, it is axiomatic that acknowledgment of past wrongs is an incred-ibly important step in making it possible to "move on." This is as true in the criminal justice system, where victims are often much more able to heal if the victimizer is genuinely remorseful, as it is in broader societal inter-actions. Emphases on the "extinguishment" or "surrender" of rights should be eliminated and a serious public education campaign embarked upon to help Canadians understand the discrimination practised against First Nations – for instance, public indignation might be provoked by the long-standing denial of voting and litigation rights to First Nations or by the typically fraudulent treaty processes that have shaped Canadian law and society. With a better sense of these injustices, which I believe would best be explained by the government itself, using concepts (such as those of human rights) familiar to Canadians, public support for revamped relationships with First Nations would surely, at the very least, not decrease. Instead of telling these stories, however, Canada voted against the *Declaration on the Rights of Indigenous People* in 2007 – one of only four countries (with three other British settler states) out of 148 to do so – despite recommendations from nearly all fronts, including its own Royal Commission on Aboriginal Peoples.[32] Mounting Aboriginal and international pressure has since resulted in adoption of the declaration, but the government has still felt it necessary to point out that the declaration is not "legally binding."[33] Overarching visions (such as those provided by James Tully and Dale Turner), legal principles (such as those highlighted by Patrick Macklem and Peter Russell), and even fairly concrete proposals (from the Royal Commission on Aboriginal Peoples) have been articulated but disregarded by the governments of Canada in favour of inaction. As the Royal Commission on Aboriginal Peoples' report explains, trying to preserve the status quo relationship, in which Aboriginal peoples' lands and resources provided the foundation for the high standards of living currently enjoyed by other Canadians, is futile.[34] Canada is shaping a political landscape that virtually guarantees that First Nations will feel as if they have no choice but to articulate their demands for territorial sovereignty in uncomfortable ways. As Celia Haig-Brown and David Nock envision the future,

> if Canada wants to justly claim to be a country committed to human rights, then perhaps the irony of acknowledging the shortcomings and calculated transgressions that have been made in our history related to land policies and legislation is the place to begin. From there the possibilities are endless. What if we became a country, like few others, that admitted its failures and frailties and built from there to address them?[35]

Part of the problem with negotiations may lie in the way that Canada and Six Nations appear to be talking about the same things – and even expressing similar sentiments on occasion – but without truly engaging in dialogue. Terre Satterfield describes how groups often seem to "talk past" each other "as though the other didn't exist."[36] In Caledonia, both Canadian and Six Nations representatives talked about the need to adhere to the law: Canada wanted the occupation to stop, and Six Nations wanted Canada to acknowledge its fraudulent land dealings. They both talked about rights: Six Nations was focused on collective land rights and the entitlement to self-determination, while Canada was concerned about individual property rights. Both claimed to be the injured party and the group that had made the largest concessions in negotiations.

Andrew Woolford explains that several dilemmas of intercultural communication can plague treaty processes and reconciliation.[37] Most crucially, while "respect" for cultural difference is asserted, the hegemonic cultural valuational model that saw this respect initially denied often lives on. By paying lip service to respect for others, the "multiculturalist" can maintain a privileged position, making real reconciliation unattainable. Woolford calls for First Nations to be treated as historically legitimate nations and for governments to make genuine apologies without thought to the legal consequences, as these will likely have more positive impacts on relationships than well-timed speeches delivered at risk-free moments such as the signing of agreements. While both sides seek material and symbolic "certainty" in agreements, Woolford sees important distinctions. In material terms, non-Aboriginal people seek safety for jobs and homes, while Aboriginal people want opportunities for economic security and community sustainability. Symbolic fulfillment for non-Aboriginal Canadians will come in the form of the feeling that things have been made right, while Aboriginal people seek recognition of unique identities. Aboriginal people tend to eschew discourses of "finality" in favour of "predictability," which reflects mutual understandings of treaty responsibilities but is not weighted by demeaning concepts of "extinguishment." First Nations have reason to mistrust non-Aboriginal governments' intentions to live up to agreements, are focused on ongoing relationships, and do not want to bind future generations to treaties that may go bad. Non-Aboriginal people seek final settlements out of fear that First Nations will continue to seek ever-greater powers and privileges.

The issues Woolford explicates are spelled out clearly in Caledonia, where the ongoing erasure of history and relationships perpetuates perceptions of injustice. Successful agreements and peaceful landscapes will depend on explicit recognition of past and ongoing mistakes as well as on distinct nationhood, as Six Nations has so often emphasized. These basic necessities for honest and healthy relationships hold across Canada and likely across the globe. As David Rossiter and Patricia Wood explain, reconciliation cannot be achieved while beliefs in the "end of history" persist: "Political, economic and social relations are sedimented in space. To move forward without excavating and facing up to each constitutive layer is, indeed, to live within a fantasy."[38]

David Usher's prescription for redressing injustices and working toward just futures also requires explicitly admitting manifold understandings of the history and geography of Canada and the power relationships built into both. He proposes to challenge the histories of exclusion that have shaped Canadian physical, discursive, and legal terrain, as we know it. By accepting that diverse concepts of power and control exist within Canada and that jurisdictions and boundaries have capacity enough for shared interests, we can use diversity as a foundation "on which people can come together for the common good."[39] The point is that the past should inform visions for the future. James (Sakéj) Youngblood Henderson, describing a constitutional vision that calls to mind Erin Manning's search for unorthodox versions of nationhood, explains that

> the incomprehensible nature of constitutional reforms requires Canadians to undertake a quest of understanding. They need to dream alternative visions. Their contrived response to these constitutional commands seeks to avoid the apparent: there is a new order possible, unknown to colonial thought or not known well enough. Canadians have a responsibility to discover the new constitutional order of Canada. They have to discover how their colonial contexts have been transformed into postcolonial government.[40]

John Borrows, too, spells out the need for new relationships, even when Aboriginal and non-Aboriginal interests seem less than compatible, and calls for a coming to terms with simultaneous traditionality, modernity, and postmodernity aspects of Aboriginal identity.[41] Although the recognition of Aboriginal rights to shape Canadian landscapes will cause significant disruption, it will set us on a path to a more just and peaceful future.[42] Borrows calls for a continuation and revitalization of the original federal relationship as agreed to in treaties, wampum, and presents, partially expressed in the written text of the Constitution and the Royal Proclamation, but more fully explicated in the oral and documentary law and history that underlies Canada's constitutional text.[43] In other words, he calls for recognition of another set of societal discourses – the ones that initially underlay Canadian–First Nations relationships but were discarded in favour of "jurisdiction" through the *Indian Act* and other justificatory instruments.[44] He cites Will Kymlicka and Wayne Norman, who point out that "it is clearly unhelpful to talk as if there is a zero-sum relationship between minority rights and citizenship; as if every gain in the direction of accommodating diversity comes at the expense of promoting citizenship."[45] In fact, Borrows says, when Aboriginal people no longer feel as though their societies are threatened they may become more willing to embrace relationships with others in Canada (though this should be neither expected nor demanded). Likewise, when non-Aboriginal peoples no longer need to worry that their resources, livelihoods, and rights are in jeopardy because expanded terms of Aboriginal citizenship are on the table, the rights secured through such interdependence may be reinforced. Intergovernmental relationships can be marked by peace, and two pertinent examples jump to mind: relationships within the

Haudenosaunee Confederacy itself and early settler–Haudenosaunee relationships. Although later abandoned in favour of colonial law and settler
priorities, early relations of interdependence, autonomy, and respect provided
possibilities for just societies.

Constitutional Possibilities

Though Canada recognized the Confederacy Council as Six Nations' governing body in the negotiations, it denied Six Nations the right to assert
authority over contested lands through the Haudenosaunee Development
Institute. Motivations for this stance likely included the belief that Six
Nations was being "unrealistic" in claiming the right to self-govern; the
perception that Natives demanding autonomy should be denied any recognition of the government's fiduciary and treaty responsibilities; a focus on the
positions of those Aboriginal people who were relatively content to belong
to Canada; and a fear of a legal vacuum if a third order of government were
created. But what might a Canadian society shaped by recognition of broad
Aboriginal rights to land and self-government actually look like? Scholars
of political science, law, and philosophy have imagined a wide range of
proposals, each based on differing conceptions of Aboriginal rights and title,
grounded in Aboriginal or Canadian law, on principles of long-standing
occupancy and management, or on some combination of these.[46] Having
examined the constitutional and legislative history of Aboriginal title in
British settler states, political scientist Peter Russell contends that

> the quest for recognition of land rights is at the centre of the modern
> Indigenous peoples' movement. The denial by occupying states of
> Indigenous peoples' ownership of the lands and waters that supported
> them for generations is the root cause of the injustice these people have
> suffered. Endeavouring to overcome this injustice is what distinguishes
> the political movement of Indigenous peoples from that of any other
> group or minority within the world's nation-states. For Indigenous
> peoples, land rights subsume their right to self-determination. The col-
> lective self whose future they wish to determine derives its identity from
> a historical relationship with a particular place on earth. Their right to
> self-determination, therefore, can be realized only when their right
> to decide how to live in that part of the earth and their responsibility to
> care for it are recognized.[47]

Highlighting the paradox according to which the courts are being asked to
question the very legitimacy of their settler states, Russell also argues that
Canada's indigenous peoples have been able to capitalize somewhat on this

country's mania for constitutional reform. Though conceding that top-down policies are simpler, Russell calls for agreements negotiated under free and fair conditions that can be dignified with the name "treaties," and he seeks a truly multinational understanding of Canada. He cites growing evidence of a positive correlation between Aboriginal peoples' control of their own land and resources and the welfare of those First Nations.[48]

Indigenous struggles the world over are connected by their demands for a new definition of nationhood and by a new recognition of Aboriginal cultures. Political philosopher James Tully argues that "modern constitutionalism" is incapable of housing cultural accommodation, calls for which are being made all over the world. He asks: "What is the critical attitude or *spirit* in which justice can be rendered to the demands for cultural recognition?"[49] He answers his own question by referring to the famed *Spirit of Haida Gwaii*, a sculpture by Haida artist Bill Reid that depicts a canoe packed with diverse inhabitants, each scuffling for recognition and acting from a unique perspective. Tully points out that societies are called "multicultural" with "no agreement on what difference this makes to the prevailing understanding of a constitutional society."[50] Indeed, as discussed in Chapter 3, the tensions inherent in Canada's claims to "multiculturality" are disconcerting. Tully insists that the Constitution be seen as an ongoing intercultural dialogue, one that respects mutual recognition and consent, both of which demand that Aboriginal peoples enjoy self-government – in short, sovereignty.[51] In his view, "the two public goods [that contemporary constitutionalism] harbours come into sharp relief ... they are the critical freedom to question in thought and challenge in practice one's inherited cultural ways, on one hand, and the aspiration to belong to a culture and place, and so to be at home in the world, on the other."[52]

Tully's vision for rethought constitutionalism speaks volumes to Six Nations' attempts to reclaim land and recognition of sovereignty. Although the accounts of Aboriginal self-determination presented in this chapter are expressed in academic terms, representatives for Six Nations in the Caledonia dispute over land have articulated their visions equally strongly and with unmistakable references to these overarching discussions. Recurring in Six Nations' discourses is the conviction that their Aboriginal "rights" are inherent and Creator-given, not delegated by the Canadian state or requiring justification by settler law, and that they are not a class of "minority" citizens with special privileges but, rather, unique and distinct peoples possessed of political systems with equal validity to those of Canada. The Haudenosaunee view treaty relationships as being of fundamental importance, and they affirm again and again the importance of dealing with Canada "in right of the Crown" to reflect this historic alliance. Though some representatives for

Six Nations in the protest or at the negotiating table may be concerned less with definitions than with outcomes, the importance of nation-to-nation relationships under the Two Row Wampum is constantly avowed. And because conversations about land and sovereignty are controlled by Canadian terminology, Six Nations activists have taken up the task of asserting the injustices done to them in language familiar to the dominant society surrounding them, speaking of rights and legalities in ways that others can understand.

We see many of the academic and theoretical arguments on offer today represented in the struggle for geographic and political space at Kanonhstaton. Matthias Koenig and Paul de Guchteneire point out that debates about the "politics of cultural recognition" and "multicultural citizenship" in culturally diverse societies address two main dilemmas.[53] First, can the recognition of difference be squared with the need for interdependence and trust in a democratic polity? This dilemma demands that constitutional arrangements establish a shared space of interaction that would still permit distinct cultural practices and identities. The second major dilemma, they say, is how to reconcile group-differentiated minority rights to self-rule with individual human rights to inclusion in the broader political body. These are largely philosophical, rather than empirical, problems, in their view. However, to Aboriginal activists, leaders, and thinkers, such as those at Six Nations, a major impasse concerns the terms of the debate itself. In this regard, the language used in discussions around sovereignty acts as a normative framework for Aboriginal declarations: "That is, they seek recognition as 'peoples' and 'nations,' with 'sovereignty' or a 'right of self-determination,' even though these terms may distort or misdescribe the claim they would wish to make if it were expressed in their own languages."[54] Tully points out – as Six Nations has so often done – that mutual recognition will be ineffective if it attempts to comprehend each culture on the same terms – that is, if it fails to rethink fundamentals of constitutionalism such as the axiomatic connection between nations and nation-states. Indigenous philosopher Dale Turner explains: "Aboriginal people's understandings of their 'rights' are constrained by contemporary constitutional discourses."[55] They view indigenous rights as not simply another class of minority rights to be defined in the context of the Canadian state but, rather, as flowing from legitimate nationhood. Important continuities exist between the old discourses that legitimized assimilation and the current Ottawa debates on Aboriginal sovereignty,[56] both of which are justified by colonial assumptions and by "unilaterally setting down limits for any political dialogue to occur."[57] Many Aboriginal people do not question that they are Canadian; it does not follow, however, that they simply embrace the status of citizens with perks:

The Aboriginal voice, in order to participate in political liberalism's dialogue about the significance of Aboriginal rights, must be able to filter out the spiritual dimension that lies at the heart of Aboriginal views of sovereignty and translate those views into the language of rights. This is what Aboriginal peoples have been trying to do since the time of contact, but the translation process itself is the problem ... Aboriginal philosophies must be forced into the language of policy in order to be deemed useful.[58]

Turner also explains that the adversarial nature of the Western European legal tradition does violence to Aboriginal understandings of political sovereignty.[59] As Gitksan and Wet'suwet'en hereditary chiefs Gisday Wa and Delgam Uukw explain, "if one culture refuses to recognize another's facts in the other culture's terms then the very possibility of dialogue between the two is drastically undermined."[60] The preamble to the *Constitution Act, 1982,* for instance, claims that Canada is founded on respect for the supremacy of God and the rule of law – a monocultural statement that "projects a singular and powerful cultural image over the Charter."[61] Emphases on the "rule of law" from Canadian representatives in Caledonia can easily be traced to national foundations such as these, which so clearly disregard the world views and systems of law that already were in place on Turtle Island when the settlers arrived. Mary Ellen Turpel delves into the paradigm that presumes that multicultural difference can be reduced to the management of "minority" issues without recognizing the inherent challenge posed by Aboriginal peoples to the entire individualistic "rights" approach to social conflict, which is clearly derived from the emphasis that Locke and Hobbes both placed on private property (that is, its protection) as the reason to enter civil society.[62] As it is, Aboriginal proposals are constrained by the individualist legal order. Visions for collective rights and Aboriginal conceptions of law are so alien to the Canadian single-state framework that simply making a claim necessitates accepting dominant legal textual and interpretive frameworks. The contemporary world of Aboriginal politics, which focuses on self-determination (and may or may not include self-government), then, is necessarily packed with references to land title, self-government, equality, and social services as well as the right to practise spiritual beliefs. However, as Turpel argues, "genuinely recognizing another People as an(other) culture is more than recognizing 'the rights' of certain persons. Aboriginal cultures are not simply groups of persons who are culturally at a prior state of development and of different races ... Aboriginal cultures are the manifestations of a different human (collective) imagination. They are no less than culturally distinct."[63]

So do Six Nations' references to treaty federalism, nation-to-nation dialogue, the Two Row Wampum, and the inherent right to self-government obscure or illuminate the debate?[64] Is it possible to recognize Six Nations' demands for self-determination without causing social upheaval? International law separating national from international competence does not exhaust sovereignty's meaning, and sovereignty can be exerted concurrently by more than one entity – this is, after all, the concept of federalism.[65] Although Canada's 1996 Royal Commission on Aboriginal Peoples' report ultimately concludes that classifications are less important than relationships, it also provides space for alternative definitions of sovereignty such as the one by Taiaiake Alfred, who suggests the Mohawk word *tewatatowie*, which means "we help ourselves."[66] The term encompasses concepts of interests, boundaries, and responsibilities related to land as expressed in the Great Law of Peace and includes respect for others and autonomy: "The people take care of themselves and the lands for which they are responsible."[67]

Does Canadian legal tradition leave room for alternative state arrangements? Law professor Patrick Macklem believes that it does. In his view, "a unique constitutional relationship exists between Aboriginal people and the Canadian state which does not exist between other Canadians and Canada."[68] He explicates key factors constituting "indigenous difference" that warrant constitutional protection: prior sovereign authority, the treaty process, and, most pressingly, occupancy prior to European arrival and the establishment of the Canadian state. While end-state theories are suitable for determining what distributive justice consists of in some cases, and historical entitlement is appropriate in others, the choice is redundant in the case of Aboriginal title. Canadian property law itself is already committed to prior occupancy as a means of assessing competing claims to land. Formal equality, therefore, requires that Aboriginal people benefit from its application (as Six Nations so often points out in references to Canada breaking its own laws). Raising the possibility of a third, Aboriginal, order of legislative authority, he explains: "The fact that Aboriginal people also belong to the broader community should not obscure the fact that this issue [of Canadian citizenship] will arise exactly when Aboriginal interests and those of the broader community are in conflict."[69] We have only to look at Caledonia and Brantford to see Macklem's predictions borne out. The "rule of law" discourse so often cited is all about terms of citizenship and Aboriginal "special" rights.

Macklem, like the Confederacy Council, calls for nation-to-nation negotiations in good faith. To him, Canadian sovereignty must – and can – constitutionally acknowledge separate territorial and jurisdictional spaces for Aboriginal societies, recognizing tight linkages between self-government and land.[70] Legal scholar Kent McNeil likewise argues that the *Constitution Act, 1982*, provides an opportunity to leave behind the notion that legislative powers were exhaustively distributed between the federal and provincial governments.[71] Decolonization of the Constitution involves envisaging space for Aboriginal governments to exercise their inherent powers by interpreting section 35(1) in an expansive way, avoiding a jurisdictional vacuum by empowering Aboriginal people to take charge of their own communities at the pace they choose.[72] Indeed, the 2000 Nisga'a Final Agreement (NFA), with its tripartite division of paramount and autonomous powers, has opened up just such a possibility. Although the issue of what kind of an "entity" the Canadian government now recognizes the Nisga'a Nation to be is still somewhat unclear, likely because the government is reluctant to face controversy where it can be avoided (if only temporarily), Emily MacKinnon argues convincingly that the Nisga'a Lisims government is a new kind of administrative unit. She also believes that the NFA "can be reconciled with Canadian federalism through section 35 of the *Constitution Act, 1982*."[73] The government currently recognizes the inherent right of self-government as an existing Aboriginal right under the Constitution, so all that remains is to negotiate and implement treaties according to this principle. The NFA was deemed not to require constitutional amendment by the courts because it was interpreted as having granted only limited powers to the Nisga'a – an approach MacKinnon argues is problematic in that "Aboriginal nations will not achieve true reconciliation until they are recognized openly as a third order of the federation." This means that

> aboriginal governments negotiate treaties in good faith, only to find that although the federal and provincial governments pay lip service to the aboriginal demands for self-government, the courts refuse such recognition of their status. The courts should either find that a third order of government may be introduced through section 35, or require a constitutional amendment process, so that the process of reconciliation can move forward.[74]

As we have seen in the long and still-continuing story of Haudenosaunee–settler relationships, the abandonment of more expansive notions of the Canadian state was, in fact, the result of a deliberate series of choices. Tracing the decisions that led to the abandonment of the treaty confederacy, Henderson draws attention to the space-shaping power of constructed law, which ignored the inherent rights of Aboriginal peoples in favour of conceptions that delegated rights from the British Crown. Europeans justified settlement of indigenous lands by applying Locke's theory that property demands the mixing of land and labour – which, however, appeared not to extend to the First Peoples managing their lands. They were believed to have no government unless allied with a European Crown. The rise of the state – linking land and polity so tightly, as we heard from Kenneth Olwig – thus accompanied the rise of colonialism.[75] Henderson, like Six Nations, calls for resumption of the treaty commonwealth, which, he feels,

> united the best of Indigenous and European traditions. It should not be characterized as a series of small-scale, routine adjustments to the context of colonialism. It was an alternative context-breaking explanation of the law of nature and nations that respected our sovereignty, our humanity, and our choices to preserve peace. The historical and legal legacy of the treaty commonwealth brings into question the necessity of colonization.[76]

Henderson's arguments concerning treaty citizenship are founded on the premise of inherent rights of Aboriginal people to their land, and they also assume that "inherent rights not specifically delegated to the sovereign or placed under its administrative jurisdiction are reserved to the Aboriginal orders."[77] For him, treaty citizenship is a "good and decent vision and an integral part of the Canadian order" that would avoid the take-it-or-leave-it propositions of merely federal citizenship and that has the potential to generate harmony through autonomous zones of power, freedom, and liberties.[78] As mentioned earlier, the Canadian government initially refused to sign the *Declaration of the Rights of Indigenous Peoples*, almost certainly out of fear of its central avowal of the inherent right to self-determination, even though UN declarations, unlike UN conventions, are not binding upon states and do not require them to report implementation progress. Ronald Niezen, who discusses the significance of the declaration's draft, points out that

> whether or not concerns over the possibility of indigenous secession are well founded is a matter of great importance. Put starkly, if these concerns are justified, then the creation of a strong foundation for indigenous self-determination could encourage new conditions of regional instability in some parts of the world; whereas if the claims are not justified, then the concerns themselves may represent a strategic obstacle to the realization of a major human rights initiative.[79]

He tracks crucial differences between Quebec's movement for independence in the 1990s and the efforts of the James Bay Cree nation to gain international rights to self-determination. The Cree were prompted by the distinct threat of environmental devastation wrought on their lands by the James Bay hydroelectric project and also by a belief in their right to determine their political destiny in the event of Quebec's secession. At the time, Quebec separatists were asserting that the borders of their province would be the borders of their new country and that they would unilaterally assume existing federal treaty obligations, removing the federal government as party to the Cree treaties. The Cree and Inuit referendums on the issue of secession showed more than a 95 percent response in favour of remaining with Canada in the event of secession.

As Niezen explains, the Cree challenged Canada's attempts to avoid the use of the word "peoples" in the draft *Declaration on the Rights of Indigenous Peoples* (Canada urged the use of terms such as "populations" or "groups") in such poignant statements as "[Canada has] decided that our rights as peoples will not exist if they simply avoid referring to us as 'peoples.'" They have also pointed out the double standard inherent in Canada's recognition of Quebec's right to self-determination and denial of the same for its Aboriginal "distinct societies" and in the use of the term "peoples" in the Constitution but not in international documents. At the same time, they have made clear that the Cree have no interest in secession from Canada but, rather, "want self-determination to be recognized so that we can finally become part of Canada."[80] Secession and independent statehood are not typically goals of indigenous groups, both for practical reasons and because of differences in the ways Natives view political and physical ties to land. They are usually "oriented more toward securing 'traditional' political identity than the trappings of statehood."[81] As Niezen points out, Deskaheh was not demanding total Haudenosaunee independence from Canada in his 1923 visit to the League of Nations; he was simply presenting statehood as an option for resolving Six Nations' grievances with Canada. Overwhelmingly, indigenous peoples are pressing for constitutional reform and separate orders of government rather than for total separation. In a description of indigenous political entities that sounds as if it had been sketched with Six Nations in mind, Niezen writes: "These entities do not fit into existing social categories. They are nations, yet do not pursue statehood. The suffering of their constituents is expressed neither in the comparatively ineffectual gestures of 'ordinary' resistance nor, so far, in more overt, politically dangerous rebellions."[82] Six Nations' most pressingly expressed concern is that its unresolved land claims be addressed by Canada, honouring the relationship of alliance that both parties agreed to centuries ago.

Indeed, the report by the Royal Commission on Aboriginal Peoples envisions sustainable relationships based on four pillars: treaties, governance, lands and resources, and economic development. Though the treaty process has been plagued by historic failures, some potential for future successes is augured by the *Constitution Act, 1982*, as well as by principles enunciated recently in the courts. The Royal Commission on Aboriginal Peoples shares Henderson's view that treaties have strong foundations in the British legal system, comparing them to the terms of union under which the provinces entered Confederation, and it asserts that "the fulfillment of the spirit and intent of the treaties is a fundamental test of the honour of the Crown and of Canada. Their non-fulfillment casts a shadow over Canada's place of respect in the family of nations."[83] The Supreme Court of Canada has recently and quite consistently – albeit slowly and at great cost to Aboriginal people – made it clear that Aboriginal and treaty rights are part of the legal system that defines (a new) "rule of law" in Canada, though built on a jurisprudential foundation that has largely ignored Aboriginal perspectives. As a commitment to a new nation-to-nation treaty process, the Royal Commission on Aboriginal Peoples recommends issuing a new Royal Proclamation that would, like the proclamation of 1763, deliver fundamental principles for treaty making and that could also serve to express Canada's regret for injuries of the past. To give it legal effect, it would be accompanied by legislation – a new way for law to shape Canadian society.

The Royal Commission on Aboriginal Peoples' specific visions for political spaces that recognize Aboriginal autonomy call for three orders of government: Aboriginal, provincial, and federal. Based on discussions with Aboriginal leaders, it concludes that many concepts of Aboriginal governance involve a nucleus of territorial jurisdiction, though there is a good deal of variety in the particular arrangements envisaged. Many First Nations' communities have expressed the conviction that outstanding land issues must be resolved before jurisdictional issues can be satisfactorily addressed. In Caledonia, as detailed previously, these issues were cited simultaneously by Six Nations, with sovereignty and land rights inseparably intertwined. The Royal Commission on Aboriginal Peoples' report includes hundreds of pages relating to areas of Aboriginal jurisdiction, how differences and overlaps between Canadian and Aboriginal law might be resolved, and various possibilities for the structures of possible Aboriginal governments, including those based on territory, those designed with the needs of urban Aboriginal people in mind, and those based on public government models (such as that of Nunavut). It recommends replacing the Department of Indian Affairs and Northern Development with a Ministry of Aboriginal Relations as well as founding an Aboriginal Parliament that would provide advice to the House of Commons and the Senate as an additional means of representing Aboriginal peoples within Canadian federalism. Finally, the commission has recommended that Canada enact legislation affirming its obligations under international human rights instruments, recognize Aboriginal peoples' rights to remedy in Canadian courts for breach of these international commitments, and support the UN *Declaration of the Rights of Indigenous Peoples*.

The Royal Commission on Aboriginal Peoples' views on the potential for treaty relationships to shape Canadian space have been both preceded and followed by legal scholars sharing the basic concepts of its vision – namely, that treaties be seen as binding constitutional documents reflecting their intended historic significance in setting out the relationship between First Nations and settlers as to the use and enjoyment of land and in forming Canada as we know it.[84] The decolonization of Canadian constitutional law through the recognition of Aboriginal sovereignty need not interpret section 35(1) as excluding all federal regulatory power. Instead, parliamentary sovereignty and the rule of law must include Aboriginal laws.[85]

In asserting rights to self-determination and treaty relationships, however, Six Nations must contend with mainstream views such as those expressed by Alan Cairns, who argues that to ask Canadians to accept and support foreign "nations" within their borders is impracticable and who asserts that the institutions of traditional federalism already represent Aboriginal peoples. Ascribing differences between Aboriginal and settler peoples primarily to the historical past, he asserts that "those who share space together must share more than space" and argues that self-government is unrealistic for Aboriginal people today because of their growing urban populations and small land bases.[86] Wayne Warry points out that although Cairns rightly views standard assimilative policies as inadequate and clearly wants to move toward a greater understanding of, and respect for, Aboriginal peoples, he nonetheless perpetuates the idea that Aboriginal cultures are well on their way to being lost, rather than recognizing that all cultures evolve. Cairns's understanding of self-government is clearly based on Eurocentric ideas, which is understandable, but he allows his fear of separate or different jurisdiction to preclude recognition of different visions for third orders of government, such as, for instance, those spelled out by the Royal Commission on Aboriginal Peoples.[87] Tom Flanagan goes further than Cairns, contending that "Aboriginal government is fraught with difficulties stemming from small size, an overly ambitious agenda, and dependence on transfer payments.[88] Flanagan likens European settlement to an inevitable, if possibly morally unjustified, takeover by a more powerful "tribe" that established legitimate sovereignty and argues that rejection of the *terra nullius* doctrine only makes sense if one is reluctant (as he is not) to distinguish between civilized and uncivilized societies. Warry points out, however, that although Flanagan may abhor the idea, "the reality is that Aboriginal cultures contained social, political, and legal processes that, though different from those found in European systems, are equivalent to those currently held by provinces and the federal government."[89] Flanagan also believes that possession and control of Turtle Island has conferred "title by prescription ... to the European discoverers and their successor states over the hundreds of years that they have controlled the New World."[90] Thus, references to inherent Aboriginal sovereignty are merely turns of phrase, without weight in either domestic or international law. To Flanagan, Aboriginal people were simply the first of many immigrant populations. He dislikes the prospect of self-government because it would be irritating to settler populations and would apparently be "a standing invitation to other racial and/or ethnic communities to demand similar corporate status."[91]

As explored in previous chapters, representatives for Six Nations in this dispute counter claims such as those of Cairns and Flanagan by pointing to the Covenant Chain and the Two Row Wampum as examples of agreements that allowed for mutual respect and interdependence yet also for autonomy. Claims that Canada deserves title to land because settlers have stayed here for several hundred years are met with reminders that the Haudenosaunee have lived here for much, much longer. And along with Aboriginal legal scholar John Borrows, the Haudenosaunee assert that their rights stem from alternative sources of law, not from the moment of first contact with Europeans.[92] Though Aboriginal people struggle to fully identify themselves as Canadian citizens because their primary interests are rarely expressed in the law or in the goals of the state, Borrows proposes in a vision strikingly similar to that of the Two Row Wampum that Aboriginal citizenship could account for differences as well as integration of Aboriginal and non-Aboriginal people's lives: "The *sui generis* doctrine expresses the confidence that there are sufficient similarities between the groups to enable them to live with their differences."[93]

Wayne Warry's *Ending Denial: Understanding Aboriginal Issues* is an extremely useful resource for anyone interested in reading a calmly reasoned, evidence-based explanation of how the logics of thinkers such as Cairns and Flanagan fall short of "solving" Aboriginal issues in Canada.[94] I do not wish to paraphrase all of his ideas here, largely because his work should be read in full, though I have borrowed several quotations, which were included earlier. Unfortunately, his work was published in 2007, and so he did not have the opportunity of directly responding to the latest, and most strongly worded, manifestation of settler angst in book form. Frances Widdowson and Albert Howard's *Disrobing the Aboriginal Industry: The Deception behind Indigenous Cultural Preservation* hit the shelves in 2008.[95] This is a disturbing book purporting to criticize not Aboriginal people themselves but, rather, the alleged "Aboriginal Industry" that supposedly exists to make money from the false claims of cultural uniqueness and that supports indefensible policy goals such as Aboriginal self-government. Aboriginal leadership is also dismissed as hopelessly corrupt due to the primitive kinship bonds that direct Aboriginal politics and resource distribution, as Widdowson and Howard see things.

Much time and many words could be usefully employed in refuting their ideas and doublespeak in detail. To take one obvious example, they claim that the 1969 White Paper, designed to force total assimilation, sought to give Aboriginal people the "same opportunities" as other Canadians.[96] They include no explanation for why it was so strongly resisted by Aboriginal people and groups despite this apparently laudable goal. They refer to treaties as "treaties," presumably using quotation marks to dismiss the significance of these intergovernmental agreements, and call the Royal Proclamation of 1763 a "proposal."[97] Widdowson and Howard assert simplistically that the basis of land claims is "ancestry" and that legal rationales have been invented to override political opposition that arises "when one group is granted privileges at the expense of another."[98] This avowal is logical if one accepts that First Nations do not deserve any recognition for having been here first or that their difference and ties to land need not necessarily find source or justification in British and Canadian law. In the Aboriginal industry that the authors describe, First Nations that assert land title are trying to take advantage of ordinary Canadians, while lawyers working for First Nations in the land claims system and in the courts are perpetuating lies and wasting money. It does not matter, then, that working within these Canadian systems is the only "legal" way for First Nations to gain any recognition for their rights (in fact, a lawyer choosing to work for First Nations people need not necessarily agree with their view of their rights – the lawyer's job is simply to argue their case as best she can). According to Widdowson and Howard, Aboriginal people should be grateful to live in such a progressive, liberal society as Canada, given the "primitive" (the authors explain that this word is not insulting but merely factual) cultures from which they came. Their ire seems to be especially directed toward a few main targets: the idea of traditional knowledge; anyone who gives credence to claims of continuing cultural difference; and the notion that First Nations may desire, and be able, to build economies compatible with both Canadian and Aboriginal cultures. Chapters focus on, for instance, the apparently endemic and incurable corruption of Aboriginal leadership, the superstitions of Aboriginal health care, and the foolishness of attempting to incorporate Aboriginal values into education.

Their chapter on land claims is most pertinent to this study, although even the authors might recognize that their comments are less relevant in

Six Nations' context. Leaving aside the sarcastic tone that they use to describe the idea of Aboriginal land "rights," Widdowson and Howard claim that it is unrealistic to expect economic development to occur on reserves. Reserve land had been specially chosen, after all, because it contained no resources desirable to the settlers.[99] It appears, then, that they expect Aboriginal people to accept being penalized twice: first, when settler governments left them tiny, undesirable patches of land to live on and, second, when those same governments explained that they should give up on these remnants of territory because they are not economically viable. *Disrobing the Aboriginal Industry* also contends that Aboriginal people lack the long-term organized planning skills to take proper part in the labour market, because their hunter-gatherer cultures are only able to react to the present moment, are unaccustomed to merit-based systems of employment, focus on "free" compensation rather than on earnings, and are confused about the difference between leisure (deliberate free time between periods of work) and idleness (unplanned free time because there is nothing to hunt or to eat). I know that these generalizations are patently untrue at Six Nations. (Although I have only briefly visited other First Nations' communities, I have an eerie feeling that they would be untrue there as well.) People at Six Nations are employed both on and off the reserve, and many are small business owners and professionals. There is absolutely no reason to assert that First Nations people are incapable of long-term planning. Indeed, Six Nations' plan for their economic future was characterized by foresight, except that they did not foresee the failings of colonial governments. In the late 1700s and early 1800s, recognizing that they could not prevent incursions of settlers on their territory and that the government would not do so, they set about to sell some parcels of land, investing the earnings, and to lease many others to farmers, typically on ninety-nine-year leases. By the time Six Nations population grew to the point that their farming economy needed more land, the leases would be up. It was not Six Nations' fault that the government took their invested money and used it for Canadian projects or that it converted the leases into fee simple title.

Unfortunately, the authors continue, we cannot simply encourage Aboriginal people to leave the reserves because they lack the skills to survive. Instead, we need to train and educate them: "The reserves will wither away when they are no longer necessary to sustain the dependent and dysfunctional native population. But such a circumstance is resisted by lawyers working for aboriginal organizations on the grounds that vacating reserve lands will jeopardize future aboriginal rights claims." This patronizing commentary suggests that the only reason Aboriginal people prefer to live on reserves is because they want cash for settling land claims down the road

(although Widdowson and Howard have asserted that such long-term planning is beyond their abilities, in any case). Indeed, Aboriginal people have
proven that they are not culturally different because they use many European
technologies and things. Therefore, they have no justification for rejecting
other aspects of European culture.[100] This suggestion makes no sense. Would
Europeans lose their distinctness from Chinese culture after adopting chop-
sticks to eat some of their meals, or even all of their meals?

Proposals to encourage and increase Aboriginal self-government are
likewise dismissed as efforts to hide "the developmental gap," resulting in
"the entrenchment of tribalism, making it difficult for most native people
to access even the basic resources needed for survival."[101] Overall, land claims
are dismissed as "stealthy" attempts to secure benefits from capitalist developments, encouraged by an avaricious troupe of lawyers and negotiators
and a judiciary tricked into recognizing Aboriginal title to land as being
about ownership. Widdowson and Howard appear to take the painfully slow
process of claims settlements as evidence that the process itself should not
exist. They assert that negotiators are elitists making a living by sucking the
assets out of future settlements before they are even reached.[102]

In Daniel Salée's insightful and concise review of *Disrobing the Aborinal
Industry,* he points out that no compelling evidence of the Aboriginal industry is ever given: "There may well be such an industry, but the mere mention
of it is insufficient to persuade the reader that it is indeed at work in shaping
Aboriginal policy."[103] As he explains, the authors make inaccurate generalizations with respect to their chosen motif – namely that a developmental
gap exists between First Nations and European cultures – despite their claim
to be historical materialists. They assume that Aboriginal people do not
know what is in their best interest and do not exercise agency. As Salée points
out, they "shut themselves analytically to the very real possibility that First
Nations communities deliberately choose cultural preservation not because
they are manipulated into doing so by the Aboriginal industry, but because
they have consciously identified it – like scores of identity based and nationalistic liberation movements around the world – as the best way to avoid
disappearing, let their claims be known, and maintain their relevance."[104]

Claims of Sovereignty on the Grand River Lands

The history surrounding the Haudenosaunee of the Grand River Territory
renders Six Nations' claims to physical and political space in the Canadian
legal context especially unique. Since the Grand River lands were part of
the enormous Haudenosaunee hunting territory even before Contact, broad
claims to Aboriginal title justified by long occupancy and use, as well as by
spiritual and cultural connections, are possible. And because a specific chunk

of this land was "given" to those of Six Nations who chose to accompany Joseph Brant in recompense for losses in the American War of Independence, and some of that land was subsequently bought or leased and not paid for, or stolen outright,[105] Six Nations awaits resolution of twenty-eight specific land claims.[106] Because Six Nations' claims are specific, addressing defined plots of land to which alleged incidents of defrauding, non-payment, and theft are attached, the task of resolving them appears to be in some ways less complicated than that of addressing large comprehensive claims, which to the Western legal mind, especially, likely seem more vague and fraught with intercultural difficulties. However, as explained previously, one of the claims awaiting resolution is in fact quite a large one, involving the 1841 purported general surrender of land, including the land that later almost became Douglas Creek Estates. Since Six Nations alleges that this general surrender was invalid, this large area of land, which is largely already developed, is implicated in the specific claims process. And, as explained in the previous chapter, Canada and Six Nations have reached a stalemate on the question of the purported 1841 general surrender for the foreseeable future. Thus, although Six Nations' land claims are "specific" as defined by the Canadian land claims system, they also have wide geographic coverage. In addition, the documents detailing (to varying degrees) the histories of each of the twenty-eight claims are extremely complex and involve varying degrees of accepted "legitimacy" on both sides. Only a few claims are viewed as being relatively straightforward by both parties, and they "merely" await decisions on how much land or money is owed in compensation.

A second complication evidenced in Six Nations' statements regarding rights and sovereignty is the considerable blurring between protesters' deeply held beliefs in their rights to the Haldimand Tract, on the one hand, regardless of sales and leases conducted with varying degrees of adherence to legality, morality, or accepted protocol, and their underlying rights as Aboriginal people to Turtle Island in general, on the other hand. There is also tremendous variance in how members of Six Nations and other nations envision rights to "the land" being recognized, the degree of compensation. they believe is owed to Six Nations as a result of past injustices, the ways they would like to see their Aboriginal rights to self-government worked out, and even the extent to which they differentiate and emphasize their various alliances to individual nations (Mohawk, Seneca, Cayuga, and so on), to Six Nations of the Grand River Territory, to the Haudenosaunee people at large, and to a broader pan-Aboriginality. Because those Haudenosaunee who settled at the Six Nations of the Grand River Territory were officially recognized as British allies in a way that other Aboriginal nations of Turtle Island were not, many Six Nations people maintain that they are not "Aboriginal" people as defined by the Canadian state. Whatever its source or identification, however, a generally and deeply felt sense of injustice in Six Nations is palpable.

The goals presented by Six Nations in their efforts to shape law and society according to their own visions and values are thus complex, though at all times the land remains central. The Haudenosaunee access a multitude of elements of pan-Aboriginal identity, including the land's significance to this identity. They also publicly articulate cultural imaginaries in opposition to colonial frameworks and histories, which often paint pictures of "factionalist" tendencies among the Haudenosaunee, talk about colonization as inevitable and/or justifiable, and define settler–Aboriginal relationships as ones of dependence rather than equality. Many of Six Nations' goals and values, such as environmental values and invocations of sacredness, are expressed in terms that surrounding settler societies can comprehend and with which they can identify. To participate more fully in public debates about Canadian constitutionalism and Aboriginal sovereignty, Six Nations representatives often articulate demands for self-determination in language that their Canadian neighbours can understand, even while echoing the insights and visions of diverse Canadian and/or Aboriginal legal scholars, political scientists, and philosophers.

I have outlined the story of the Haudenosaunee and their relations with settler societies. Keeping in mind my own location within these settler societies, I have also advanced my understanding of the importance of discursive analysis to the act of unearthing buried power relations and ideological underpinnings implicated in representations of "truth" and "history." Since discursive regimes are so inseparable from projects to claim both legitimacy and actual space, the dispute at Caledonia is revelatory not only of the histories and geographies of its particular location but also of broader epistemologies and ontologies. What people say about the world consists of more than just words – these truth claims actually mould law, landscape, and society. I have told a Caledonia story, demonstrating how spokespersons for Canada and for Six Nations in this dispute over land access and represent certain discursive strategies and themes in order to further their respective conceptions of "landscape," weaving identity and polity together in complex ways. Both parties seek to shape the land according to their particular visions of law, justice, economy, and the future. Yet this investigation has also revealed ways in which Euro-Canadian discourses bury the histories and relationships that Six Nations invokes as fundamental and crucial to its existence. I have also sought to show how these discursive moves are contoured not only with self-image and value systems for Canada and Six Nations but also with struggles over the very meaning of landscape and nationhood the world over. The dispute in Caledonia over a particular patch of land is intimately linked to Six Nations' demands for recognition. As Michael Coyle has warned, solutions will not be found in status quo approaches.[107] Instead, innovative dialogues must be shaped, reflecting a genuine commitment to recognizing both the legitimacy and the land rights of First Nations.

On this basis, and with the support of many others before me, I have contended that Canada is not taking seriously its responsibilities to reconfigure and decolonize its relationships with First Nations, and I have briefly outlined a possible response, which is simple in concept though certainly difficult to accomplish. First and foundationally, Canada needs to unabashedly accept that reality is not monolithic; that differing and equally legitimate perspectives of history exist; and that more is at stake in disputes over land than the land itself. That said, as discussed throughout this book, land rights are foundational and must be resolved, and while these claims are being addressed, relationships built up, and treaties rewritten, Canada must also acknowledge its obligation to truly "consult and accommodate" First Nations with land under claim. This does not mean paying lip service to the concept, as has occurred with the Grand River Notification Agreement, but genuine consideration for First Nations' visions and plans. If one prefers "practical" justifications for these steps, then take the argument that costly and socially damaging protests and litigation will certainly continue under the business-as-usual approach. From a moral standpoint, fashioning new discourses and practices is crucial if Canada is ever to claim national dignity, legitimacy, and honour. Underlying these projects, and therefore most important, the roots of the conflicts between the Original People and the settler societies must be honestly accepted – roots in racism, illegality, theft, broken promises, and denial, as manifested again and again in the discourses constituting the dispute in Caledonia today. If these realities are glossed over – as they have been in Caledonia, through citations of Canadian law, Canadian history, Canadian value systems and epistemologies, and Canadian visions for economy, development, justice, and society – it seems clear that the story of striving for healthy and mutually respectful relations in "our home and native land" will not end well and that conflicts over the right to shape Canadian landscapes will continue apace.

I have focused in this chapter on treaties and constitutional possibilities, and I believe these broader forums to be the most important, efficient, and symbolically and materially appropriate spaces to shape society through law. The local scale, however, is far from inconsequential. Smaller-scale proposals for increased recognition of Aboriginal rights to shape Canadian space vary widely and deserve attention. Some suggestions explicitly address Canadian legal obligations to consult and accommodate where Aboriginal interests are affected, while others appear to take these for granted, calling for planning to involve indigenous perspectives so that "justice might be won through state action and not in spite of it."[108] Despite acknowledging the power of developmentalism as an ideology and the acrimonious nature of tensions between indigenous peoples and modern nation-states regarding rights to land and natural resources, some call for "community-based planning" rather than prescriptive agendas. In my view, larger-scale changes will be necessary in concert with such schemes, for summons to community-based planning do not provide a motivation for local non-indigenous communities to participate in co-operative planning processes if broader state regulations do not require them to do so. Co-management – a sharing of responsibility – is also identified as a possible mechanism for integrating Aboriginal and state systems of resource management. Some call for the right of Aboriginal people to co-management of natural resources to be entrenched in the Constitution,[109] and others hail it as a response to repeated Aboriginal demands for self-determination.[110] Others discuss the potential and the reality of social entrepreneurship as an approach to economic development that is capable of recognizing land as both the vital "place" of the nation and the foundation on which indigenous communities can rebuild their economies, thus meeting several objectives at once.[111]

In my view, Six Nations' historical and geographical context is unique in ways that *currently* make it more difficult to shape local spaces with consideration for Haudenosaunee economy and autonomy. The fertility and desirability of the Grand River lands, as related previously, has made settlement rapid. Six Nations is now located in the most populated area of Canada, the Golden Horseshoe, and development of nearby towns and municipalities shows no signs of slowing down – indeed, growth is now actually *mandated* in many areas by Ontario's *Places to Grow Act*.[112] However, if the nation's land grievances are resolved in such a way as to restore even part of its original land base in the Haldimand Tract or to earmark non-contiguous lands to increase the size of Six Nations' territory, the potential for a strong collective economy appears enormous, given Six Nations' large, growing, and educated population and central location. Many other First Nations in Canada are caught in a different bind; with less developed and desirable lands in isolated locations, the potential for even relative economic autonomy is much more limited.

I am getting ahead of myself here. The settlement of outstanding land grievances and the (re)acquisition of its own "places to grow" – and here I refer to both geographical and political spaces – are first-order necessities for Six Nations. Assimilation into Canada is not a realistic option. Given the persistence of Haudenosaunee political traditions and the momentum gained in recent years through the reclamation effort, language reinforcement, increased recognition of the Confederacy Council, and efforts at cooperation between the Confederacy and Elected Band Councils, assimilation simply will not occur. The Haudenosaunee will maintain their ability to actively adapt and change social and organizational structures to shape their collective future.[113] It is up to the Crown to decide whether to recognize its relationship with the Haudenosaunee now or later, as it seems unlikely that Six Nations will ever relinquish its sovereignty or cease to assert its rights to justice regarding its land grievances.

There are signs of local change, however. A major expressway planned since the 1980s in Hamilton, located just north of Caledonia, was protested by activists from both within and outside Six Nations. Non-Native protesters hoped that Six Nations' land rights might hold sway against the environmentally damaging development. Susan Hill points out that though the highway construction went ahead, agreements negotiated between the Haudenosaunee and the city of Hamilton, made possible by focusing on co-operation rather than confrontation, "have resulted in a unique partnership (and series of partnerships) based upon Haudenosaunee ethics and treaty principles," including articulations of Haudenosaunee land ethics and protection for as much land as possible.[114] The agreement "clearly delineates the position of Hamilton as a government of Canada bound by the ancient covenants of the Crown. Of extreme historical significance, this agreement marked the first time a government of Canada had recognized the governing authority of the Haudenosaunee Confederacy Council since 1924."[115] In this way, the challenges of, and opportunities for, accommodation were acknowledged, and solutions were arrived at that respected future generations. The current negotiations in Caledonia are an opportunity for recognition and respect, and, in this regard, an important step was taken when the government recognized the authority of the Confederacy Council as the negotiating body.

Instead of continuing to erase historical, geographical, and cultural realities, Canada must acknowledge that the Grand River lands have been seeded with racism, fraud, and denial. With new Canadian perspectives of recognition and respect in mind, Hill asks: "So as the governments of Canada and the Haudenosaunee Grand Council continue down this river, what exists in their shared history to use as a base for reconstructing healthy relationships between the Haudenosaunee and the Crown? Where might this river lead us if we travel it together in peace and friendship? What will our shared forever look like?"[116]

Conclusion

I began this research hoping to answer the question, "How have cultural values regarding land as a resource been acted upon and publicly elucidated in the Caledonia land dispute communications and negotiations?" I wanted to find out how this conflict over land began, why it appeared that it would not be resolved quickly, and what it was really all about. I felt that it must have something to do with "culture." It certainly does, though not in the somewhat simplistic way I had anticipated. As the discursive analysis I undertook revealed, assertions regarding "culture" and "rights" stake claims to particular constructions of the world. What might appear to be a "culture clash" or a dispute over land is in fact both at the same time, with questions of legitimacy, nationhood, justice, and law all mixed up in between. Epistemologies – the ways we learn about and view the world – shape ontologies – what we believe about the world – and categorizations of events, people, and ways of knowing work together to dictate social and legal "landscapes" according to certain logics. We can see the workings of competing frameworks in Caledonia, and we know that larger and deeper cultural imaginaries underlie them. In examining the discourses constituting, and constituted by, the dispute in Caledonia, and in paying attention to the Canadian spaces that have resulted from processes such as these, we are able to understand more about the unsustainable inequalities embedded in the relationships between Canada and First Nations.

At its most visible level, this dispute is about ownership and rights to a particular patch of land in Caledonia, Ontario, called Douglas Creek Estates, a partially built neighbourhood of new houses in a rapidly growing town. The solution seems simple enough: check the paperwork and problem solved. However, news releases, public statements, letters, meeting minutes, information pamphlets, and other texts circulated by those involved quickly reveal multiple layers of dialogue and debates nested and entangled. At the start of this particular dispute, the Grand River Haudenosaunee had already been contesting the purported surrender of this land for over a hundred and fifty years. Even the federal land claims process finally established in the 1970s proved inadequate and uncommitted to actually addressing the land grievances of Six Nations and other Original People. Though little understood by the surrounding settler communities, this protest and occupation of land in Caledonia is merely the latest assertion of Six Nations' land rights and nationhood.

And the public conversations between Canada and Six Nations that constitute the dispute have quickly morphed into double-edged debates over the "rule of law" and the right to protest. These debates have provided opportunities for Haudenosaunee representatives to point out that as a nation that has never ceded sovereignty in word or in battle, Six Nations has its own system of law and that Canada is breaking its own law in continuing to develop on contested lands and failing to attend to long-standing land claims. However, making claims such as "the law does not apply to us" to colonial societies largely ignorant of the Aboriginal foundations of their country has proven to be problematic. Canadian citizens unaware of these histories or of the implications of the Canadian Constitution's recognition of Aboriginal land and self-government rights are understandably frightened by the spectres raised by Aboriginal protests, which appear to be both illegal and threatening to settler property rights, incomes, and ways of life. Indeed, failures to address Six Nations' land rights issues reflect continuing colonial policy favouring settlers over Native people. As their First Nations allies became less necessary to the settlers, British-Canadian law and society were gradually formed in ways that ignored the initial treaties and relationships built around reciprocity and respect. The physical landscape of the Grand River was shaped according to settler norms of development, pushing Six Nations from their settled villages along the river onto an area of land known today as an Indian reserve. In a legal framework that premises underlying Crown sovereignty and the illegitimacy of Haudenosaunee government, how can Six Nations' land rights be fairly addressed?

At the heart of the dispute, then, is a much broader and deeper debate about identity and nationhood. Are the persons physically occupying the land in Caledonia protesters or criminals? Is the Confederacy Council the legitimate governing body of a still-sovereign nation or a cultural relic that must be pandered to as a matter of political expediency? Is Canada a multicultural state of hard-working and honest immigrants or a society built around the erasure of the people whose territory it now occupies? Do individualistic capitalist economies reflect the demands of reality or are they deliberately chosen systems of managing land and resources to which alternatives exist? And, most important, who gets to decide, and why?

The public discourses constituting this dispute thus expose ongoing historical erasures crucial to Canadian colonial and space-making projects. The narratives presented by Six Nations and by Canada reveal fundamental differences in the way the land is viewed both as resource and property and as a foundational prerequisite for nationhood. The story of the land – and the identities both discursively and physically embedded in it – exposes crucial dishonesties in Canada's national persona and calls for a renewal of ancient relationships between peoples who must find a way to shape the landscape together.

The story told by Six Nations in this dispute in Caledonia is one in which land figures prominently as an entity intensely bound to Haudenosaunee law, identity, and international diplomacy, and it is to be protected for future generations. Collective landownership and societal rights are tied together and, in turn, are fastened to sovereignty and nationhood. Six Nations' spokespersons repeatedly emphasize the ways in which rights to the land were eroded and ignored as the Covenant Chain alliance relationship was discarded by British and Canadian governments. The reclamation of Kanonhstaton, "the protected place," has catalyzed ongoing political dialogues within Six Nations regarding governance structures as well as environmental and economic visions for the territory. Protest and negotiation spokespersons underscore the need to view the story of the Grand River lands within their larger contexts of colonial history and not as black-and-white questions of documented "facts" written and controlled by the colonial government.

Six Nations activists and representatives have utilized a variety of strategies to publicly articulate their views. Discursive approaches range from the utilization of Six Nations' and mainstream media through interviews and press releases; to letters written to various government officials at all levels; to informal newsletters disseminated widely over e-mail and the Internet; and to public signage and radio and video documentaries. Other approaches are more "physical": open protests and land occupations; barricades complete with flags; the removal of half-built homes; and the use of wampum and the wearing of traditional ceremonial dress. Spokespersons have often negotiated the swirling waters of identity and activism by articulating assertions for land, spirituality, and sovereignty in language and symbols to which surrounding societies can relate. Referring to the imposition of the Elected Band Council in 1924, "borrowing" liberal society's "rights" discourse, reminding Canadians of Six Nations' alliance in war, pointing out the need for Haudenosaunee "places to grow," and accessing societal concerns about environmental degradation are some of the approaches that Six Nations' discourses have taken to finding "common ground" with mainstream understandings. Yet some differences seem too fundamental to be discursively rearticulated in the name of cross-cultural communication: differences relating to, for example, the spiritual importance of land; differing ontologies and epistemologies; uniquely Haudenosaunee systems for knowing (and thinking about) time and history; and the continuing existence and relevance of Haudenosaunee law.

Representatives for Canada in this dispute have offered a public narrative highlighting patience, tolerance, and the primacy of business interests and Canadian property law. Land is individually owned and serves as a site for orderly development and economic growth, while landscapes are to be managed along with populations to accomplish these priorities. Positive contemporary and future relationships between Six Nations and surrounding communities are emphasized over historical treaties between the Crown and the Haudenosaunee. Canada acknowledges the need to address outstanding land claims, focusing on the ownership of disputed land as indicated by documentation kept by the Department of Indian Affairs. The Haudenosaunee of Six Nations are presented as part of Canadian multiculturalism with special rights, not as a people with legitimate claims to nationhood.

Lessons learned the hard way at Ipperwash and Oka have resulted in discursively diplomatic techniques that reframe Six Nations' demands as "issues" with regrettably little relevance to the modern world of racelessness and liberal universalities. Representing the dispute as one of "rule of law" and property ownership rather than as one encompassing crucial issues of constitutional rights and territorial jurisdiction has served to criminalize activists and trivialize the Confederacy Council. As a result of the focus on economic hardships faced by the developers and Caledonians, the reclamation came to be seen as a drain on government coffers – like Native people themselves. The end goal of societal "normalcy" offers up images of tidy neighbourhoods accepting the status quo of Canadian peace, order, and good government, which masks the racist realities and the ways in which Six Nations' routines have been denied and suppressed. Claims to intercultural dialogue under the auspices of formal negotiation frameworks are belied by refusals to acknowledge the legitimacy of Haudenosaunee thought frameworks and histories. Physically, Canadian views have manifested themselves in the failed attempt to "remove" the protesters from the disputed land, thereby marking Douglas Creek Estates as an actual territorial battleground. The provincial police – a tangible materialization of Canadian law – have complicated dichotomies by directing attention toward aggressive non-Natives protesting the protest, and, all the while, the *Places to Grow Act* is shaping the Grand River landscape according to Canadian development prerogatives.[1]

So how is this dispute, which is ostensibly about land, really about "culture"? As I can attest from countless conversations, many Canadians would no doubt argue, usually with the best of intentions, that First Nations should "get with the program," stop trying to assert difference, blend into Canadian society and economy, and forget about long-past injustices related to land and sovereignty – they should realize that they are "no different from the rest of us." Here I must refer to James Clifford once more. He untangles some of the difficulties inherent in conflicts between Aboriginal peoples and settler states, in which issues of "culture" are so irretrievably central. As he explains, "in the conflict of interpretations, concepts such as 'tribe,' 'culture,' 'identity,' 'assimilation,' 'ethnicity,' 'politics,' and 'community'" can themselves be on trial.[2] This dispute is nothing less than a clash between master narratives tying land to polity, nationhood, and the right to shape the future. As such, it is contoured to global efforts to recontextualize rights to self-determination, as expressed through the management of lands and resources, from Western hegemonic norms to alternative visions. The Haudenosaunee of Six Nations on the Grand River Territory are not the only Original People in Canada or in North America to challenge ongoing colonialism, assimilation, and historical erasures, nor are the Aboriginal people of Turtle Island unique in this work. The fact that the openly racist and colonial discourses that originally justified Western supremacy and sovereignty have been refashioned into liberal economic discourses prescribing undifferentiated universal progress (according to Euro-American norms) does not make these conversations any less hegemonic, only less candid and more difficult to challenge. Canadian imaginaries of normalcy and order prevent us from acknowledging racialized attitudes and legislation. These erasures are continuing obstacles to decolonization.

Discourse analysis is an explicitly political project. I have tried to demonstrate the linkages among the discourses, histories, and identities as these stories are told and as they are inscribed on landscapes and political bodies, reflective of broader grapplings with identity. "Ontopology" is about how what we know and where we know it are connected. Along the way, I have developed ideas as to whether Six Nations and Canada could have expressed their viewpoints in ways that might have minimized conflict, speeded reconciliation, and mobilized public support for fair resolution. I have notions about the ways that a just Grand River landscape might be shaped for all who have staked claim to it. All of these concepts are inescapably shaped by what I consider to be my deeply Canadian world view. Many researchers, theorists, and philosophers before me have argued for new ways of shaping Canadian–First Nations relationships. In this book, I have sought to demonstrate how this dispute over land in Caledonia reproduces broader and deeper conflicts over history and the right to tell it. Inequalities are literally built into the land – Indian Reserve 40, hemmed in by settler societies all around.

The research for this book focused on 2006 and 2007, the first two years of the dispute. It is now 2011, and the story has not simplified at all. Caledonia is largely peaceful on the surface, and the physical occupation of Douglas Creek Estates has been reduced to a bare minimum, but tensions remain. Barricades have been resurrected for brief periods. Occasionally, someone will attempt to raise a Canadian flag across from or next to Kanonhstaton. There have been marches of Six Nations people and supporters to the site to raise awareness of their ongoing concerns as well as marches of Caledonia "grannies" citing two-tier justice. A group called Canadian Advocates for Charter Equality, founded by Gary McHale, Mark Vandermaas, and Jeff Parkinson, continues to call for the enforcement of the rule of law and has had charges laid against various members of the Ontario Provincial Police (OPP) (and it is in turn being sued by the OPP for defamation). The Canadian Advocates for Charter Equality has been especially involved in a class action lawsuit launched by business and property owners against the former OPP Commissioner Gwen Boniface and a former Cayuga Detachment commander of the OPP. The parties are seeking to add Her Majesty in right of Ontario (the Province of Ontario) as a party defendant for the actions of various ministers of the provincial Crown. The action was certified as a class proceeding in February 2010. Although the lawsuit is not officially targeted at Six Nations, the images on the main page of the class action website are photos of protesters burning a historic bridge in Caledonia and blockading the roads.

In another lawsuit, Dave Brown and Dana Chatwell, occupants of the home immediately adjacent to Douglas Creek Estates and most negatively impacted by the protest, sued the OPP and the Ontario government, seeking $7 million for failing to protect their safety and their home from the protesters. The Crown held that it was not liable for the disturbance of their peace and accused them of exacerbating the situation at times. Media reports on their struggles have been mixed, but it is clear that the couple and Dana's teenage son suffered from their home's position next to Douglas Creek Estates, especially at the height of tensions when protesters and barricades prevented them from freely accessing their home, and from the OPP's strategy, which appears to have exacerbated, rather than lessened, their difficult situation. The case was quietly settled out of court for an undisclosed sum in early 2010, though neither the OPP nor Ontario publicly admitted to any wrongdoing. The property was purchased by Ontario, and their house was immediately razed to the ground. Janie Jamieson said that she would have preferred to see the homeowners' allegations examined more closely in court and that by putting blame on the OPP political leaders had abandoned their responsibility to focus on the land claims rather than on intercommunity conflict.[3] Wherever the relative burden of accountability lies, Brown and Chatwell's lives were undeniably severely disrupted.

And, yet, many new homes continue to be built in Caledonia, which is still a desirable place to live despite the upheaval and the unsettled land claims. These homes are constructed on land legally purchased by builders and developers, with legitimate building permits granted by Canadian government offices. Gary McHale ran in the 2008 federal election in the Caledonia riding under an independent ticket but received little support. He was forbidden to campaign within 100 metres of the former Douglas Creek Estates. Ken Hewitt, a well-known spokesperson in the Caledonia Citizens Alliance, a group primarily organized by prominent business people, which sought to be the recognized voice for Caledonians and to end the occupation, was voted mayor of Haldimand County in the municipal elections of 2010. Although Gary McHale and two of his close associates, Merlyn Kinrade and Doug Fleming, also ran for positions on the County Council, they were not elected.

Conflicts over law, responsibility, and landownership have been playing out more informally in the controversy over shops set up to sell cigarettes on disputed land. The "smoke shops," which are basically trailers selling untaxed cigarettes and typically carrying names such as "Broken Promises Smoke Shop," are met with mixed feelings by both Native and non-Native locals. Some people welcome the cheaper source of tobacco and support the shops as manifestations of ongoing land rights disputes; some do not. Opinions on the subject are by no means robustly correlated with Native or non-Native identity. For instance, there are Canadians who are supportive of the shops because they believe that cigarettes are too highly taxed and/or they agree with Six Nations' grievances, and there are Haudenosaunee who oppose the shops, arguing that shop owners are simply using land claims as a smokescreen to run big money-making rackets and/or that the shops reflect poorly on Six Nations.

The bulk of the visible controversy, however, has shifted from Caledonia to Brantford, where work stoppages have been an ongoing reality for local builders. The courts have been busy with litigation related to the protests, with injunctions against protesters announced and then put on hold, then renewed. The parties involved, the Haudenosaunee Development Institute and the city of Brantford, were told by the courts to participate in "good faith talks." When talks failed to produce results, the injunctions were strengthened, and Justice Harrison Arrell explained that "good faith negotiations can only take place if there are no work stoppages."[4] The decision was appealed by the Haudenosaunee Development Institute. A developer sued the city of Brantford for $10 million for misrepresentation and breach of disclosure relating to property purchased by the firm for development. When asked for proof of release from Six Nations prior to the purchase, Brantford had inaccurately told the developer there was no claim on the land. The company withdrew its injunction against Six Nations protesters. Meanwhile, Six Nations' Elected Band Council resumed litigation against the Crown for a full accounting of all sales, leases, and trust fund transactions carried out on behalf of Six Nations. As explained in earlier chapters, the litigation had been initiated in 1995, then put on hold in favour of negotiated approaches.

The Confederacy Council continues to participate in negotiations, although proceedings are often stalled for months on end. In interviews in 2009, both federal representative Ronald Doering and Confederacy Chief Allen MacNaughton seemed exhausted, but both expressed hope that negotiations would produce solutions. At one point, MacNaughton publicly announced his intention to step down as lead negotiator for the Confederacy, but a replacement could not be found. In November 2009, Doering explained that Six Nations' claims against Canada were legitimate and that setting a deadline on the negotiations was not an option. Responding to a question relayed from a Caledonia citizen through Mayor Marie Trainer as to why reserves were not simply eliminated and First Nations peoples allowed to become part of mainstream communities, Doering explained: "People who say that probably don't recognize that Aboriginal people have constitutional treaty rights protected in the constitution. That is something we cannot change and neither can the courts."[5] Efforts have been made to appoint a mediator to smooth the negotiating process, but no one can be agreed upon. Floyd and Ruby Montour, an elderly Six Nations couple well known to Brantford builders and local media for their conspicuous part in numerous work stoppages across the city, have quailed in the face of ongoing development, arrests, and injunctions and have sometimes received little support for their work stoppages from other Haudenosaunee people. They too have decided to carry on, although they have turned themselves in to police when charged with mischief and for disobeying court-ordered injunctions.

Led by interim director Hazel Hill, the Haudenosaunee Development Institute – to all appearances controversial both within and outside Six Nations – continues to press for official recognition of Six Nations' rights to consultation and accommodation regarding projects on disputed land. There is also dissatisfaction with Ontario's new harmonized sales tax, which took effect in July 2010 and established procedures for First Nations to claim tax exemption in certain circumstances. Elected Band Chief Bill Montour has called the tax, which would allow point-of-sale exemptions only on reserve land, a step toward "ghettoizing" Six Nations: "They are trying to ghettoize our people saying, 'You stay on reserve where you belong and that's it.' I think that's distasteful, I think it's unconstitutional. If I live off reserve I am not any less Mohawk than living on reserve."[6]

Five years after the stoppage of construction at Douglas Creek Estates, there have been countless arrests on all sides of the dispute. Many of these charges have been dismissed for various reasons. Some people claiming association with Six Nations' land reclamation activities have been openly condemned by the community leadership for their violent actions, and some claiming alliance with "Caledonia citizens" have been equally denounced by their supposed supporters. Racism born of fear, ignorance, and defensiveness has been painfully on display at times among both Natives and non-Natives. The scars from verbal and physical clashes will not heal quickly, and serious physical injuries have also been incurred on both sides.

At the same time, Six Nations' dispute with the Canadian government is more visible than it has ever been, with the Haudenosaunee gaining many supporters both nationally and internationally. Locally, an organization called Two Row Understanding through Education (TRUE) held public meetings for several years in Brantford, starting in 2006, with the goal of increasing awareness of the complicated history of local Haudenosaunee–settler relations. In November 2008, it held a session focusing on the term "rule of law." In November 2009, a large contingent of non-Native "allies" to Six Nations held a march in downtown Brantford. Some local city councillors supportive of Six Nations have been willing to risk censure by their colleagues for their views and actions. Although later shifted from his post as provincial minister of Aboriginal affairs, Brad Duguid signed an official agreement with Six Nations Elected Band Chief Bill Montour to improve communications between Ontario and the Haudenosaunee. There was local talk that Duguid was "too good" and that strong performance in the portfolio of the Ontario Ministry of Aboriginal Affairs was inevitably followed by reposting to a portfolio of higher priority to the Ontario government. One Six Nations elected councillor commented: "As soon as we seem to be getting somewhere with a Minister of Aboriginal Affairs there's always a cabinet shuffle and they're gone. We had the same kind of good working relationship with Michael Bryant and we were moving ahead and then he was gone."[7] In December 2009, the Olympic torch passed through Six Nations. In common with many Canadian communities, there were supporters and dissenters. As happened in the East Vancouver neighbourhood where I currently live, the torch was rerouted as a concession to the demonstrators.

This book is not the first to be published about the dispute in Caledonia. In October 2010, while this manuscript was under final review stages at UBC Press, Christie Blatchford's *Helpless: Caledonia's Nightmare of Fear and Anarchy, and How the Law Failed All of Us* was published by Doubleday Canada. I strongly urge anyone reading this book to read Blatchford's as well and to form their own opinion of it. Written in her characteristically engaging style (I have read Blatchford's columns in the *Globe and Mail* for years), *Helpless* chronicles some of the events in Caledonia from the perspective of many of the townspeople. As the title clearly indicates, it essentially argues that the OPP and, indeed, the Canadian government, failed to deal with the dispute according to the "rule of law." Blatchford conducted many interviews, and the book has an intensely personal touch, inviting readers to sympathize with the difficulties posed to Caledonians by the occupation at Douglas Creek Estates and to condemn the lawlessness of the occupiers. I benefited greatly from a thorough read. Blatchford employs a different analytical frame than I do here, and it is always helpful to test one's own conclusions through someone else's eyes. She also provides additional, albeit often indirect and very likely unintentional, support for many of the arguments I make in this book, especially those about the power of words to shape "reality."

Blatchford takes pains to provide at the outset a series of disclaimers explaining what her book is not about, and her statements are accurate. The book is not about Aboriginal land claims, the horrors of the residential school system, or the dubious merits of the reserve system. She says: "I do not in any way make light of these issues, and they are, in one way or another, in the background of everything that occurred in Caledonia. But *Helpless* is about what happened to the rule of law – the dry legal term for the noble arrangement a civilized society makes with its citizens, rendering us all equal before and bound by the same laws – in that town and environs."[8] In broad strokes, I agree with many of Blatchford's conclusions: that the way Caledonia was handled was deeply affected by the events at Ipperwash; that the dispute was often marked by violence; and that the government's response was inadequate. I viewed with embarrassment the simplistic charges of "racism" that have been leveled at her since the publication of *Helpless*, and the actions that prevented her from speaking at the University of Waterloo, for instance, in November 2010. It is obvious that Blatchford did not *intend* a racist perspective, and any reasoned critique of *Helpless* cannot simply rely on that crude charge.

Blatchford's perspective is openly avowed throughout the book as being one that favours the "rule of law." This lens is also palpable in less explicit, but certainly no less deliberate, ways – Blatchford is a careful writer, and she loses no opportunity to argue her case. For instance, she quotes one Caledonia resident, discussing the OPP's failure to remove the protesters on 20 April 2006, who compared the police to his grandparents who had "fought against the Germans in Germany for this, for law and order." Yet, he laments, the police in Caledonia had retreated in the face of opposition. His grandparents "would have just marched on." Although a comparison between the occupation and the Nazi regime is left unstated, Blatchford often works in this way through anecdotes and through the words of others to impliedly discredit the entire protest, despite stating that her official target is the OPP.

There is, of course, nothing inherently wrong with this approach. What I specifically take issue with is that, although Blatchford pointedly sets out to write a book that is not about Aboriginal land claims, this goal is quite simply impossible if one's topic is Caledonia. One of the main points I sought to demonstrate in this book is that what is left unsaid is often just as important as what is said. (I also question some of her facts – to take one obvious example, her claim that no one builds houses in Caledonia any more is patently untrue.) Blatchford certainly did not need to decide whether the dispute over Douglas Creek Estates was justified in order to write her book – I am likewise in no position to make any final ruling on this subject, and I do not attempt to do so. My argument is rather that the situation is much more complicated than *Helpless* implies, and my intent is to illuminate the ways that Caledonia is involved in a bigger picture, rather than the ways it can be illogically simplified. By bracketing the underlying history and focusing almost entirely on the failures of the OPP to oust the protesters and to restore the "rule of law" in Caledonia, the entire premise of the dispute is dismissed as illegitimate. Many of the deeply troubling events that Blatchford writes about have also been described in these pages, but where *Helpless* appears to accept at face value the government's position that Douglas Creek Estates was validly surrendered by Six Nations in 1841, I argue that this conclusion itself is borne of deeply embedded cultural assumptions that must at least be thought about before they are accepted.

At all turns, the story of Caledonia resists simplification and asks for considered thought. Even its main characters are complicated, often displaying evidence of the uneasy tensions inherent in the relationships between Six Nations and the surrounding communities and country, both at the individual and the collective level. This is true of people on both "sides" of the dispute and those who occupy uncomfortable but very real ground in the middle. "Agreeing" with one aspect of the occupation does not make it impossible to condemn another part. Having ambivalent feelings toward Aboriginal self-government does not make it impossible to recognize the underlying injustices perpetrated on First Nations in Canada; sharing moments of common understanding does not preclude disagreeing more generally; and acknowledging the understandable frustration of Caledonians, and the lives that have arguably been irreparably damaged, still leaves room for understanding Six Nations' own understandable frustration and distress, which has occurred over a much longer period of time. Without coming to terms with complexity, there is no way to move forward.

I hope it has been clear throughout this book that I have not set out to present either the Haudenosaunee or Canada as flawless heroes or malevolent villains or all Canadian–First Nations relationships as entirely negative or positive. Rather, my point is that when we take the time to scrutinize the conversations enacted in a dispute such as this one, we see that "the law" is far from a neutral instrument, and we can and must, at the very least, question its trajectory. Exchanges regarding citizenship, "equality," rights, and the law are constantly occurring in Caledonia. What kind of a society is being moulded along the Grand River by the acrimonious and seemingly endless web of litigation and counter-litigation between individuals, groups, businesses, and government? The inheritance of cultural imaginaries predicated on colonial assumptions, *Indian Act* legislation, and racialized interactions has shaped a Canada in which First Nations' continuing cultural differences have resulted in government attempts to control, ignore, and valorize.[9] These efforts are unrealistic and unsustainable. In telling this story and in calling attention to the shifty and shifting ways in which hegemonic imaginaries and power relations have sneaked into the discourses surrounding this dispute over land, I have pointed out that changing the trajectory of Canadian relationships with First Nations will take conscious effort.

To many people living within Canadian borders, this is a country of peaceful, good-humoured, and harmonious diversity built by immigrants seeking better lives for themselves. That has largely been my "reality." To others sharing this geographical area but shut out of its political spaces, "reality" has meant a state characterized by essentially monocultural Euro-American identities dictated by colonizers defining better lives for other people. These multiple realities are both true and false, and plenty of physical and discursive space is taken up by the no man's land in between. If Six Nations is to have its fair shake at justice in a society that claims integrity, then cultural, historical, and national differences must be saluted and honesty must determine how we shape the land together. We already have the constitutional and legal tools at our disposal to formalize new relationships. Section 35(1) formalizes Aboriginal and treaty rights, and numerous Supreme Court of Canada rulings have directed consultation and accommodation with First Nations regarding land rights, calling for negotiations rather than litigated solutions, which inevitably escalate tensions and create winners and losers. The report by the Royal Commission on Aboriginal Peoples provides a stunningly detailed vision of the ways in which Aboriginal sovereignty and nationhood could be recognized without destroying currently healthy aspects of relationships between Canadians and First Nations people.[10] I do not claim the legal and constitutional expertise to design a shared sustainable future that would recognize multiple sovereignties in Canada – our shared village, our Kanata. Yet surely common ground is possible. Perhaps, for insight, we could look to the Confederacy formed under the Tree of Peace.

Appendix 1: Key Persons

Barrett, Toby	Member of Provincial Parliament (MPP) (Conservative, opposition) for Haldimand-Norfolk riding, 1995–present.
Boniface, Gwen	Ontario Provincial Police (OPP) Commissioner until resignation in October 2006; succeeded by Julian Fantino.
Boyko, Lorne	Haldimand County Councillor, Ward 6 (Dunnville, Canborough).
Bryant, Michael	Ontario Minister of Aboriginal Affairs (Liberal) appointed on 30 October 2007.
Coolican, Murray	Succeeded Jane Stewart as principal Ontario representative at negotiations on 7 May 2007; succeeded by Tom Molloy in September 2008.
Coyle, Michael	Federal fact finder appointed 24 March 2006; released report on 7 April 2006.
Crombie, David	Liaison between non-Aboriginal Caledonia community and negotiation table; appointed 15 September 2007.
Detlor, Aaron	Lawyer and spokesperson for Haudenosaunee Development Institute.

Doering, Ronald	Assistant federal negotiator to Barbara McDougall; later succeeded McDougall as principal negotiator.
Fantino, Julian	OPP Commissioner, October 2006–present.
Finley, Diane	Member of Parliament (MP) for Haldimand-Norfolk riding (Conservative), which includes Caledonia (adjacent to Six Nations' territory).
Flanagan, Anne-Marie	Spokesperson for David Ramsay.
General, David	Six Nations Elected Council Chief until 21 November 2007; succeeded by Bill Montour.
Grice, Craig	Haldimand County Councillor, Ward 3 (Caledonia, parts of Oneida and Seneca).
Hill, Hazel	Principal spokesperson for protesters at site; representative for Six Nations at lands' side table in negotiations; interim director for Haudenosaunee Development Institute.
Hill, Leroy	Cayuga Bear Clan Subchief (Hohahe:s); one of the Confederacy Council's main representatives and spokespersons at the negotiations.
Jamieson, Janie	Initial reclamation leader, along with Dawn Smith.
Levac, Dave	MPP (Liberal) for Brant riding (including Six Nations), 1999–present.
MacNaughton, Allen	Mohawk Chief (Tekarihoken), the Confederacy Council's main representative and spokesperson at the negotiations.
Marshall, David	Ontario Superior Court Justice; issued numerous injunctions and court orders against protesters but was eventually overruled by the Ontario Court of Appeal.
McDougall, Barbara	Main federal negotiator until replaced by Ron Doering.
McGuinty, Dalton	Premier of Ontario, 2003–present.
Molloy, Tom	Principal Ontario representative in negotiations, appointed 18 July 2008 to replace Murray Coolican.

Montour, Bill	Six Nations Elected Band Chief beginning 21 November 2007.
Montour, Ruby	Dedicated and vocal protester in Caledonia and Brantford.
Monture, Phil	Principal Six Nations' land claims researcher and representative at the negotiations.
Peterson, David	Former Ontario Premier appointed 30 April 2006 to help resolve standoff; stepped down 14 June 2006.
Powless, Clyde	Frequent spokesperson for protesters at the Douglas Creek Estates site.
Prentice, Jim	Federal Minister of Indian Affairs and Northern Development (Conservative) until 14 August 2007; succeeded by Chuck Strahl.
Ramsay, David	Ontario Minister Responsible for Aboriginal Affairs (Liberal) until October 2007; succeeded by Michael Bryant.
Sloat, Buck	Haldimand County Councillor, Ward 2 (Cayuga, Rainham) until 2010.
Smith, Dawn	Initial reclamation leader along with Janie Jamieson.
St. Amand, Lloyd	MP (Liberal, opposition) for Brant riding (including Six Nations), 2004–08.
Stewart, Jane	Principal Ontario negotiator at talks until May 2007; succeeded by Murray Coolican.
Strahl, Chuck	Minister of Indian Affairs and Northern Development (Conservative), 14 August 2007–10.
Trainer, Marie	Haldimand County Mayor.

Appendix 2: Timeline of Events

1987
18 June   Hamilton–Port Dover Plank Road claim submitted by Six Nations to Canada.

1992
unknown date   Henco Homes (development company) purchases land in Caledonia, including future Douglas Creek Estates.

1994
December   Six Nations serves notice of action on Canada and Ontario demanding accounting of all sale and lease money.

2004
14 September   Six Nations, Canada, and Ontario agree to explore potential for out-of-court settlement.

2005
14 June   Ontario passes the *Places to Grow Act*, slating areas in Haldimand Tract for intensified development.

25 October   Day-long shutdown of Douglas Creek Estates construction by Six Nations' Land Claims Awareness Group, led by Dawn Smith and Janie Jamieson.

| 16 November | Land Claims Awareness Group hands out information pamphlets to 3,000 drivers on highway near Douglas Creek Estates. |

2006

28 February	Construction at Douglas Creek Estates is halted; occupation of site begins.
5 March	Henco Industries obtains interim injunction ordering protesters to remove barricades and allow construction to resume; protesters ignore injunction.
16 March	Ontario Superior Court Justice David Marshall sets 22 March deadline for protesters to leave site in order to avoid arrest for contempt of court.
24 March	First federal response to protest: appointment of Michael Coyle as "fact finder."
27 March	Confederacy Council officially states support for reclamation.
17 April	Elected Band Council councillors vote to designate the Confederacy Council as lead negotiators.
20 April	Ontario Provincial Police (OPP) officers raid protest site at 4:30 a.m. but withdraw after about four hours when masses of Six Nations and other supporters arrive in support; in response, protesters set fires and erect blockades on Argyle Street, Highway 6 bypass, and the Canadian National railway line; sixteen protesters are arrested but later released.
22 April	Representatives from Six Nations, Canada, and Ontario agree to appoint principal representatives within two weeks for negotiations to resolve the Douglas Creek Estates/Plank Road claim.
24 April	Hundreds of Caledonia residents gather at the Argyle Street South blockade to vent frustration over dispute; OPP officers form police line between crowd and protesters.
25 April	Haldimand County Mayor Marie Trainer is taken to task for racist comments regarding Six Nations members.
29 April	Former Ontario premier David Peterson is appointed by the Ontario government to help resolve the standoff.

3 May	Barbara McDougall and Ron Doering are appointed as federal representatives; Jane Stewart is appointed as provincial representative in the negotiations.
16 May	Part of Argyle Street barrier is removed by protesters.
17 May	Ontario government imposes moratorium on development at Douglas Creek Estates.
19 May	Some Caledonia residents set up their own blockade across Highway 6 to prevent protesters from reaching Douglas Creek Estates.
22 May	Violent clashes between large crowds of protesters and residents on Victoria Day; attempt by protesters to remove Argyle Street barricade is aborted; act of vandalism on power transformer blacks out much of Caledonia and Six Nations; Haldimand County Council declares state of emergency.
23 May	Argyle Street South reopened after protesters remove barricade; OPP clears away remaining Caledonia protesters.
24 May	Power is restored to most of the area by this time.
30 May	Caledonia's Emergency Financial Assistance Program commences.
8 June	Mayor Marie Trainer lifts state of emergency.
9 June	Camera operator from Hamilton television station CHTV is taken to hospital after scuffle with protesters who confiscated a camera; additional clashes between protesters and Caledonians occur in parking lot adjacent to Douglas Creek Estates.
12 June	Ontario refuses to attend negotiations because of the incident involving the television station CHTV.
13 June	Highway 6 barrier removed; Premier McGuinty says Ontario will return to negotiations.
14 June	David Peterson leaves talks.
15 June	Negotiations resume due to the removal of barricades.
16 June	Ontario government signs agreement in principle to purchase Douglas Creek Estates land from Henco Homes and announces additional homeowner and business assistance funding; Ontario releases *Growth Plan*

	for the Greater Golden Horseshoe, pursuant to *Places to Grow Act,* which appeared one year earlier.
22 June	Ontario agrees to pay Henco Homes $12.3 million for Douglas Creek Estates land; amount is later amended to $15.8 million for land and compensation, plus $4 million to other builders with plans for the site; MacNaughton, McDougall, and Stewart sign a "Negotiation Framework" agreeing to negotiations according to the Covenant Chain and Two Row Wampum.
11 June	Protesters remove barricade blocking the entrance to Douglas Creek Estates site.
27 June	Creation of various side tables to assist the main table in the negotiations, including archaeology and appearance, Douglas Creek Estates Plank Road lands, consultation issues, and education.
7 August	Further altercations between protesters and Caledonians.
8 August	Superior Court Justice David Marshall tells Ontario to halt negotiations until court order to remove the Native occupiers from the site is enforced.
11 August	Government of Ontario announces that it will appeal Justice Marshall's ruling at the Ontario Court of Appeal.
25 August	Ontario Court of Appeal rules that protesters can continue to occupy the Douglas Creek Estates site; negotiations subsequently continue.
30 August	Three protesters hurt in fire in unfinished house on Douglas Creek Estates; Premier Dalton McGuinty says he does not want protesters to settle in for the winter.
15 October	About 400 attend the "March for Freedom" rally organized near the Douglas Creek Estates by Gary McHale who called for 20,000 to attend; rally condemned in advance by various Canadian politicians; about 750 supporters attended Potluck for Peace, which was organized simultaneously by protesters at Kanonhstaton.
18 October	Ontario commits to hold off developing provincially held lands to the south of Six Nations' territory.
20 October	Ron Doering tells a Caledonia meeting that Ottawa has informed Six Nations that it does not have legal title to Douglas Creek Estates; Ontario Premier McGuinty

	announces intention to ask Ottawa to compensate the province for costs arising from the dispute.
30 October	Julian Fantino replaces Gwen Boniface as OPP commissioner.
31 October	Federal Minister of Indian Affairs Jim Prentice refuses to meet with Ontario Minister Responsible for Indian Affairs David Ramsay because of criticism directed at Ottawa by Ramsay and McGuinty.
3 November	Federal negotiators present Canada's official position on ownership of Plank Road lands (including Douglas Creek Estates) at the negotiations.
14 November	Six Nations negotiators present their views on the historical background of lands under dispute at the negotiations.
3 December	Rally held by about thirty people who want to raise a Canadian flag near Kanonhstaton.
14 December	Ontario Court of Appeal issues final quashing of injunction against protesters; states that Justice Marshall erred in earlier ruling.
16 December	Gary McHale and Mark Vandermaas arrested at third flag rally of about 150 people as they try to cross "no-go" zone to reach occupied site.

2007

1 January	Elected Band Council returns keys to historic council house to Confederacy Council.
20 January	Another rally organized by Gary McHale; OPP warns that breaching police line will result in arrests.
25 January	Federal negotiators present federal legal response to Six Nations' presentation of 14 November 2006.
19 March	Financial compensation details released for homeowners adjacent to the Douglas Creek Estates site.
29 March ,	Jim Prentice announces $26.4 million toward Ontario's costs incurred as a result of the occupation as well as an expanded negotiations mandate to address all of Six Nations' claims.

12 April	Julian Fantino implies that the OPP will not support a renewal of Caledonia's policing contract if divisive rallies are allowed to continue in town.
7 May	Ontario announces Murray Coolican to replace Jane Stewart as principal Ontario negotiator.
23 May	Protesters occupy development site in town of Hagersville south of Caledonia.
30 May	Federal government issues $125 million offer for four of Six Nations' outstanding land claims.
6 June	Confederacy Council provides official response to $125 million offer (neither accepts nor rejects); unofficial and publicly stated response is a rejection of the offer.
12 June	Government of Canada announces Specific Claims Action Plan in attempt to speed claims across country; plan does not apply to the unique Six Nations' negotiations.
21 June	Ontario converts the Secretariat of Aboriginal Affairs into a stand-alone ministry; David Ramsay becomes minister of Aboriginal affairs.
1 September	Haudenosaunee Development Protocol released by newly created Haudenosaunee Development Institute.
13 September	Canada votes against the UN *Declaration on the Rights of Indigenous Peoples* at General Assembly; builder Sam Gualtieri injured at Caledonia's Stirling Street protest site after two sides agree to pause both protest and building.
15 September	David Crombie appointed by federal minister of Indian affairs to be community liaison official linking non-Aboriginal community and negotiators.
20 September	Nine protesters arrested for continuing to demonstrate at Caledonia Stirling Street development after deal was made with the Confederacy to allow development.
18 October	Ontario commits to hold off developing some provincially owned lands in region while negotiations continue.
21 November	Bill Montour elected Band Chief at Six Nations, pledges to work more closely with the Confederacy Council and to treat the Elected Band Council as an administrative body.

2 December	Gary McHale injured and charged with mischief in demonstration against cigarette shops operated by Six Nations residents; five Six Nations people also eventually charged with mischief.
12 December	Federal government issues $26 million offer to compensate for flooding of Six Nations' lands in construction of the Welland Canal.

Notes

Introduction

1 *An Act to Amend and Consolidate the Laws Respecting Indians,* assented to 12 April 1876, Library and Archives Canada, http://epe.lac-bac.gc.ca/100/205/301/ic/cdc/aboriginaldocs/stat/html/1876ap12.htm.

2 *British Columbia v. Imperial Tobacco Ltd.,* [2005] 2 S.C.R. 473 at para. 58.

Chapter 1: "Rule of Law"

1 Ontario Provincial Police (OPP), "First Nations Land Claim Dispute – Caledonia," 3 April 2006, Caledonia Wakeup Call, http://caledoniawakeupcall.com/OPPRelease.html.

2 OPP, "Protesters Removed from Caledonia Housing Development," 20 April 2006, Caledonia Wakeup Call, http://caledoniawakeupcall.com/OPPRelease.html.

3 John Paul Zronik, "Inside the Occupation," *Brantford Expositor,* 5 May 2006, A1.

4 Quoted in ibid.

5 Marissa Nelson, "Rude Awaking for Young Protester," *Hamilton Spectator,* 21 April 2006, A1.

6 Hazel E. Hill, "Hazel's Update of April 12, 2007," 12 April 2007 [used with permission; on file with author]. Many appreciative thanks go to Hazel E. Hill for her permission to quote from her communications about the dispute in Caledonia, which were initially distributed via e-mail.

7 Hazel E. Hill, "Hazel's Update," 23 April 2007, 5 [used with permission; on file with author].

8 Ibid.

9 Lynda Powless, "Six Nations at the Cross Roads: Douglas Creek Reclamation – A Pictorial History" (Ohsweken, ON: Turtle Island News Publications, 2006).

10 Ibid., 29.

11 Marissa Nelson, "Protesters Observe Raid Anniversary: Natives Challenged OPP and Retained Position on Occupied Site," *Hamilton Spectator,* 20 April 2007, A12.

12   For instance, Canadian Press, "Six Nations Protesters Occupy Home Building Site in Caledonia," *Brantford Expositor*, 1 March 2006, A5.

13   Claims were launched in the 1970s. Eventually, in the 1990s, the Six Nations' Elected Council pressed a lawsuit in an attempt to force the Crown to provide a full accounting of land sales and of the proceeds that were to have been placed in a fund for the Six Nations' benefit. The Crown's stall tactics meant that the case made virtually no progress over several years. The Six Nations eventually placed the litigation in abeyance in 2005, when the federal government promised that progress would be made in negotiations.

14   The term "claims" is problematic to many both within and outside First Nations circles because it frames issues in the legal terms of the colonizers. The term land "rights" is often preferred.

15   I owe this terminology of mapping and unmapping to Sherene Razack, whose book *Race, Space, and the Law: Unmapping a White Settler Society* (Toronto: Between the Lines, 2002) has inspired me (and, I hope, my work) in many ways.

16   *Canada Act 1982* (U.K.), 1982, c. 11.

17   Michel Foucault, *L'Ordre du Discours* (Paris: Gallimard, 1971); Michel Foucault, *Discipline and Punish: The Birth of the Prison* (New York: Vintage, 1995).

18   The term "text" is used broadly to apply to various forms and verbal and written language as well as, for instance, websites and television programs, which also incorporate other elements as part of their overall message. Michel Foucault, *Archaeology of Knowledge*, translated from the French by A.M. Sheridan Smith (London: Tavistock, 1972), 49.

19   Mainly Norman Fairclough, *Analysing Discourse: Textual Analysis for Social Research* (London and New York: Routledge, 2003).

20   Jan Blommaert and Chris Bulcaen, "Critical Discourse Analysis," *Annual Review of Anthropology* 29 (2000): 447-66, 447-48.

21   Similarly, Ernest Laclau and Chantal Mouffe theorize the political process in terms of the "logic of difference," which creates differences and divisions, and the "logic of equivalence," which works to subvert them. Ernest Laclau and Chantal Mouffe, *Hegemony and Socialist Strategy: Towards a Radical Democratic Politics* (London: Verso, 1985).

22   Several groups could be characterized as "protesters" over the course of this dispute. In the interests of simplicity, however, I reserve this term (unless otherwise specified) for the Six Nations people who worked actively on the reclamation effort in some capacity. Many non-Six Nations and non-Native people also rallied to this cause by attending the protest site, where they spoke publicly in support of the reclamation and of Six Nations' claims to continuing sovereignty, but I generally do not give voice to their statements in this book.

23   James Paul Gee, *An Introduction to Discourse Analysis: Theory and Method* (London and New York: Routledge, 2005).

24   Richard Delgado, "Storytelling for Oppositionists and Others: A Plea for Narrative," in Richard Delgado and Jean Stefancic, eds., *Critical Race Theory: The Cutting Edge*, 60-70 (Philadelphia: Temple University Press, 2000), 61.

25   Ibid.

26   Daniel Nolan, "Finley: Send Cops to Clear Out Natives: MP Wants Caledonia Returned to 'Normalcy,'" *Hamilton Spectator*, 9 June 2006, A9.

27   Canadian Press, "Developer Says He's Done Nothing Wrong As Native Protesters Occupy Subdivision," *Brantford Expositor*, 2 March 2006, A4.

28   Mike Pearson, "Natives Defy Arrest Warrant," *Grand River Sachem*, 24 March 2006, 1.

29   Mike Pearson, "Fact Finder Arrives," *Grand River Sachem*, 31 March 2006, 1.

30 Mike Pearson, "Moratorium Shocks Henco Lawyer," *Grand River Sachem*, 26 May 2006, 18.

31 Mike Pearson, "Standoff Taught Police, Province," *Brantford Expositor*, 25 August 2006, A1.

32 Buck Sloat, "Problems Are Far from Over," *Grand River Sachem*, 30 June 2006, 4.

33 Toby Barrett, "One Law for All – Period," *Grand River Sachem*, 3 August 2007, 10.

34 Jim Windle, "John Tory's 'Friendly but Firm' Comments Draw Ire," *Tekawennake*, 12 September 2007, 7.

35 Canada, "Federal Legal Response to Haudenosaunee/Six Nations' Presentation of November 14, 2006," 25 January 2007, 13 [used with permission; on file with the author].

36 Quoted in Jim Knisley, "Provincial Negotiator Reports Progress in Land Talks," *Grand River Sachem*, 15 September 2006, 3.

37 *Henco Industries Ltd v. Haudenosaunee Six Nations Confederacy Council*, [2006] OJ No. 3285 (QL), (Ontario Superior Court of Justice) (Marshall J.).

38 Ibid.

39 Alex Dobrota and Hayley Mick, "Caledonia Tensions Heat Up as Judge Orders End to Talks: Ontario Court Orders Natives Off Disputed Land to Restore 'the Rule of Law,'" *Globe and Mail*, 9 August 2006, A1.

40 Deirdre Healey and Barb McKay, "Natives Disregard Judge's Decision: Vow to 'Maintain Position' for Now," *Hamilton Spectator*, 9 August 2006, A1.

41 Mike Pearson, "Arrest Warrants to Be Addressed," *Grand River Sachem*, 7 July 2006, 1.

42 Hazel E. Hill, "Update July 25, 2006," 25 July 2006, 1 [used with permission; on file with author].

43 Paul Legall, "Judge Continues Hearing: Protester Claims His Land Ownership Constitutes Conflict of Interest," *Hamilton Spectator*, 17 March 2006, A4.

44 *Henco Industries Limited v. Haudenosaunee Six Nations Confederacy Council*, (2006) 82 O.R. (3d) 721, 277 D.L.R. (4th) 274, 240 OAC 119 (ON C.A.), para. 136.

45 Ibid., paras. 117-18.

46 Ibid., para. 122.

47 Chinta Puxley, "Caledonia Judge Overruled," *Brantford Expositor*, 15 December 2006, A1.

48 Mike Pearson, "Natives Shut Down Home Construction," *Grand River Sachem*, 3 March 2006, 1.

49 Pearson, "Natives Defy Arrest Warrant," 12.

50 Mike Pearson, "Natives Staying the Course," *Grand River Sachem*, 10 March 2006, 1.

51 Susan Gamble, "Protesters Stand Firm: Deadline Passes to Leave Caledonia Construction Site," *Brantford Expositor*, 23 March 2006, A1.

52 Gregory Bonnell, "Police Presence, Court Order Fail to Deter Protesters," *Brantford Expositor*, 30 March 2006, A4.

53 Mike Pearson, "Natives Rally for Sovereignty," *Grand River Sachem*, 28 July 2006, 1.

54 Quoted in Mike Pearson, "Natives Committed to Land Rights," *Grand River Sachem*, 23 June 2006, 9.

55 Hazel E. Hill, "Update from Grand River October 19, 2006," 19 October 2006, 1 [used with permission; on file with author].

56 Sandra Muse, "2006: Janie Jamieson Looks Back on History," *Tekawennake*, 3 January 2007, 7.

57 Hill, "Update from Grand River October 19, 2006," 1.

58 Jim Windle, "Progress at the Table Slow but Showing Fruit," *Tekawennake*, 24 October 2007, 4.

59   Six Nations "Iroquois" Confederacy, *Six Nations Confederacy Council Land Rights Statement*, as adopted in Council, 4 November 2006, published in *Tekawennake*, 22 November 2006, 8, Turtle Island Native Network, http://www.turtleisland.org/news/news-sixnations.htm.

60   Ibid. [emphasis added].

61   *Haida Nation v. British Columbia (Minister of Forests)*, [2004] 3 S.C.R. 511; *Taku River Tlingit First Nation v. British Columbia (Project Assessment Director)*, [2004] 3 S.C.R. 550; *Mikisew Cree First Nation v. Canada (Minister of Canadian Heritage)*, [2005] 3 S.C.R. 388.

62   Windle, "Progress at the Table."

63   Haudenosaunee Men's Council of the Grand River, "Six Nations: How We Got Here," pamphlet [on file with author].

64   Hill, "Hazel's Update of April 12, 2007," 1-2.

65   Allen MacNaughton, "Confederacy Optimistic, but Wants Halt to Development on Crown Lands within Track," *Grand River Sachem*, 14 September 2007, 7.

66   Quoted in Dana Brown, "Montour Vows New Era of Communication," *Hamilton Spectator*, 20 November 2007, A6.

67   Christie Blatchford, *Helpless: Caledonia's Nightmare of Fear and Anarchy, and How the Law Failed All of Us* (Toronto: Doubleday Canada, 2010), 137-38.

68   Dawn Martin-Hill, *Sewatokwa'tshera't: The Dish with One Spoon* (Brantford: Lock3 Media, 2008).

69   Though a detailed examination of these events is unfortunately outside the scope of this book, the conflict that began in Caledonia has indeed spread to other places, most notably the city of Brantford, where at the time of this writing in January 2010 conflicts over development continue to intensify within and outside of the courts.

70   Paul Morse, "Court Orders Protesters Out: Natives Must Leave by Thursday," *Hamilton Spectator*, 22 April 2006, A3.

71   Michael-Allen Marion, "City Rejects Playing Host to Meeting, Lack of Native Representation Cited as Concern," *Brantford Expositor*, 15 June 2006, A1.

72   Canadian Press, "GRCA Projects Moving Forward without Six Nations Consultation," *Brantford Expositor*, 15 November 2006, A4.

73   Jim Knisley, "Developers Cautious," *Grand River Sachem*, 4 August 2006, 9.

74   Jim Windle, "Mayor Hancock Set to Protect Relationship with Six Nations/New Credit," *Tekawennake*, 6 December 2006, 1.

75   John Paul Zronik, "Six Nations Not Being Notified of Development in Brant County, Complains Confederacy Chief," *Brantford Expositor*, 20 December 2006, A3.

76   Leroy Hill, "Canada Owes Us Millions," *Brantford Expositor*, 11 January 2007, A10.

77   Neil Dring, "Natives Stall Another Housing Project," *Grand River Sachem*, 25 May 2007, 1.

78   James Wallace, "Documents Obtained by Osprey News Puts Price Tag on Settling Caledonia Dispute: Ottawa to Offer $125 Million," *Brantford Expositor*, 31 May 2007, A1.

79   Dring, "Natives Stall."

80   Jim Windle, "Trainer Wants to Meet with PM Harper on Land Claims Resolution," *Tekawennake*, 11 July 2007, 2.

81   Trevor Bomberry, "Letter to Brantford Mayor Mike Hancock," 28 September 2007 [used with permission; on file with author].

82   Mike Pearson, "Six Nations Protesters Hold Information Picket," *Grand River Sachem*, 17 August 2007, 1.

83   Many of these protesters acted without the approval of either the Elected Band Council or the Confederacy Council.

84 Katie Dawson, "'Remember Us' March Leads to One Arrest," *Grand River Sachem*, 12 October 2007, 3.

85 Hazel E. Hill, "Update from Grand River," 25 September 2007, 3-4 [used with permission; on file with author].

86 Susan Gamble, "City Breaking the Law: Protesters," *Brantford Expositor*, 4 August 2007, A3.

87 Mike Pearson, "Contempt Charges Unclear," *Grand River Sachem*, 28 July 2006, 1.

88 Wade Hemsworth, "'Everybody's Watching': Six Nations Residents Blame All Levels of Government for Not Stepping Forward and Resolving Land Claims," *Hamilton Spectator*, 21 April 2006, A8.

89 Michael Coyle, "Results of Fact-Finding on Situation at Caledonia," 7 April 2006, report, Caledonia Wakeup Call, http://www.caledoniawakeupcall.com.

90 Ibid., 17-18 [emphasis added].

91 Ibid., 24.

92 Ibid., 25.

Chapter 2: Places to Grow

1 *Places to Grow Act*, S.O. 2005, c. 13, para. 1.

2 Slogan on website, https://www.placestogrow.ca/.

3 *Places to Grow Act*, Preamble.

4 Ibid.

5 Ibid.

6 Ibid.

7 Ibid.

8 *Places to Grow Act*, section 6.

9 Ontario Ministry of Public Infrastructure Renewal, *Growth Plan for the Greater Golden Horseshoe* (Toronto: Ministry of Public Infrastructure Renewal, 2006), https://www.placestogrow.ca.

10 Ibid., 6 and 7.

11 Ibid., 45-47.

12 Six Nations Council, "Six Nations of the Grand River Community Profile," 2007, Six Nations Council, http://www.sixnations.ca/CommunityProfile.htm.

13 Thanks to Cole Harris for this concise and evocative phrase, which I borrow from his fascinating account of land appropriation from the First Nations living in what is now British Columbia, Canada.

14 Donald Bourgeois, "The Six Nations: A Neglected Aspect of Canadian Legal History," *Canadian Journal of Native Studies* 6, no. 2 (1986): 252-70, 256.

15 Charles Johnston, ed., *The Valley of the Six Nations: A Collection of Documents on the Indian Lands of the Grand River* (Toronto: Champlain Society for the Government of Ontario, University of Toronto, 1964), 994.

16 Susan Hill, "The Clay We Are Made Of: An Examination of Haudenosaunee Land Tenure on the Grand River Territory" (Ph.D. dissertation, Trent University, Peterborough, 2006), 242.

17 Robert Surtees, "Land Cessions, 1763-1830," in Donald Smith and Edward Rogers, eds., *Aboriginal Ontario: Historical Perspectives on the First Nations*, 92-121 (Toronto: Dundurn, 1994), 97; Hill, "The Clay We Are Made Of," 240; Johnston, *The Valley of the Six Nations*, xxxiv.

18   Hill, "The Clay We Are Made Of," 243; Johnston, *The Valley of the Six Nations*, xxxv.

19   Haldimand Proclamation, B222, 1071, Haldimand Papers, National Archives of Canada, cited in Johnston, *The Valley of the Six Nations*, 50-51.

20   In a 1701 treaty, the lands had already been acknowledged as having been part of Haudenosaunee territory long before the settlers arrived.

21   Sidney Harring, *White Man's Law: Native People in Nineteenth-Century Canadian Jurisprudence* (Toronto: University of Toronto Press, 1998), 36.

22   Hill, "The Clay We Are Made Of," 233; Johnston, *The Valley of the Six Nations*, xxxviii.

23   Hill, "The Clay We Are Made Of," 246.

24   Ibid., 249.

25   Deborah Jean Doxtator, "What Happened to the Iroquois Clans? A Study of Clans in Three Nineteenth Century Rotinonhsyonni Communities" (Ph.D. dissertation, University of Western Ontario, London, 1997), 220; Charles Johnston, "The Six Nations in the Grand River Valley, 1784–1847," in Smith and Rogers, *Aboriginal Ontario*, 167-81, 170.

26   Johnston, *The Valley of the Six Nations*, 170.

27   Bourgeois, "The Six Nations," 259.

28   Harring, *White Man's Law*, 36-37.

29   Hill, "The Clay We Are Made Of," 260; Johnston, *The Valley of the Six Nations*, xxxix.

30   Simcoe's Patent of the Grand River Lands to the Six Nations, 14 January 1793, reprinted in Johnston, *The Valley of the Six Nations*, 73-74.

31   Hill, "The Clay We Are Made Of," 265; Johnston, *The Valley of the Six Nations*, xxxix.

32   Sally Weaver, "The Iroquois: The Consolidation of the Grand River Reserve in the Mid-Nineteenth Century, 1847–1875," in Smith and Rogers, *Aboriginal Ontario*, 182–212, 182; Hill, "The Clay We Are Made Of," 267.

33   Six Nations Lands and Resources, "Six Nations of the Grand River: Land Rights, Financial Justice, Creative Solutions," Claims Summary, Ohsweken, 2006, booklet handed out by Six Nations Lands and Resources Department, http://www.hamilton.ca/NR/rdonlyres/0FCA0BC2-A78F-47AC-9577-016BB397F1D7/0/SixNationsClaimsBooklet.pdf.

34   Harring, *White Man's Law*, 39.

35   Robert Surtees, "The Iroquois in Canada," in Francis Jennings, ed., *The History and Culture of Iroquois Diplomacy: An Interdisciplinary Guide to the Treaties of the Six Nations and Their League*, 67–83 (Syracuse: Syracuse University Press, 1985), 76.

36   Johnston, *The Valley of the Six Nations*, xliv; Harring, *White Man's Law*, 39.

37   Hill, "The Clay We Are Made Of," 270-72.

38   Johnston, *The Valley of the Six Nations*, xlvi; Harring, *White Man's Law*, 9.

39   Surtees, "Land Cessions," 112.

40   Doxtator, "What Happened to the Iroquois Clans?" 224.

41   John Noon, *Law and Government of the Grand River Iroquois* (New York: Viking Fund, 1949), 97; Johnston, *The Valley of the Six Nations*, xviv.

42   Edward Rogers, "The Algonquian Farmers of Southern Ontario," in Smith and Rogers, *Aboriginal Ontario*, 122-66, 152; Harring, *White Man's Law*, 37.

43   Hill, "The Clay We Are Made Of," 279.

44   Doxtator, "What Happened to the Iroquois Clans?" 128.

45   Harring, *White Man's Law*, 39; Johnston, "The Six Nations," 173; Johnston, *The Valley of the Six Nations*, l.

46   Hill, "The Clay We Are Made Of," 282.

47   See Barbara Martindale, *Caledonia: Along the Grand River* (Winnipeg: Natural Heritage Books, 1995).

48 Ibid., 112-20.
49 Roger Carpenter, *The Renewed, the Destroyed, and the Remade: The Three Thought Worlds of the Huron and the Iroquois, 1609-1650* (East Lansing, MI: Michigan State University Press, 2004), 136.
50 Johnston, "The Six Nations," 176; Robert Porter, "Building a New Longhouse: The Case for Government Reform within the Six Nations of the Haudenosaunee," *Buffalo Law Review* 46 (1998): 805-945, 823.
51 Hill, "The Clay We Are Made Of," 117.
52 Doxtator, "What Happened to the Iroquois Clans?" 10.
53 Johnston, *The Valley of the Six Nations*, lxviv and lxxvii.
54 Porter, "Building a New Longhouse," 900.
55 Russell Barsh, "Canada's Aboriginal Peoples: Social Integration or Disintegration?" *Canadian Journal of Native Studies* 14, no. 1 (1994): 1-46, 2.
56 Sharon Venne, "Understanding Treaty 6: An Indigenous Perspective," in Michael Asch, ed., *Aboriginal and Treaty Rights in Canada: Essays on Law, Equality, and Respect for Difference*, 173-207 (Vancouver: UBC Press, 1997).
57 Kent McNeil, "Envisaging Constitutional Spaces for Aboriginal Governments" *Queen's Law Journal* 95 (1994): 95-137, 114. *Constitution Act, 1867*, (U.K.), 30 & 31 Vict., c. 3, reprinted in R.S.C. 1985, App. II, No. 5.
58 Harring, *White Man's Law*, 40.
59 Johnston, "The Six Nations," 178; Johnston, *The Valley of the Six Nations*, xliv.
60 Hill, "The Clay We Are Made Of," 290; Harring, *White Man's Law*, 45.
61 Paul Williams and Curtis Nelson, "Kaswentah," January 1995, research report prepared for the Royal Commission on Aboriginal Peoples, *For Seven Generations: An Information Legacy of the RCAP*, CD-ROM, Libraxus, 1997, part III.
62 Harring, *White Man's Law*, 45.
63 Hill, "The Clay We Are Made Of," 292.
64 See Six Nations Lands and Resources, "Six Nations of the Grand River."
65 Harring, *White Man's Law*, 49.
66 Ibid., 58; Hill, "The Clay We Are Made Of," 305-8.
67 Johnston, *The Valley of the Six Nations*, lxxxviv; Harring, *White Man's Law*, 59.
68 Johnston, *The Valley of the Six Nations*, lxxiii; Harring, *White Man's Law*, 59.
69 Harring, *White Man's Law*, 24.
70 Ibid., 31.
71 According to Harring, the term "reserve" is misleading because Six Nations does not view its land this way and also because the term was not part of the original Haldimand grant. The word has legal meaning implying "reservation" of lands not sold in the treaty process, but the Six Nations' situation is distinct from that of other First Nations in Canada. However, the Canadian government later passed legislation applying to reserves that they considered to apply to Six Nations as well, and it is in this sense that the term is used. See Harring, *White Man's Law*, 311.
72 Johnston, "The Six Nations," 178; Harring, *White Man's Law*, 52.
73 The town of Jarvis, which is about twenty minutes south of Caledonia, is named for Samuel Jarvis. Harring, *White Man's Law*, 53.
74 Hill, "The Clay We Are Made Of," 308-11; Johnston, "The Six Nations," 178; Williams and Nelson, "Kaswentah," part iii.
75 Six Nations Band Council, "Backgrounder: The Six Nations Plank Road Claim in Brief" [used with permission; on file with author].

76 Weaver, "The Iroquois: The Consolidation," 180-85.
77 Hill, "The Clay We Are Made Of," 316, 350, and 352; Weaver, "The Iroquois: The Consolidation," 188.
78 Weaver, "The Iroquois: The Consolidation," 185.
79 Doxtator, "What Happened to the Iroquois Clans?" 247.
80 Hill, "The Clay We Are Made Of," 300.
81 Doxtator, "What Happened to the Iroquois Clans?" 235.
82 It was restructured in 2003 and renamed the Six Nations Lands and Resources Department.
83 *Six Nations of the Grand River Band v. The Attorney General of Canada and Her Majesty the Queen in Right of Ontario,* 7 March 1995, Court File no. 406/95.
84 Charting the complex histories and discourses that have been generated as a result of the suburbanization of productive agricultural land (through the building of detached housing developments such as Douglas Creek Estates) would amount to a fascinating examination of Euro-American reverence for individual property and orderly society. Unfortunately, this project falls outside the scope of this book.
85 Personal communication with members of Grand River communities, June 2008.
86 Hazel E. Hill, "Update from Grand River: Hazel Hill," *Tekawennake,* 14 November 2007, 14.
87 Quoted in John Paul Zronik, "Inside the Occupation," *Brantford Expositor,* 5 May 2006, A1.
88 Editorial, "Developer Warned Months Ago about Six Nations Land," *Hamilton Spectator,* 9 March 2006, A6.
89 Unknown author, "Honour Six Nations Land Claims: Do Not Buy or Sell Unsettled Land," information pamphlet, 2006 [used with permission; on file with author].
90 Dawn Martin-Hill, *Sewatokwa'tshera't: The Dish with One Spoon,* film (Brantford: Lock3 Media, 2008).
91 Editorial, "Developer Warned."
92 Haudenosaunee Men's Council of the Grand River, "Six Nations: How We Got Here," pamphlet [used with permission; on file with author] [emphasis in original].
93 John Paul Zronik, "Brant Expansion Influenced by Others," *Brantford Expositor,* 8 July 2006, A12.
94 Brant Riding Intergovernmental Committee, "Meeting Minutes," 17 March 2007 [used with permission; on file with author].
95 Ibid., 1-2.
96 Ibid., 2.
97 Vincent Ball, "Confederacy Objects to City's Land Deal," *Brantford Expositor,* 7 May 2007, A1.
98 Jim Windle, "Developers Disappointed at Onondaga Longhouse," *Tekawennake,* 5 September 2007, 2.
99 Peter Russell, *Recognizing Aboriginal Title: The Mabo Case and Indigenous Resistance to English-Settler Colonialism* (Toronto: University of Toronto Press, 2005), 253 and 267. *Calder v. British Columbia (Attorney General),* [1973] S.C.R. 313.
100 John Borrows, *Recovering Canada: The Resurgence of Indigenous Law* (Toronto: University of Toronto Press, 2002), 119.
101 Borrows, *Recovering Canada,* 236.
102 Ibid., 12.
103 Harring, *White Man's Law,* 5.
104 John Hylton, *Aboriginal Self-Government in Canada: Current Trends and Issues* (Saskatoon: Purich, 1999), 50.

105 McNeil, "Envisaging Constitutional Spaces," 97.

106 Ibid., 108. *Guerin v. the Queen*, [1984] 2 S.C.R. 335.

107 *Sui generis* means unique, in a class of its own. The term is often used in legal circles to describe the special nature of treaties with First Nations peoples. *Simon v. the Queen*, [1985] 2 S.C.R. 387. Royal Commission on Aboriginal Peoples (RCAP), *Royal Commission Report on Aboriginal Peoples* (Ottawa: Indian and Northern Affairs Canada, 1996), 2, Indian and Northern Affairs Canada, http://www.ainc-inac.gc.ca/ap/rrc-eng.asp; Patrick Macklem, *Indigenous Difference and the Constitution of Canada* (Toronto: University of Toronto Press, 2001), 144.

108 *R. v. Sparrow*, [1990] 1 S.C.R. 1075. Harring, *White Man's Law*, 5; Patrick Macklem, "First Nations Self-Government and the Borders of the Canadian Legal Imagination," *McGill Law Journal* 36 (1990): 382-456, 446.

109 Macklem, *Indigenous Difference*, 58; Russell, *Recognizing Aboriginal Title*, 242.

110 McNeil, "Envisaging Constitutional Spaces," 95 and 133.

111 Michael Coyle, *Addressing Aboriginal Land and Treaty Rights in Ontario: An Analysis of Past Policies and Options for the Future*, Ipperwash Inquiry Research Report, 2005, 25, Ipperwash Inquiry, http://www.attorneygeneral.jus.gov.on.ca/inquiries/ipperwash/policy_part/research/index.html.

112 *Delgamuukw v. British Columbia*, [1997] 3 S.C.R. 1010, 153 D.L.R. (4th) 193 [*Delgamuukw*].

113 Russell, *Recognizing Aboriginal Title*, 342.

114 RCAP, *Royal Commission Report on Aboriginal Peoples*, 2; Macklem, *Indigenous Difference*, 90.

115 Tom Flanagan, *First Nations? Second Thoughts* (Montreal and Kingston: McGill-Queen's University Press, 2000), 63 [emphasis added].

116 *Delgamuukw*, para. 186.

117 Russell, *Recognizing Aboriginal Title*, 342.

118 Macklem, *Indigenous Difference*, 282.

119 Emily MacKinnon, *The Nisga'a Final Agreement and Canadian Federalism: Asymmetrical Design* (Vancouver: UBC Faculty of Law, 2010), 4-5 [unpublished paper].

120 *Haida Nation v. British Columbia (Minister of Forests)*, [2004] 3 S.C.R. 511 [*Haida Nation*]; *Taku River Tlingit First Nation v. British Columbia (Project Assessment Director)*, [2004] 3 S.C.R. 550; *Mikisew Cree First Nation v. Canada (Minister of Canadian Heritage)*, [2005] 3 S.C.R. 388.

121 *Haida Nation*, para. 53.

122 Six Nations Lands and Resources, "Six Nations of the Grand River," 14-15.

123 Indian and Northern Affairs Canada, "Background to the Grand River Notification Agreement," *Ontario Region – Agreements* (Ottawa: Indian and Northern Affairs Canada, 2005), 1, http://www.lmtac.com/handbook2006/Example%2023.pdf.

124 Cindi Katz, "On the Grounds of Globalization: A Topography for Feminist Political Engagement," *Signs* 26, no. 4 (2001): 1213-34.

125 Ibid., 1228.

126 Jacques Derrida, *Specters of Marx: The State of Debt, the Work of Mourning, and the New International*, translated by Peggy Kamuf (London and New York: Routledge, 1994), 82.

127 See Hill, "The Clay We Are Made Of," 409. The word means "we are of the Ohswe:ken-kind of clay" and refers to the people of the Six Nations of the Grand River Territory.

128 Kenneth Olwig, "Landscape as a Contested Topos of Place, Community, and Self," in Paul Adams, Steven Hoelscher, and Karen Till, eds., *Textures of Place: Exploring Humanist Geographies*, 93-119 (Minneapolis: University of Minnesota Press, 2001), 93.

129   Ibid.
130   Ronald Niezen, "Recognizing Indigenism: Canadian Unity and the International Movement of Indigenous Peoples," *Comparative Studies in Society and History* 42, no. 1 (2000): 119-48, 119.
131   Kenneth Olwig, *Landscape, Nature, and the Body Politic: From Britain's Renaissance to America's New World* (Madison: University of Wisconsin Press, 2002), xxiv.
132   Ibid., 125.
133   Ibid., 216.
134   Paul Memmott and Stephen Long, "Place Theory and Place Maintenance in Indigenous Australia," *Urban Policy and Research* 20, no. 1 (2002): 39-56.
135   Ibid., 40.
136   Donald Moore, Anand Pandian, and Jake Kosek, "The Cultural Politics of Race and Nature: Terrains of Power and Practice," in Donald Moore, Jake Kosek, and Anand Pandian, eds., *Race, Nature, and the Politics of Difference*, 1-70 (Durham: Duke University Press, 2003), 11.
137   Ibid., 12.
138   Ibid., 32.
139   Stuart Hall, "Cultural Identity and Diaspora," in Jonathan Rutherford, ed., *Identity, Community, Culture, Difference*, 222-37 (London: Lawrence and Wishart, 1990), 225, as cited in Moore, Kosek, and Pandian, *Race, Nature, and the Politics of Difference*, 40.
140   Sherene Razack, *Race, Space, and the Law: Unmapping a White Settler Society* (Toronto: Between the Lines, 2002), 9.
141   Ibid. Bruce Braun, "'On the Raggedy Edge of Risk': Articulations of Race and Nature after Biology," in Moore, Kosek, and Pandian, *Race, Nature, and the Politics of Difference*, 175-203.
142   James Clifford, *The Predicament of Culture: Twentieth-Century Ethnography, Literature, and Art* (Cambridge, MA: Harvard University Press, 1988), 6.
143   Bruce Braun, *The Intemperate Rainforest: Nature, Culture, and Power on Canada's West Coast* (Minneapolis: University of Minnesota Press, 2002), 19.
144   Ibid., 23.
145   Cole Harris, *Making Native Space: Colonialism, Resistance, and Reserves in British Columbia* (Vancouver: UBC Press, 2002); Cole Harris, "How Did Colonialism Dispossess? Comments from an Edge of Empire," *Annals of the Association of American Geographers* 94, no. 1 (2004): 165-82.
146   Harris, "How Did Colonialism Dispossess?" 165.

Chapter 3: "Us" and "Them"

1   Daniel Nolan, "Finley: Send Cops to Clear Out Natives: MP Wants Caledonia Returned to 'Normalcy,'" *Hamilton Spectator*, 9 June 2006, A9.
2   Corporation of Haldimand County, "A Message to the Citizens of Haldimand County Regarding Recent Local Calls for Action Regarding the Demonstration at Douglas Creek Estates in Caledonia," 24 April 2006, press release, Haldimand County website, http://www.haldimandcounty.on.ca/MediaReleases.aspx.
3   Michael-Allen Marion, "Conservative MPP Lays Blame for Standoff with Liberals," *Brantford Expositor*, 21 April 2006, C3.
4   Cheryl Bauslaugh, "'It Was Pretty Hot and Heavy': Haldimand Mayor Still Hopes for Peaceful Resolution to Protest," *Brantford Expositor*, 21 April 2006, C3.

5 Ontario Ministry of Aboriginal Affairs, "Progress Being Made on Caledonia Situation," 28 April 2006, press release, Ontario Secretariat of Aboriginal Affairs, http://www.aboriginalaffairs.gov.on.ca/english/news/2006/news_060428_2.asp.

6 Ontario Provincial Police (OPP), "Key to Successful Negotiations and Community Safety: Understanding, Mutual Respect and Meaningful Dialogue," 23 September 2006, press release, Caledonia Wakeup Call, http://www.caledoniawakeupcall.com/OPPRelease.html.

7 Murray Coolican, "Re: Ontario's Response to June 6 2007 Letter from Haudenosaunee/Six Nations," 12 June 2007, 1 [used with permission; on file with author].

8 Corporation of Haldimand County, "Haldimand County Council Statement re: Douglas Creek Estates Occupation," 16 May 2006, press release, http://www.haldimandcounty.on.ca/MediaReleases.aspx.

9 Cheryl Bauslaugh, "Six Nations Protesters Reopen Part of Hwy. 6," *Brantford Expositor*, 16 May 2006, A4.

10 Jennifer Graham, "Talks on Caledonia Occupation on Hiatus," *Brantford Expositor*, 24 April 2006, A1.

11 Greg McArthur, "Caledonia Natives Set to Remove One Blockade," *Globe and Mail*, 22 May 2006, A1.

12 Matt Kruchak, Barb McKay, and Marissa Nelson, "Caledonia Erupts: Emergency Declared, Schools Closed: Fists Fly as Natives and Non-Natives Take to the Streets," *Hamilton Spectator*, 23 May 2006, A1.

13 Colin Freeze and Oliver Moore, "Caledonia Tensions Reach Boiling Point," *Globe and Mail*, 23 May 2006, A1.

14 Kruchak, McKay, and Nelson, "Caledonia Erupts," 1. Mayor Trainer had requested army presence on 20 April as well.

15 Susan Gamble, "Haldimand Mayor Pins Vandalism on Natives: Damage to Power Station Could Reach $2 Million: Trainer," *Brantford Expositor*, 27 May 2006, A1.

16 Corporation of Haldimand County, "Mayor Declares 'State of Emergency,'" 22 May 2006, press release, http://www.haldimandcounty.on.ca/MediaReleases.aspx.

17 Marissa Nelson, "Local Folk Broker Barricade Deal: A Small Group of Caledonia and Native Residents Take Charge and Find a Way to Move Ahead," *Hamilton Spectator*, 24 May 2006, A6.

18 Corporation of Haldimand County, "Mayor Declares 'State of Emergency'"; Corporation of Haldimand County, "County Establishes Emergency Shelter and Emergency Telephone Number," 23 May 2006 [used with permission; on file with author]; County of Haldimand County, "Power Restored in Haldimand County," 24 May 2006 [used with permission; on file with author]; Corporation of Haldimand County, "State of Emergency Due to the Power Outage Remains in Effect," 25 May 2006 [used with permission; on file with author], all of these documents are press releases available at http://www.haldimandcounty.on.ca/MediaReleases.aspx.

19 Corporation of Haldimand County, "Mayor Marie Trainer Declares an End to State of Emergency in Haldimand County," 8 June 2006, press release, http://www.haldimandcounty.on.ca/MediaReleases.aspx.

20 John Paul Zronik, "Natives Remove Main Barricade: Protesters Put Focus on Land Claims," *Brantford Expositor*, 24 May 2006, A1.

21 Office of the Premier of Ontario, "Ontario Premier Dalton McGuinty Today Issued the Following Statement Regarding the Events in Caledonia," 22 May 2006, press release, http://www.premier.gov.on.ca/news/event.php?ItemID=4699&Lang=EN.

22 Indian and Northern Affairs Canada and Ontario Secretariat of Aboriginal Affairs, "Joint Statement by Minister Jim Prentice and Minister David Ramsay," 11 June 2006, press release, Secretariat of Aboriginal Affairs, http://www.aboriginalaffairs.gov.on.ca/english/news/2006/news_060611.asp.

23 Keith Leslie, "Caledonia Talks Back On," *Brantford Expositor*, 14 June 2006, A1.

24 Canadian Press, "Native Protesters Remove Barricade in Caledonia," *Brantford Expositor*, 12 July 2006, A5.

25 Corporation of Haldimand County, "A Message to the Citizens of Haldimand County Regarding the Current Demonstration at Douglas Creek Estates in Caledonia," 22 April 2006, press release, http://www.haldimandcounty.on.ca/MediaReleases.aspx.

26 John Burman, "Henco Gets $12.3 Million for Land: McGuinty Implores Native Protesters to Leave Douglas Creek Estates Property," *Hamilton Spectator*, 23 June 2006, A5.

27 Toby Barrett, "A Plan for Land Dispute," *Grand River Sachem*, 5 May 2006, 8.

28 Mike Pearson, "Barricades Down, Negotiations Set for Thursday," *Grand River Sachem*, 16 June 2006, 11.

29 Cheryl Bauslaugh, "Safety Measures Eyed for Caledonia School," *Brantford Expositor*, 17 August 2006, A1.

30 Hazel E. Hill, "Update July 25, 2006," 25 July 2006, 2, mass e-mail [used with permission; on file with author].

31 Corporation of Haldimand County, "Douglas Creek Estates Demonstration Chronology of Events," 30 January 2007, 2, press release, http://www.haldimandcounty.on.ca/MediaReleases.aspx.

32 Indian and Northern Affairs Canada and Ontario Secretariat of Aboriginal Affairs, "Joint Statement by Minister Jim Prentice and Minister David Ramsay," 11 June 2006, press release, Secretariat of Aboriginal Affairs, http://www.aboriginalaffairs.gov.on.ca/english/news/2006/news_060611.asp.

33 Mike Pearson, "Anger, Frustration Lead to Revolt," *Grand River Sachem*, 28 April 2006, 9.

34 Corporation of Haldimand County, "Province Offers Assistance to Haldimand County," 28 April 2006 [used with permission; on file with author]; Corporation of Haldimand County, "Province Commits to Communications and Business Assistance," 1 May 2006 [used with permission; on file with author]; Corporation of Haldimand County, "Haldimand County Council Passes Two Motions Regarding Douglas Creek Estates Issue," 9 May 2006 [used with permission; on file with author], all of these documents are press releases available at http://www.haldimandcounty.on.ca/MediaReleases.aspx.

35 Corporation of Haldimand County, "Douglas Creek Estates Demonstration Chronology of Events," 30 January 2007, 2, press release, http://www.haldimandcounty.on.ca/MediaReleases.aspx, 2.

36 Corporation of Haldimand County, "A Message to the Citizens of Haldimand County Regarding the Demonstration at Douglas Creek Estates in Caledonia," 22 April 2006 [used with permission; on file with author]; Corporation of Haldimand County, "A Message to the Citizens of Haldimand County Regarding the Demonstration at Douglas Creek Estates in Caledonia," 23 April 2006, press releases, http://www.haldimandcounty.on.ca/MediaReleases.aspx.

37 Susan Gamble, "Dispute Is Dividing Community: Mayor," *Brantford Expositor*, 25 April 2006, A7.

38 Sandra Muse, "Haldimand Deputy Mayor Wants Healing to Begin," *Tekawennake*, 31 May 2006, 4.

39 Scott Smith, "Townsfolk Getting Testy over Blockades," *Tekawennake*, 26 April 2006, 2.

40 Zronik, "Natives Remove Main Barricade," A1.

41 Mike Pearson, "Feds Working to Resolve Standoff: Finley," *Grand River Sachem*, 12 May 2006, 3.

42 Jim Knisley, "County Seeks Answers," *Grand River Sachem*, 12 May 2006, 5.

43 Craig Grice, "Spotlight on Caledonia," *Grand River Sachem*, 7 December 2007, 6.

44 Laura Nader, "Controlling Processes: Tracing the Dynamic Components of Power," *Current Anthropology* 38, no. 5 (1997): 711; Laura Nader, "Current Ilusions and Delusions about Conflict Management: In Africa and Elsewhere," *Law and Social Inquiry* 27, no. 3 (2002): 573-94.

45 Paul Legall and Daniel Nolan, "Mayor Lands in Hot Water: Apologizes to Natives," *Hamilton Spectator*, 26 April 2006, A1.

46 Corporation of Haldimand County, "A Message from Haldimand County Council Regarding Remarks Made by the Mayor on Tuesday Morning April 25, 2006," 25 April 2006, press release, http://www.haldimandcounty.on.ca/MediaReleases.aspx.

47 Jim Knisley, "Marie Muzzled," *Grand River Sachem*, 28 April 2006, 3.

48 Sandra Muse, "Haldimand Council Can't Seem to Muzzle Mayor Trainer," *Tekawennake*, 31 May 2006, 1.

49 Sandra Muse, "Numerous Events Lead to Escalation of Racial Tensions," *Tekawennake*, 24 May 2006, 17.

50 Ontario Secretariat of Aboriginal Affairs, "Province Appoints David Peterson to Help Resolve Caledonia Situation," 29 April 2006, press release, http://www.aboriginalaffairs. gov.on.ca/english/news/2006/news_060429.asp.

51 Daniel Nolan, "E-mail Threatens Lacrosse Game; Caledonia Citizens Are Being Called on to 'Restrict Access' to Six Nations Match," *Hamilton Spectator*, 6 June 2006, A2.

52 Corporation of Haldimand County, "Haldimand County Caledonia Centre Remains Open to Everyone," 7 June 2006, press release, http://www.haldimandcounty.on.ca/ MediaReleases.aspx.

53 Buck Sloat, "Problems Are Far from Over," *Grand River Sachem*, 30 June 2006, 4.

54 Diane Finley, "Governments Working Hard for Resolution," *Brantford Expositor*, 24 April 2006, A9.

55 Office of the Premier of Ontario, "Ontario Premier Dalton McGuinty ..." press release, http://www.premier.gov.on.ca/news/event.php?ItemID=4699&Lang=EN.

56 OPP, "Tolerance Encouraged in Caledonia," 8 August 2006 [used with permission; on file with author].

57 Indian and Northern Affairs Canada and Ontario Secretariat of Aboriginal Affairs, "Joint Statement," 2.

58 OPP, "Canada Day Celebrations," 29 June 2006, press release, Caledonia Wakeup Call, http://www.caledoniawakeupcall.com/OPPRelease.html.

59 Paul Legall, "Police Cars in Hagersville Put Natives on 'High Alert,'" *Hamilton Spectator*, 4 March 2006, A5.

60 Zronik, "Natives Remove Main Barricade," A1.

61 Wilma Green, "Road to the Reclamation," CD and accompanying transcript (Ohsweken: CKRZ FM Radio, 21 December 2007), 46.

62 Marissa Nelson and Joan Walters, "RCMP Specialists at Land Dispute: Spectator Exclusive," *Hamilton Spectator*, 2 August 2006, A1.

63 Dierdre Healey and Barb McKay, "Natives Disregard Judge's Decision: Vow to 'Maintain Position' for Now," *Hamilton Spectator*, 9 August 2006, A1.

64 Chinta Puxley, "Caledonia Braces for Showdown," *Brantford Expositor*, 14 October 2006, A1.

65 Leroy Hill, "Canada Owes Us Millions," *Brantford Expositor*, 11 January 2007, A10.

66 Michael-Allen Marion, "Hundreds Protest Government Inaction over Native Occupation in Caledonia," *Brantford Expositor*, 16 October 2006, A1, Caledonia WakeUp Call, http://www.caledoniawakeupcall.com/. This reference to Ipperwash appears to call for police to kill protesters, given that the 1995 occupation of Ipperwash Provincial Park culminated in the OPP shooting protester Dudley George, whose death led to a public inquiry and report that – among other conclusions – essentially called for less politicized and militarized police action.

67 Hayley Mick, "Polarizing Figure Takes on Native Protesters: Caledonia Fight Becomes Full-Time for Christian with Troubled Background," *Globe and Mail*, 20 January 2007, A15.

68 Chinta Puxley, "Head of OPP Quits," *Brantford Expositor*, 29 July 2006, A1.

69 OPP, "Key to Successful Negotiations," 1, press release, Caledonia Wakeup Call, http://www.caledoniawakeupcall.com/OPPRelease.html.

70 Sandra Muse, "CHTV Scolded by Indian Affairs Minister," *Tekawennake*, 9 August 2006, 1.

71 Katie Dawson, "March Back at DCE," *Grand River Sachem*, 13 October 2006, 1.

72 Corporation of Haldimand County, "For Immediate Release," 13 October 2006, press release, Haldimand County, http://www.haldimandcounty.on.ca/MediaReleases.aspx.

73 Corporation of Haldimand County, "Re: CaledoniaWakeUpCall.com Website Misrepresentation," 6 November 2006, press release, Haldimand County, http://www.haldimandcounty.on.ca/MediaReleases.aspx.

74 Diane Finley, "No Need for Rally Says MP," *Grand River Sachem*, 13 October 2006, 4.

75 Chinta Puxley, "Caledonia Braces for Showdown," *Brantford Expositor*, 14 October 2006, A1.

76 Katie Dawson, "McHale Leads March," *Grand River Sachem*, 20 October 2006, 1.

77 Daniel Nolan, "Mayor Urges Organizer to Cancel Second Caledonia March," *Hamilton Spectator*, 14 December 2006, A14.

78 Corporation of Haldimand County, "Caledonia Land Dispute," 19 January 2007, press release, Haldimand County, http://www.haldimandcounty.on.ca/MediaReleases.aspx

79 Hazel E. Hill, "Update from Grand River October 19, 2006," 19 October 2006, 1, mass e-mail [used with permission; on file with author].

80 Jim Windle, "McHale's Flag Flap Flops," *Tekawennake*, 24 January 2007, 1.

81 Graham, "Talks on Caledonia Occupation on Hiatus," A1.

82 Dana Brown, "OPP Stop Flap over Flags in Caledonia," *Hamilton Spectator*, 4 December 2006, A9.

83 Daniel Nowlan, "Mayor Urges Organizer to Cancel Second Caledonia March," *Hamilton Spectator*, 14 December 2006, A14.

84 OPP, "Rally Is Irresponsible," 18 January 2007, press release, Caledonia Wakeup Call, http://www.caledoniawakeupcall.com/OPPRelease.html.

85 Katie Dawson, "Natives Shout 'Go Home Gary,'" *Grand River Sachem*, 26 January 2007, 1.

86 Chinta Puxley, "Resolving Caledonia Dispute Requires 'Patience,'" *Brantford Expositor*, 26 February 2007, A1.

87 Toby Barrett, "Unhappy Anniversary Caledonia – February 28," *Grand River Sachem*, 23 February 2007, 8.

88 Ontario Secretariat of Aboriginal Affairs, "Media Advisory – Minister Responsible for Aboriginal Affairs and Haldimand County Mayor Available to Media," 25 September 2006, press release [used with permission; on file with author].

89 Daniel Nolan, "Caledonia Convoy Set to Roll Today," *Hamilton Spectator*, 2 May 2007, A10.

90 Juanita Sundberg. "Placing Race in Environmental Justice Research in Latin America," *Society and Natural Resources* 21, no. 7 (2008): 569-82, 579.

91 Ibid., 573.

92 See Peter Russell, *Recognizing Aboriginal Title: The Mabo Case and Indigenous Resistance to English-Settler Colonialism* (Toronto: University of Toronto Press, 2005), for a comparative study of settler states' gradual movements toward acknowledgment of the fallacy of *terra nullius*.

93 Edward Said, *Culture and Imperialism* (New York: Vintage, 1994), 78.

94 Michel Foucault, as explained in Norman Fairclough, *Analysing Discourse: Textual Analysis for Social Research* (London and New York: Routledge, 2003).

95 Howard Winant, *The World Is a Ghetto: Race and Democracy since World War II* (New York: Basic, 2001), xiv.

96 Teun van Dijk, *Elite Discourse and Racism* (Newbury Park: Sage, 1993).

97 Ibid., 9.

98 Rodney Bobiwash, "The Sacred and the Profane: Indigenous Lands and State Policy," in Jill Oakes, Rick Riewe, Kathi Kinew, and Elaine Maloney, eds., *Sacred Lands: Aboriginal World Views, Claims, and Conflicts*, 203-13 (Edmonton: Canadian Circumpolar Institute Press, 1996), 208.

99 Ibid., 207.

100 van Dijk, *Elite Discourse and Racism*, 50.

101 Ibid., 77.

102 Jan Blommaert and Jef Verschueren, *Debating Diversity: Analysing the Rhetoric of Tolerance* (London and New York: Routledge, 1998).

103 Michael Clyne, "Establishing Linguistic Markers of Racist Discourse," in Christina Schaffner and Anita Wenden, eds., *Language and Peace*, 111-18 (Amsterdam: Harwood, 1999), 118.

104 James (Sakéj) Youngblood Henderson, "Postcolonial Ghost Dancing: Diagnosing European Colonialism," in Marie Battiste, ed., *Reclaiming Indigenous Voice and Vision*, 57-76 (Vancouver: UBC Press, 2000), 65.

105 Audrey Kobayashi and Linda Peake, "Racism Out of Place: Thoughts on Whiteness and an Antiracist Geography in the New Millennium," *Annals of the Association of American Geographers* 90, no. 2 (2000): 392-403.

106 Winant, *The World Is a Ghetto*, 289.

107 Patricia Ofner, "The Indian in Textbooks: A Content Analysis of History Books Authorized for Use in Ontario Schools" (MA thesis, Lakehead University, 1983).

108 Chris Cunnean, "The Criminalization of Indigenous People," in Tania Das Gupta, Carl James, Roger Maaka, Grace-Edward Galabuzi, and Chris Andersen, eds., *Race and Racialization: Essential Readings*, 266-74 (Minneapolis: University of Minnesota Press, 2007); Elizabeth Furniss, "Challenging the Myth of Indigenous Peoples' 'Last Stand' in Canada and Australia: Public Discourse and the Conditions of Silence," in Annie Coombes, ed., *Rethinking Settler Colonialism: History and Memory in Australia, Canada, Aotearoa New Zealand, and South Africa*, 172-92 (Manchester: Manchester University Press, 2002), 190.

109 Robert Harding, "Historical Representations of Aboriginal People in the Canadian News Media," *Discourse and Society* 17, no. 2 (2006): 205-35.

110   Ibid., 206.
111   Daniel Francis, "The Imaginary Indian: The Image of the Indian in Canadian Culture," in Das Gupta et al., *Race and Racialization*, 234-39, 236.
112   Ibid.
113   Pierre Trudeau, as cited in ibid., 238.
114   Ibid.
115   Ibid., 239.
116   Jennifer Reid, *Louis Riel and the Creation of Modern Canada: Mythic Discourse and the Postcolonial State* (Albuquerque, NM: University of New Mexico Press, 2008).
117   Ibid., 5.
118   Erin Manning, *Ephemeral Territories: Representing Nation, Home, and Identity in Canada* (Minneapolis: University of Minnesota Press, 2003), xvii.
119   Maria de la Salette Correia, "Peace, Order, and Good Government at Oka 1990: A Limited Anthropological Analysis," in Jill Oakes, Rick Riewe, Kathi Kinew, and Elaine Maloney, eds., *Sacred Lands: Aboriginal World Views, Claims, and Conflicts*, 69-76 (Edmonton: Canadian Circumpolar Institute Press, 1996), 75 [emphasis in original].
120   Ibid., 74.
121   Geoffrey York and Loreen Pindera, *People of the Pines: The Warriors and the Legacy of Oka* (New York: Little Brown, 1991), 430, as cited in de la Salette Correia, "Peace, Order, and Good Government," 74.
122   Ibid., 75.
123   Ibid., 71.
124   Royal Commission on Aboriginal Peoples, *Royal Commission Report on Aboriginal Peoples* (Ottawa: Indian and Northern Affairs Canada, 1996), vol. 2, 2, Indian and Northern Affairs Canada, http://www.ainc-inac.gc.ca/ap/rrc-eng.asp.
125   Patrick Macklem, "First Nations Self-Government and the Borders of the Canadian Legal Imagination," *McGill Law Journal* 36 (1990): 382-456 at 423. *Constitution Act, 1867*, (U.K.), 30 & 31 Vict., c. 3, reprinted in R.S.C. 1985, App. II, No. 5.
126   Ernest Bramsted and K.J. Melhuish, eds., *Western Liberalism: A History in Documents from Locke to Croce* (London: Longman, 1978).
127   Michael Lee Ross, *First Nations Sacred Sites in Canada's Courts* (Vancouver: UBC Press, 2005), 177-78.
128   John Borrows, *Recovering Canada: The Resurgence of Indigenous Law* (Toronto: University of Toronto Press, 2002), 114.
129   Ibid., 117.
130   Andrew Woolford, *Between Justice and Certainty: Treaty Making in British Columbia* (Vancouver: UBC Press, 2005).
131   Nader, "Controlling Processes," 714-15.
132   Asha Varadharajan, "The 'Repressive Tolerance' of Cultural Peripheries," in Marie Battiste, ed., *Reclaiming Indigenous Voice and Vision*, 142-49 (Vancouver: UBC Press, 2000), 144.
133   Theresa McCarthy, "'It Isn't Easy': The Politics of Representation, 'Factionalism,' and Anthropology in Promoting Haudenosaunee Traditionalism at Six Nations" (Ph.D. dissertation, McMaster University, 2006).
134   Sherene Razack, *Looking White People in the Eye: Gender, Race, and Culture in Courtrooms and Classrooms* (Toronto: University of Toronto Press, 1998), 9, as cited in McCarthy, "'It Isn't Easy,'" 45 and 40.
135   Ozay Mehmet, *Westernizing the Third World: The Eurocentricity of Economic Development Theories* (London and New York: Routledge, 1999).

136 Ibid., 11.
137 Arturo Escobar, *Encountering Development: The Making and Unmaking of the Third World* (Princeton: Princeton University Press, 1995), 59.
138 Ibid., 60.
139 Peter Usher, "Environment, Race and Nation Reconsidered: Reflections on Aboriginal Land Claims in Canada," Wiley Lecture, *Canadian Geographer* 47, no. 4 (2003): 365-82.
140 Deborah Jean Doxtator, "Inclusive and Exclusive Perceptions of Difference: Native and Euro-based Concepts of Time, History, and Change," in Germaine Warkentin and Carolyn Podruchny, eds., *Decentring the Renaissance: Canada and Europe in Multidisciplinary Perspective 1500-1700*, 33-47 (Toronto: University of Toronto Press, 2001), 43.
141 Peter Usher, Frank Tough, and Robert Galois, "Reclaiming the Land: Aboriginal Title, Treaty Rights, and Land Claims in Canada," *Applied Geography* 12 (1992): 109-32, 121.
142 Mary Ellen Turpel, "Aboriginal Peoples and the Canadian Charter: Interpretive Monopolies, Cultural Differences," in Richard Devlin, ed., *First Nations Issues*, 40-73 (Toronto: Emond Montgomery, 1991).
143 David Rossiter and Patricia Wood, "Fantastic Topographies: Neo-liberal Responses to Aboriginal Land Claims in British Columbia," *Canadian Geographer* 49, no. 4 (2005): 352-67, 352.
144 Sidney Harring, *White Man's Law: Native People in Nineteenth-Century Canadian Jurisprudence* (Toronto: University of Toronto Press, 1998), 7.
145 Ibid., 34.
146 Ibid., 35.
147 Ibid., 54.
148 Ibid., 60.
149 Ibid., 61.
150 *Places to Grow Act*, S.O. 2005, c. 13.
151 Donald Moore, Anand Pandian, and Jake Kosek, "The Cultural Politics of Race and Nature: Terrains of Power and Practice," in Donald Moore, Jake Kosek, and Anand Pandian, eds., *Race, Nature, and the Politics of Difference*, 1-70 (Durham: Duke University Press, 2003), 42.

Chapter 4: A History of Sovereignty
1 James Clifford, *The Predicament of Culture: Twentieth-Century Ethnography, Literature, and Art* (Cambridge, MA: Harvard University Press, 1988), 289.
2 The Haudenosaunee Confederacy is commonly known to settler societies as the famed Iroquois Confederacy or the League of the Iroquois.
3 See Susan Hill, "The Clay We Are Made Of: An Examination of Haudenosaunee Land Tenure on the Grand River Territory" (Ph.D. dissertation, Department of Native Studies, Trent University, Peterborough, 2006), 83-112, for a more detailed overview of the Great Law of Peace, from which this account primarily borrows.
4 Robert Porter, "Building a New Longhouse: The Case for Government Reform within the Six Nations of the Haudenosaunee," *Buffalo Law Review* 46 (1998), 805-945, 900.
5 These first Mohawk chiefs carried, then later passed on, the titles of Ayenwatha and Tekarihoken. The current Six Nations Confederacy chief, Allan McNaughton, still bears the name Tekarihoken.
6 Mary Becker, "We Are an Independent Nation: A History of Iroquois Sovereignty," *Buffalo Law Review* 46 (1998): 981-1001, 983.

7 Mary Becker, "Iroquois and Iroquoian in Canada," in Bruce Morrison and Roderick Wilson, eds., *Native Peoples: The Canadian Experience*, 229-47 (Don Mills: Oxford University Press, 2004), 236; Charles Johnston, *The Valley of the Six Nations: A Collection of Documents on the Indian Lands of the Grand River* (Toronto: Champlain Society for the Government of Ontario, University of Toronto, 1964), xxx.

8 Susan Hill, personal communication, June 2008; Deborah Jean Doxtator, "What Happened to the Iroquois Clans? A Study of Clans in Three Nineteenth Century Rotinonhsyonni Communities" (Ph.D. dissertation, University of Western Ontario, London, 1997), 56; Hill, "The Clay We Are Made Of," 121-24.

9 Susan Hill, "'Traveling Down the River of Life Together in Peace and Friendship, Forever': Haudenosaunee Land Ethics and Treaty Agreements as the Basis for Restructuring the Relationship with the British Crown," in Leanne Simpson, ed., *Lighting the Eighth Fire: The Liberation, Resurgence and Protection of Indigenous Nations*, 1-34 (Winnipeg: Arbeiter Ring, 2008).

10 Horatio Hale, *The Iroquois Book of Rites*, edited by William Fenton (Toronto: University of Toronto Press, 1963), 33-34 and 189.

11 Roger Carpenter, *The Renewed, the Destroyed, and the Remade: The Three Thought Worlds of the Huron and the Iroquois, 1609-1650* (East Lansing, MI: Michigan State University Press, 2004), 118.

12 Donald Bourgeois, "The Six Nations: A Neglected Aspect of Canadian Legal History," *Canadian Journal of Native Studies* 6, no. 2 (1986): 252-70, 256.

13 Hill, "The Clay We Are Made Of," 183.

14 The term "Aboriginal title" is also one that serves a purpose in Canadian constitutional law that does not always coincide with Aboriginal conceptions of their connection to their lands.

15 James Tully, *Strange Multiplicity: Constitutionalism in an Age of Diversity* (Cambridge: Cambridge University Press, 1995), 71.

16 Indigenous definitions and employments of the term "sovereignty" are explored elsewhere in this book and more fully in Taiaiake Alfred's *Peace, Power, Righteousness: An Indigenous Manifesto* (Don Mills, ON: Oxford University Press, 1999). The European concept described here is from Hobbes's *Leviathan*.

17 Sidney Harring, *White Man's Law: Native People in Nineteenth-Century Canadian Jurisprudence* (Toronto: University of Toronto Press, 1998), 18.

18 This discussion of the Two Row Wampum and following treaties is based on Hill, "'Traveling Down the River of Life,'" 1-45.

19 John Borrows, *Recovering Canada: The Resurgence of Indigenous Law* (Toronto: University of Toronto Press, 2002), 126.

20 Paul Williams and Curtis Nelson, "Kaswentah," January 1995, research report prepared for the Royal Commission on Aboriginal Peoples, *For Seven Generations: An Information Legacy of the RCAP*, CD-ROM, Libraxus, 1997.

21 Hill, "The Clay We Are Made Of," 191.

22 For a discussion of this, see Williams and Nelson, "Kaswentah."

23 Ibid., part iii.

24 Treaty Minutes, Pennsylvania Council Minutes, 16 June 1744, 4: 706-9, as cited by Hill, "Traveling Down the River of Life Together," 34.

25 Becker, "We Are an Independent Nation," 993.

26 Hill, "The Clay We Are Made Of," 222.

27 Johnston, *The Valley of the Six Nations*, 70.

28 Ibid., 70.

29 Robert Surtees, "Land Cessions, 1763-1830," in Donald Smith and Edward Rogers, eds., *Aboriginal Ontario: Historical Perspectives on the First Nations*, 92-121 (Toronto: Dundurn, 1994), 95.

30 Royal Commission on Aboriginal Peoples (RCAP), *Royal Commission Report on Aboriginal Peoples* (Ottawa: Indian and Northern Affairs Canada, 1996), vol. 2, Indian and Northern Affairs Canada, http://www.ainc-inac.gc.ca/ap/rrc-eng.asp.

31 Surtees, "Land Cessions," 96; Hill, "The Clay We Are Made Of," 227.

32 Bourgeois, "The Six Nations," 256.

33 Hill, "The Clay We Are Made Of," 228.

34 Williams and Nelson document incredible continuity in these assertions of sovereignty. A few examples include a visit to Queen Anne in 1710 during which the Haudenosaunee were treated as allies and leaders; a 1788 visit to London by Joseph Brant demanding a proper deed to the Grand River lands; and a delegation in 1930 that the British Parliament refused to greet due to Canadian protests.

35 Bourgeois, "The Six Nations," 260.

36 Doxtator, "What Happened to the Iroquois Clans?" 144; Hill, "The Clay We Are Made Of," 324.

37 Porter, "Building a New Longhouse," 921 [emphasis in original].

38 Patrick Macklem, *Indigenous Difference and the Constitution of Canada* (Toronto: University of Toronto Press, 2001), 13-14.

39 Patrick Macklem, "First Nations Self-Government and the Borders of the Canadian Legal Imagination," *McGill Law Journal* 36 (1990): 382-456, 423.

40 RCAP, *Royal Commission Report on Aboriginal Peoples*, vol. 3.

41 *St. Catherine's Milling and Lumber Co v. The Queen*, (1888) 14 App. Cas. 46 (J.C.P.C.).

42 Tom Flanagan, *First Nations? Second Thoughts* (Montreal and Kingston: McGill-Queen's University Press, 2000), 62; Peter Russell, *Recognizing Aboriginal Title: The Mabo Case and Indigenous Resistance to English-Settler Colonialism* (Toronto: University of Toronto Press, 2005), 113.

43 Bruce Clark, *Native Liberty, Crown Sovereignty: The Existing Aboriginal Right of Self-Government in Canada* (Montreal and Kingston: McGill-Queen's University Press, 1990), 12; Harring, *White Man's Law*, 140.

44 Michael Coyle, *Addressing Aboriginal Land and Treaty Rights in Ontario: An Analysis of Past Policies and Options for the Future*, Ipperwash Inquiry Research Report, Toronto, 2005, 20, Ipperwash Inquiry, http://www.attorneygeneral.jus.gov.on.ca/inquiries/ipperwash/policy_part/research/index.html; Michael Coyle, *Addressing Aboriginal Land and Treaty Rights in Ontario: An Analysis of Past Policies and Options for the Future*, Ipperwash Inquiry Research Report, 25, Ipperwash Inquiry, http://www.attorneygeneral.jus.gov.on.ca/inquiries/ipperwash/policy_part/research/index.html.

45 Harring, *White Man's Law*, 147.

46 Hill, "The Clay We Are Made Of," 327 and 361; Sally Weaver, "The Iroquois: The Grand River Reserve in the Late Nineteenth and Early Twentieth Centuries, 1875-1945," in Smith and Rogers, *Aboriginal Ontario*, 213-57, 234; *An Act for Conferring Certain Privileges on the More Advanced Bands of the Indians of Canada, with the View of Training Them for the Exercise of Municipal Powers*, Chapter 28, assented to 19 April 1884, Library and Archives Canada, http://epe.lac-bac.gc.ca/100/205/301/ic/cdc/aboriginaldocs/m-stat.htm.

47 Williams and Nelson, "Kaswentah."

48 Weaver, "The Iroquois," 245.

49   Deskahe (Levi General), speech given in London, August 1923, as cited in Williams and Nelson, "Kaswentah."

50   Ronald Niezen, "Recognizing Indigenism: Canadian Unity and the International Movement of Indigenous Peoples," *Comparative Studies in Society and History* 42, no. 1 (2000): 119-48, 124-25.

51   Unknown author, "Indians at San Francisco," *Brantford Expositor*, 27 April 1945; Russell, *Recognizing Aboriginal Title*, 150.

52   Williams and Nelson, "Kaswentah," part ii.

53   Doxtator, "What Happened to the Iroquois Clans?" 242; Hill, "The Clay We Are Made Of," 357-60 and 379; Williams and Nelson, "Kaswentah," part ii.

54   Weaver, "The Iroquois," 248; Hill, "The Clay We Are Made Of," 388.

55   For a detailed account of the marginal Dehorners' movement at Six Nations, see E. Brian Titley, *A Narrow Vision: Duncan Campbell Scott and the Administration of Indian Affairs in Canada* (Vancouver: UBC Press, 1986).

56   Ibid., 134.

57   Ibid.

58   Hill, "The Clay We Are Made Of," 389.

59   Alan McMillan and Eldon Yellowhorn, eds., *First Peoples in Canada* (Vancouver: Douglas and McIntyre, 2004), 95; Weaver, "The Iroquois," 250.

60   Dale Turner, *This Is Not a Peace Pipe* (Toronto: University of Toronto Press, 2006), 12; William Bogart, *Good Government? Good Citizens? Courts, Politics, and Markets in a Changing Canada* (Vancouver: UBC Press, 2005), 101; Peter Usher, Frank Tough, and Robert Galois, "Reclaiming the Land: Aboriginal Title, Treaty Rights, and Land Claims in Canada," *Applied Geography* 12 (1992): 109-32, 123; *Constitution Act, 1982* (U.K.), 1982, c. 11, s. 59.

61   Alan Cairns, *Citizens Plus: Aboriginal Peoples and the Canadian State* (Vancouver: UBC Press, 2000), 67.

62   Timothy Appleby, "Mayor Hangs on Despite Caledonia," *Globe and Mail*, 14 November 2006, A18.

63   Chinta Puxley and Jennifer Ditchburn, "Stop Acting Like Kids, Politicians Scolded," *Brantford Expositor*, 2 November 2006, A1.

64   Chinta Puxley, "Bill for Caledonia Standoff at $55 Million: PC Leader," *Brantford Expositor*, 27 September 2006, A1.

65   Sue Bailey, "Politicians Point Fingers, Dodge Duties, Critics Say," *Brantford Expositor*, 21 April 2006, C2.

66   Diane Finley, "Governments Working Hard for Resolution," *Brantford Expositor*, 24 April 2006, A9.

67   Karen Howlett, "Standoff at Caledonia: McGuinty Comes under Fire in Legislature as Natives Resist Predawn OPP Raid," *Globe and Mail*, 21 April 2006, A1.

68   Daniel Nolan, "E-mail Threatens Lacrosse Game; Caledonia Citizens Are Being Called On to 'Restrict Access' to Six Nations Match," *Hamilton Spectator*, 6 June 2006, A2.

69   Indian and Northern Affairs Canada, "Michael Coyle Appointed to Undertake a Fact-Finding Initiative in Relation to the Situation in Caledonia," 24 March 2006," press release, Indian and Northern Affairs Canada, http://www.ainc-inac.gc.ca/ai/mr/nr/j-a2006/2-02758-eng.asp.

70   Michael-Allen Marion, "Confederacy Chiefs Call for Talks on Land Claims: Throw Support behind Caledonia Housing Development Occupation," *Hamilton Spectator*, 28 March 2006, A1.

71 Michael Coyle, *Results of Fact-Finding on Situation at Caledonia* (Ottawa: Government of Canada, 7 April 2006), 16.

72 Jim Prentice, "Letter to Six Nations 'Iroquois' Confederacy," 17 April 2006.

73 Jim Windle, "St. Amand Says Talks Must Continue," *Tekawennake*, 16 August 2006, 3.

74 Toby Barrett, "Dispute Is Talk of the Land," *Grand River Sachem*, 25 August 2006, 4.

75 Hazel E. Hill, "Grand River Update from Hazel Hill, March 10, 2007," 10 March 2007, mass e-mail [used with permission; on file with author].

76 Hazel E. Hill, "Hazel's Update of April 12, 2007," 12 April 2007, mass e-mail [used with permission; on file with author].

77 Hazel E. Hill, "Grand River Update from Hazel Hill, March 10, 2007," mass e-mail [used with permission; on file with author].

78 Ibid.

79 Chinta Puxley, "'Too Many Voices' Hindering Caledonia Talks: Six Nations Chief," *Brantford Expositor*, 14 March 2007, A1.

80 Dana Brown, "Montour Vows New Era of Communication," *Hamilton Spectator*, 20 November 2007, A6.

81 Department of Justice Canada, "Canada's Position on the History of the Surrender of the Plank Road Lands (including the Douglas Creek Estates): Summary of the Narrative Presented by Michael McCulloch to the Plank Road Lands Side Table," 3 November 2006, 1 [used with permission; on file with author].

82 Tania Murray Li, "Masyarakat Adat, Difference, and the Limits of Recognition in Indonesia's Forest Zone," in Donald Moore, Jake Kosek, and Anand Pandian, eds., *Race, Nature, and the Politics of Difference*, 380-406 (Durham, NC: Duke University Press, 2003), 404.

83 Theresa McCarthy, "'It Isn't Easy': The Politics of Representation, 'Factionalism,' and Anthropology in Promoting Haudenosaunee Traditionalism at Six Nations" (Ph.D. dissertation, Department of Anthropology, McMaster University, 2006), 89.

84 Oren Lyons, "The American Indian in the Past," in Oren Lyons and John Mohawk, eds., *Exiled in the Land of the Free: Democracy, the Indian Nations, and the U.S. Constitution*, 13-42 (Santa Fe, NM: Clear Light, 1991), 39; McCarthy, "It Isn't Easy," 99.

85 Leroy Little Bear, "Jagged Worldviews Colliding," in Marie Battiste, ed., *Reclaiming Indigenous Voice and Vision*, 77-85 (Vancouver: UBC Press, 2000), 77.

86 Voice of the Grand, "Talk of the Nation" (Ohsweken: CKRZ FM Radio, 1999), as cited in McCarthy, "It Isn't Easy," 76.

87 McCarthy, "It Isn't Easy," 90.

88 Theresa McCarthy, "Mobilizing the Metanarrative of Iroquois Factionalism and the Kanonhstaton Land Reclamation in the Grand River Territory" (unpublished paper, University of Buffalo, 2008), 3 [used with permission; on file with author].

89 McCarthy, "It Isn't Easy," 4.

90 Canadian Press, "Finley Floats a Suggestion," *Brantford Expositor*, 5 April 2007, A15.

91 Keith Leslie and Tobi Cohen, "Prentice Cancels Meeting on Caledonia Standoff," *Brantford Expositor*, 1 November 2006, A1.

92 Ontario Secretariat of Aboriginal Affairs, "Statement from Minister Ramsay – Minister Responsible for Aboriginal Affairs," 31 October 2006, press release, Secretariat of Aboriginal Affairs, http://www.aboriginalaffairs.gov.on.ca/english/news/2006/news_061101.asp.

93 Allen MacNaughton, "Press Release from Six Nations Confederacy Council," *Grand River Sachem*, 10 November 2006, 4.

94   Puxley and Ditchburn, "Stop Acting Like Kids, Politicians Scolded," A1.

95   Karen Howlett, "Ottawa Accepts Leadership Role in Effort to Quell Caledonia Dispute," *Globe and Mail*, 15 November 2006, A7.

96   Paul Legall, "Natives Vow to Continue Protest After Court Blow," *Hamilton Spectator*, 10 March 2006, A8.

97   Leroy Hill, "Canada Owes Us Millions," *Brantford Expositor*, 11 January 2007, A10.

98   Hazel E. Hill, "Update from Grand River October 19, 2006," 19 October 2006, 1, mass e-mail [used with permission; on file with author].

99   Hill, "Canada Owes Us Millions," A10.

100 John Paul Zronik, "All Quiet at Occupation Site, but Protest Takes Personal Toll," *Brantford Expositor*, 24 February 2007, A12.

101 Susan Gamble, "Some 'Divine Intervention,'" *Brantford Expositor*, 31 August 2006, A5.

102 Hazel E. Hill, "Update from Grand River," 25 September 2007 [used with permission; on file with author].

103 Marissa Nelson, "Clan Mothers Seek UN's Help; Doreen Silversmith Says 'Genocidal Practices' of Canada Must Stop," *Hamilton Spectator*, 3 May 2006, A6.

104 Marissa Nelson, "Rude Awaking for Young Protester," *Hamilton Spectator*, 21 April 2006, A1.

105 Mike Pearson, "Fact Finder Arrives," *Grand River Sachem*, 31 March 2006, 1.

106 Corporation of Haldimand County, "Haldimand County Council Statement re: Douglas Creek Estates Occupation," 16 May 2006, press release, Haldimand County, http://www.haldimandcounty.on.ca/MediaReleases.aspx.

107 Mike Pearson, "Talks Fail to End Protest; Henco Industries Considering Legal Action Against OPP," *Grand River Sachem*, 21 April 2006, 7.

108 Prentice, "Letter to Six Nations 'Iroquois' Confederacy." The implication that the government would only negotiate if the protesters were removed, of course, turned out to be an empty threat. Negotiations were actually stepped up after the 20 April raid and the construction of the blockades, bearing out the initial premise of the protesters: only direct action gets attention from the government.

109 Allen MacNaughton, Barbara McDougall, and Jane Stewart, "Negotiation Framework," 22 June 2006 [used with permission; on file with author].

110 Indian and Northern Affairs Canada, "Exploration Resolution Process: Joint Statement of Canada, Ontario, and Six Nations," 5 April 2006, press release, Indian and Northern Affairs Canada, http://www.ainc-inac.gc.ca/ai/mr/nr/j-a2006/snjs-eng.asp; Chinta Puxley, "McGuinty Wants Ottawa to Pay Up," *Brantford Expositor*, 21 October 2006, A1.

111 Marie Battiste, "Introduction," in Battiste, *Reclaiming Indigenous Voice and Vision*, xvi-xxx, xix.

112 Bruce Braun, *The Intemperate Rainforest: Nature, Culture, and Power on Canada's West Coast* (Minneapolis: University of Minnesota Press, 2002), 23.

113 Cole Harris, "How Did Colonialism Dispossess? Comments from an Edge of Empire," *Annals of the Association of American Geographers* 94, no. 1 (2004): 165-82, 179.

114 Daniel Clayton, "Captain Cook and the Spaces of Contact at 'Nootka Sound," in Jennifer Brown and Elizabeth Vilbert, eds., *Reading beyond Words: Contexts for Native History*, 95-123 (Peterborough, ON: Broadview, 1996), 120.

115 Peter Usher, "Environment, Race, and Nation Reconsidered: Reflections on Aboriginal Land Claims in Canada," Wiley Lecture, *Canadian Geographer* 47, no. 4 (2003): 365-82; Usher, Tough, and Galois, "Reclaiming the Land," 117.

116 Ibid.

117 Usher, "Environment, Race, and Nation Reconsidered," 368.

118 Mary Ellen Turpel, "Aboriginal Peoples and the Canadian Charter: Interpretive Monopolies, Cultural Differences," in Richard Devlin, ed., *First Nations Issues*, 40-73 (Toronto: Emond Montgomery, 1991), 57.

119 Sharon Venne, "Understanding Treaty 6: An Indigenous Perspective," in Michael Asch, ed., *Aboriginal and Treaty Rights in Canada: Essays on Law, Equality, and Respect for Difference*, 173-207 (Vancouver: UBC Press, 1997), 197.

120 Ibid., 205.

121 Evelyn Peters, "Aboriginal People and Canadian Geography: A Review of the Recent Literature," *Canadian Geographer* 44, no. 1 (2000): 44-55.

122 Dale Turner, "From Valladolid to Ottawa: The Illusion of Listening to Aboriginal People," in Jill Oakes, Rick Riewe, Kathi Kinew, and Elaine Maloney, eds., *Sacred Lands: Aboriginal World Views, Claims, and Conflicts*, 53-68 (Edmonton: Canadian Circumpolar Institute Press, 1996), 64.

123 Linda Tuhiwai Smith, *Decolonizing Methodologies: Research and Indigenous Peoples* (London and New York: Zed Books, 1999).

124 Ibid., 33.

125 Ibid., 34.

126 Jake Thomas, 1996, as cited in McCarthy, "It Isn't Easy," 177.

127 Deborah Jean Doxtator, "Inclusive and Exclusive Perceptions of Difference: Native and Euro-based Concepts of Time, History, and Change," in Germaine Warkentin and Carolyn Podruchny, eds., *Decentring the Renaissance: Canada and Europe in Multidisciplinary Perspective 1500-1700*, 34-47 (Toronto: University of Toronto Press, 2001), 34.

128 Ibid., 36.

129 Ibid., 41.

130 Coyle, *Addressing Aboriginal Land and Treaty Rights*, 55.

131 Turner, *This Is Not a Peace Pipe*, 72.

132 Tom Deer, as cited in McCarthy, "It Isn't Easy," 69.

133 Michael Asch and Norman Zlotkin, "Affirming Aboriginal Title: A New Basis for Comprehensive Claims Negotiations," in Asch, *Aboriginal and Treaty Rights in Canada*, 208-29, 214-16.

134 Michael Lee Ross, *First Nations Sacred Sites in Canada's Courts* (Vancouver: UBC Press, 2005), 177-78.

135 Usher, Tough, and Galois, "Reclaiming the Land," 111.

136 Rodney Bobiwash, "The Sacred and the Profane: Indigenous Lands and State Policy," in Jill Oakes, Rick Riewe, Kathi Kinew, and Elaine Maloney, eds., *Sacred Lands: Aboriginal World Views, Claims, and Conflicts*, 203-13 (Edmonton: Canadian Circumpolar Institute, 1996), 206.

137 David C. Natcher, "Land Use Research and the Duty to Consult: A Misrepresentation of the Aboriginal Landscape," *Land Use Policy* 18, no. 2 (April 2001): 113-22.

138 Bobiwash, "The Sacred and the Profane," 206.

139 Usher, Tough, and Galois, "Reclaiming the Land," 122-24.

140 Bonita Lawrence, "Gender, Race, and the Regulation of Native Identity in Canada and the United States: An Overview," *Hypatia* 18, no. 2 (2003): 3-31, 24.

141 *Places to Grow Act*, S.O. 2005, c. 13.

142 Lawrence, "Gender, Race," 4.

143 Mary Becker, "Iroquois and Iroquoian in Canada," in Bruce Morrison and Roderick Wilson, eds., *Native Peoples: The Canadian Experience*, 229-47 (Don Mills: Oxford University Press, 2004), 240-41.

144 McCarthy, "It Isn't Easy," 116.

145 Oren Lyons and John Mohawk, "Introduction," in Lyons and Mohawk, eds., *Exiled in the Land of the Free*, 2-12; Williams and Nelson, "Kaswentah."

146 Oren Lyons, "The American Indian in the Past," in Lyons and Mohawk, eds., *Exiled in the Land of the Free*, 13-42, 16.

147 Ibid., 42.

148 Tully, *Strange Multiplicity*, 127-28, 209.

149 Borrows, *Recovering Canada*, 126; Turner, *This Is Not a Peace Pipe*, 54.

150 Williams and Nelson, "Kaswentah."

151 Tully, *Strange Multiplicity*, 39.

152 Smith, *Decolonizing Methodologies*, 81.

153 Ibid., 51.

154 Oren Lyons, "The Seventh Generation Yet Unborn," *Futurist* 22, no. 2 (1988): 60.

155 Gerald (Taiaiake) Alfred, *Heeding the Voices of Our Ancestors: Kahnawake Mohawk Politics and the Rise of Native Nationalism* (Don Mills, ON: Oxford University Press, 1995).

156 Ibid., 181.

157 Ibid., 184.

158 Donald Moore, Anand Pandian, and Jake Kosek, "The Cultural Politics of Race and Nature: Terrains of Power and Practice," in Donald Moore, Jake Kosek, and Anand Pandian, eds., *Race, Nature, and the Politics of Difference*, 1-70 (Durham, NC: Duke University Press, 2003), 42.

159 Terre Satterfield, *Anatomy of a Conflict: Identity, Knowledge, and Emotion in Old-Growth Forests* (Vancouver: UBC Press, 2002), 160-61.

160 Hank Johnston, Enrique Larana, and Joseph Gusfield, "Identities, Grievances, and New Social Movements," in Hank Johnston, Enrique Larana, and Joseph Gusfield, eds., *New Social Movements: From Ideology to Identity*, 3-35 (Philadelphia: Temple University Press, 1994), 23, as cited in Satterfield, *Anatomy of a Conflict*, 9.

161 Satterfield, *Anatomy of a Conflict*, 137.

162 Ibid., 149.

163 Ibid., 158.

164 Ibid., 157.

165 Ibid., 103.

166 Lyons, "The Seventh Generation Yet Unborn," 60.

167 Alfred, *Heeding the Voices of Our Ancestors*, 188.

168 Bobiwash, "The Sacred and the Profane," 205.

169 Ibid., 205.

170 William Carroll and Robert Ratner, "Master Frames and Counter-Hegemony: Political Sensibilities in Contemporary Social Movements," *Canadian Review of Sociology* 33, no. 4 (1996): 407-35 at 420.

Chapter 5: In Search of Justice

1 Allen MacNaughton, Barbara McDougall, and Jane Stewart, "Negotiation Framework," 22 June 2006 [used with permission; on file with author].

2 Michael-Allen Marion, "Confederacy Chiefs Call for Talks on Land Claims: Throw Support behind Caledonia Housing Development Occupation," *Hamilton Spectator*, 28 March 2006, A1.

3 Susan Gamble, "Ontario Still Wants to See Negotiated Settlement: Minister," *Brantford Expositor,* 21 April 2006, C2.
4 Indian and Northern Affairs Canada, "Michael Coyle Appointed to Undertake a Fact-Finding Initiative in Relation to the Situation in Caledonia," 24 March 2006, press release, Indian and Northern Affairs Canada, http://www.ainc-inac.gc.ca/ai/mr/nr/j-a2006/2-02758 -eng.asp.
5 Canadian Press, "Peterson to Help Solve Land Dispute: Former Premier Says He Can't Guarantee He'll Have Success," *Brantford Expositor,* 1 May 2006, A1.
6 Jim Prentice, "Letter to Six Nations 'Iroquois' Confederacy," 17 April 2006 [used with permission; on file with author].
7 Ronald Doering was to later assume the lead negotiating role when Barbara McDougall stepped down.
8 Indian and Northern Affairs Canada, "Barbara McDougall Appointed as Federal Representative in Caledonia Talks," 3 May 2006," press release, Indian and Northern Affairs Canada, http://www.ainc-inac.gc.ca/ai/mr/nr/m-a2006/2-02763-eng.asp.
9 Barb McKay, "Land Negotiators Join Talks," *Hamilton Spectator,* 4 May 2006, A8.
10 John Paul Zronik, "Levac Takes Shot at Tory Rival," *Brantford Expositor,* 4 October 2007, A4.
11 Mike Pearson, "Talks Fail to End Protest: Henco Industries Considering Legal Action against OPP," *Grand River Sachem,* 21 April 2006, 7.
12 Susan Gamble, "Whose Land Is It, Anyway?" *Brantford Expositor,* 8 May 2006, A1.
13 Hazel E. Hill, "Update from Grand River," 18 July 2006, 2, mass e-mail [used with permission; on file with author].
14 Angela Pacienza, "Premier to Caledonia Residents: Be Patient: Asks for More Time to Resolve Dispute," *Brantford Expositor,* 11 May 2006," A1.
15 David Ramsay, "Letter from David Ramsay to Haudenosaunee Six Nations Confederacy Council," 17 May 2006 [used with permission; on file with author].
16 Indian and Northern Affairs Canada and Ontario Secretariat of Aboriginal Affairs, "Joint Statement by Minister Jim Prentice and Minister David Ramsay," 11 June 2006, 1-2, press release, Secretariat of Aboriginal Affairs, http://www.aboriginalaffairs.gov.on.ca/english/ news/2006/news_060611.asp.
17 Toby Barrett, "What's on Negotiating Table?" *Grand River Sachem,* 28 July 2006, 14.
18 Daniel Nolan, "Six Nations Evidence Due," *Hamilton Spectator,* 21 October 2006, A15.
19 Ontario Secretariat of Aboriginal Affairs, "Haudenosaunee/Six Nations-Canada-Ontario Main Negotiation Table Update," 27 July 2006, press release, http://www. aboriginalaffairs.gov.on.ca/english/news/2006/news_060727.asp.
20 The mineral resources are extensive, especially gypsum.
21 Six Nations Lands and Resources, "Six Nations of the Grand River: Land Rights, Financial Justice, Creative Solutions," November 2006, 14, booklet handed out by Six Nations Lands and Resources Department, http://www.hamilton.ca/NR/rdonlyres/0FCA0BC2 -A78F-47AC-9577-016BB397F1D7/0/SixNationsClaimsBooklet.pdf. The Plank Road claim was filed on 23 June 1987 and is registered under File no. B-8260-322.
22 Ibid., 19. The 1841 Purported General Surrender claim was filed on 28 September 1989 and is registered under File no. B-8260-381.
23 Ibid., 21.
24 Six Nations Band Council, "Backgrounder: The Six Nations Plank Road Claim in Brief," 2007, Six Nations of the Grand River [used with permission; on file with author].
25 Ronald Doering, "Letter: Re: Plank Road Side Table," 18 September 2006 [used with permission; on file with author].

26 Nolan, "Six Nations Evidence Due," A15.
27 Department of Justice Canada, "Canada's Position on the History of the Surrender of the Plank Road Lands (including the Douglas Creek Estates): Summary of the Narrative Presented by Michael McCulloch to the Plank Road Lands Side Table," 3 November 2006, 1 [used with permission; on file with author].
28 Ibid., 2.
29 Ibid., 4.
30 Ibid., 5.
31 Ibid., 12.
32 Hazel E. Hill, "Update from Grand River, November 16, 2006," 16 November 2006, 1, mass e-mail [used with permission; on file with author].
33 The Dish with One Spoon, as explained in Chapter 1, refers to a practice of sharing lands and resources so that there is enough for everyone, including future generations.
34 Hill, "Update from Grand River, November 16, 2006," 3.
35 Government of Canada, "Federal Legal Response to Haudenosaunee/Six Nations' Presentation of November 14, 2006," 25 January 2007 [used with permission; on file with author].
36 Phil Monture, "Hamilton/Port Dover Plank Road Update," 6 December 2006, Caledonia Wakeup Call, http://www.caledoniawakeupcall.com/updates/061206mnn.html.
37 Ibid., 4.
38 Ibid., 5.
39 Government of Canada, "Federal Legal Response to Haudenosaunee/Six Nations' Presentation of November 14, 2006," 25 January 2007, 13 [used with permission; on file with author].
40 Ibid., 6.
41 Department of Justice Canada, "Canada's Position," 3 November 2006 [used with permission; on file with author].
42 Hazel E. Hill, "Hazel's Update of April 12, 2007," 12 April 2007, 1, mass e-mail [used with permission; on file with author].
43 Toby Barrett, "One Law for All – Period," *Grand River Sachem*, 3 August 2007, 10; Mike Pearson, "A State of Emergency Declared after Town Left in the Dark," *Grand River Sachem*, 26 May 2006, 3.
44 Chinta Puxley, "McGuinty Wants Ottawa to Pay Up," *Brantford Expositor*, 21 October 2006, A1.
45 Ontario Secretariat of Aboriginal Affairs, "Statement from Minister Ramsay – Minister Responsible for Aboriginal Affairs," 31 October 2006, press release, http://www.aboriginalaffairs.gov.on.ca/english/news/2006/news_061101.asp.
46 Ontario Secretariat of Aboriginal Affairs, "Six Nations (Caledonia) Costs to Date," 16 February 2007, press release, http://www.aboriginalaffairs.gov.on.ca/english/news/2006/news_061102.asp.
47 Hazel E. Hill, "Update from Grand River, October 19, 2006," 19 October 2006, 2, mass e-mail [used with permission; on file with author].
48 Leroy Hill, "Canada Owes Us Millions," *Brantford Expositor*, 11 January 2007, A10.
49 Gillian Livingston, "Ontario Considers Financial Help in Native Occupation," *Brantford Expositor*, 13 April 2006, A5.
50 Ontario Secretariat of Aboriginal Affairs, "Progress Being Made on Caledonia Situation," 28 April 2006, press release, Secretariat of Aboriginal Affairs, http://www.aboriginalaffairs.gov.on.ca/english/news/2006/news_060428_2.asp.

51 Corporation of Haldimand County, "Province Commits to Communications and Business Assistance," 1 May 2006, press release, Haldimand County, http://www.haldimandcounty.on.ca/MediaReleases.aspx.

52 Corporation of Haldimand County, "Haldimand County Council Passes Two Motions Regarding Douglas Creek Estates Issue," 9 May 2006, press release, Haldimand County, http://www.haldimandcounty.on.ca/MediaReleases.aspx.

53 Corporation of Haldimand County, "Province Provides Local Businesses with Emergency Financial Relief Program," 26 May 2006, press release, Haldimand County, http://www.haldimandcounty.on.ca/MediaReleases.aspx.

54 Corporation of Haldimand County, "Haldimand County Opens Local Business Emergency Relief Assistance Office," 29 May 2006, press release, Haldimand County, http://www.haldimandcounty.on.ca/MediaReleases.aspx.

55 Sandra Muse, "Judge Playing Dangerous Game, Says Janie Jamieson," *Tekawennake*, 31 May 2006, 1-2.

56 Ontario Secretariat of Aboriginal Affairs, "Significant Progress Made in Caledonia Dispute," 16 June 2006, press release, Secretariat of Aboriginal Affairs, http://www.aboriginalaffairs.gov.on.ca/english/news/2006/news_060616.asp.

57 Ontario Ministry of Economic Development. "Ontario Provides Financial Assistance Program for Caledonia Area Businesses," 16 June 2006, press release, Caledonia Wakeup Call, http://www.caledoniawakeupcall.com/updates/060616omedt.html.

58 Mike Oliviera and Steve Erwin, "Ontario Buys Out Caledonia Developer," *Brantford Expositor*, 17 June 2006, A1.

59 Ibid.

60 Corporation of Haldimand County, "News Release from the Council of the Corporation of Haldimand County," 9 July 2007, press release, Haldimand County, http://www.haldimandcounty.on.ca/MediaReleases.aspx.

61 Frederieka Van Driel, "Ontario's Approach to Land Claims," *Tekawennake*, 1 November 2006, 2.

62 Chinta Puxley and Jennifer Ditchburn, "Stop Acting Like Kids, Politicians Scolded," *Brantford Expositor*, 2 November 2006, A1.

63 Toby Barrett, "Government Can't Ignore Its Role," *Grand River Sachem*, 13 July 2007, 4.

64 John Paul Zronik, "Haldimand Held Hostage: Trainer," *Brantford Expositor*, 10 July 2007, A1.

65 Katie Dawson, "Finley Meets with Rotary Club," *Grand River Sachem*, 16 March 2007, 33.

66 Hill, "Update from Grand River October 19, 2006," 2-3 [used with permission; on file with author].

67 Hill, "Hazel's Update of April 12, 2007," 2.

68 The Plank Road claim was not addressed in the offer.

69 Ontario Ministry of Aboriginal Affairs, "Statement by Ontario's Principal Representative Regarding Provincially Owned Lands near Six Nations Reserve," 26 October 2007, press release, Ministry of Aboriginal Affairs, http://www.aboriginalaffairs.gov.on.ca/english/news/2007/oct26nr_07.asp.

70 Allen MacNaughton, "Statement: Chief Allen MacNaughton Six Nations Confederacy Council Negotiating Team Response to Canada," 5 December 2006, 1, press release [used with permission; on file with author].

71 James Wallace, "Documents Obtained by Osprey News Puts Price Tag on Settling Caledonia Dispute: Ottawa to Offer $125 Million," *Brantford Expositor*, 31 May 2007, A1.

72 Christopher Maughan, "Caledonia Offer 'a Slap in the Face,'" *Brantford Expositor*, 1 June 2007, A1.

73 Jim Windle, "Talks End – Negotiations Finally Begin: Money Not the Issue, Land Should Be Returned," *Tekawennake*, 6 June 2007, 1.

74 Ibid., 2.

75 Ibid.

76 Ronald Doering, "Letter to Chief Allen MacNaughton," 13 June 2007, 1-3 [used with permission; on file with author].

77 Editorial, "Caledonia Protesters Target Osgoode Hall, Say Claims Money Used to Construct Building," *Hamilton Spectator*, 22 August 2007, A10.

78 Hill, "Update from Grand River November 16, 2006," 4.

79 Daniel Nolan, "Caledonia Negotiations Near Turning Point," *Hamilton Spectator*, 23 February 2007, A10.

80 Daniel Nolan, "McDougall, Stewart Join Team: Peterson Suggests Province Buy Protest Site," *Hamilton Spectator*, 11 May 2006, A6.

81 Government of Canada, "Federal Legal Response," 1.

82 Ibid., 13.

83 *Declaration of Rights of Indigenous Peoples*, adopted by General Assembly Resolution 61/295 on 13 September 2007, United Nations, http://www.un.org/esa/socdev/unpfii/en/drip.html.

84 Indian and Northern Affairs Canada, "Statement by Canada's New Government Regarding the United Nations Declaration on the Rights of Indigenous Peoples," 12 September 2007, 1, press release, Indian and Northern Affairs Canada, http://www.ainc-inac.gc.ca/ai/mr/nr/s-d2007/2-2936-eng.asp.

85 Indian and Northern Affairs Canada, "Canada Endorses the United Nations Declaration on the Rights of Indigenous Peoples," 12 November 2010, press release, Indian and Northern Affairs Canada, http://www.ainc-inac.gc.ca/ai/mr/nr/s-d2010/23429-eng.asp.

86 Chinta Puxley, "Caledonia Visit Top Priority: Bryant," *Brantford Expositor*, 1 November 2007, A1.

87 Chinta Puxley, "'Too Many Voices' Hindering Caledonia Talks: Six Nations Chief," *Brantford Expositor*, 14 March 2007, A1.

88 Hazel E. Hill, "Hazel's View from the Table," *Tekawennake*, 27 June 2007, 7.

89 Haudenosaunee Development Institute, "Haudenosaunee Development Protocol," 1 September 2007, 1 [used with permission; on file with author].

90 Ibid., 2.

91 Allen MacNaughton, "Feds and Provinces Leave Table," *Grand River Sachem*, 21 September 2007, 9.

92 Jim Windle, "Optimism for Christmas Settlement," *Tekawennake*, 5 December 2007, 10.

93 Paul Legall, "Builder Calls Natives' Fees 'Mafia Shakedown,'" *Hamilton Spectator*, 14 September 2007, A1.

94 Paul Legall, "Six Nations Warns of Legal Action over Permits," *Hamilton Spectator*, 10 October 2007, A1.

95 Hazel E. Hill, "Update from Grand River," 25 September 2007, 2 [used with permission; on file with author].

96 Ibid.

97 Michael-Allen Marion, "City Can't Comply with Protocol: Mayor. Municipalities Must Follow Ontario Laws in Granting Permits to Developers," *Brantford Expositor*, 13 September 2007, A4.

98 Legall, "Builder Calls Natives' Fees 'Mafia Shakedown,'" A1.
99 Jim Windle, "Tensions at the Negotiations Noticeable," *Tekawennake*, 24 October 2007, 5.
100 Katie Dawson, "Six Nations Responds to Government," *Grand River Sachem*, 26 October 2007, 1.
101 Ibid.
102 Six Nations "Iroquois" Confederacy, "Rotienneson Urge the Public to Keep the Peace," 17 October 2007, 1-2 [used with permission; on file with author]; Dawson, "Six Nations Responds to Government," 1.
103 Jim Windle, "Bryant Brings His Wallet to Caledonia – Rejects HDI," *Tekawennake*, 28 November 2007, 2.
104 Hazel E. Hill, "Update from Grand River: Hazel Hill," *Tekawennake*, 14 November 2007, 8.
105 Jim Knisley, "Doering Says Negotiations Can't Go On Forever," *Grand River Sachem*, 7 December 2007, 3.
106 Indian and Northern Affairs Canada, "Statement from Canada's Representatives in Six Nations Talks," 12 December 2007, press release, Indian and Northern Affairs Canada, http://www.ainc-inac.gc.ca/ai/mr/nr/s-d2007/2-2980-eng.asp.
107 Indian and Northern Affairs Canada, "Frequently Asked Questions: Canada's Offer to Six Nations Welland Canal Flooding Claim," 21 January 2008, press release, Indian and Northern Affairs Canada, http://www.ainc-inac.gc.ca/ai/mr/nr/s-d2007/2-2980-faq -eng.asp.
108 Ronald Doering, "Senior Federal Negotiator's Speaking Points: Welland Canal Flooding," 12 December 2007, 2.
109 James Bradshaw, "Six Nations to 'Consider' $26-Million Offer in Welland Dispute," *Globe and Mail*, 13 December 2007, A16.
110 Michael-Allen Marion, "Six Nations Offered $26M to Settle One Land Claim," *Brantford Expositor*, 13 December 2007, A1.
111 Daniel Nolan, "Ottawa Offers $26m for Claims; Welland Feeder Canal/Dunnville Dam," *Hamilton Spectator*, 13 December 2007, A7.
112 Bradshaw, "Six Nations to 'Consider' $26-Million Offer in Welland Dispute," A16.
113 Marion, "Six Nations Offered $26M," A1.
114 Murray Campbell, "A Standoff by the Numbers," *Globe and Mail*, 1 March 2007, A14.
115 Kate Harries, "Records Show Caledonia Land Never Given Up, Natives Say: On Anniversary of Occupation, Chiefs Contend Confederacy Leaders in Past Only Leased Areas," *Globe and Mail*, 1 March 2007, A14.
116 John Paul Zronik, "Twelve Months Later, There Is No End in Sight to the Dispute over Native Land Claims. 'This Is Going to Take a Long Time,' Says a Federal Negotiator," *Brantford Expositor*, 24 February 2007, A1.
117 Andrew Woolford, *Between Justice and Certainty: Treaty Making in British Columbia* (Vancouver: UBC Press, 2005).
118 James Clifford, *The Predicament of Culture: Twentieth-Century Ethnography, Literature, and Art* (Cambridge, MA: Harvard University Press, 1988), 10.
119 Cole Harris, *Making Native Space: Colonialism, Resistance, and Reserves in British Columbia* (Vancouver: UBC Press, 2002); Michael Coyle, *Addressing Aboriginal Land and Treaty Rights in Ontario: An Analysis of Past Policies and Options for the Future*, Ipperwash Inquiry Research Report, 2005, Ipperwash Inquiry, http://www.attorneygeneral.j us.gov.on.ca/ inquiries/ipperwash/policy_part/research/index.html; Woolford, *Between Justice and*

Certainty, 10, 61, 88; Michael Asch and Norman Zlotkin, "Affirming Aboriginal Title: A New Basis for Comprehensive Claims Negotiations," in Michael Asch, ed., *Aboriginal and Treaty Rights in Canada: Essays on Law, Equity, and Respect for Difference*, 208-29 (Vancouver: UBC Press, 1997).

120 Asch and Zlotkin, "Affirming Aboriginal Title," 211-12.

Chapter 6: Constitutional Territory

1 Bruce Clark, *Native Liberty, Crown Sovereignty: The Existing Aboriginal Right of Self-Government in Canada* (Montreal and Kingston: McGill-Queen's University Press, 1990), 198.

2 Ibid., 198.

3 Ibid., 202.

4 Ibid., 204.

5 Patrick Macklem, "What's Law Got to Do with It? The Protection of Aboriginal Title in Canada," *Osgoode Hall Law Journal* 35, no. 1 (1997): 125-37.

6 Ibid., 132.

7 Ibid., 134.

8 Ibid., 136.

9 Ibid.

10 Patrick Macklem, *Indigenous Difference and the Constitution of Canada* (Toronto: University of Toronto Press, 2001), 269.

11 Peter Usher, Frank Tough, and Robert Galois, "Reclaiming the Land: Aboriginal Title, Treaty Rights, and Land Claims in Canada," *Applied Geography* 12 (1992): 109-32; Macklem, *Indigenous Difference*, 175-76.

12 As cited in Macklem, *Indigenous Difference*, 273. *Delgamuukw v. British Columbia*, [1997] 3 S.C.R. 1010, 153 D.L.R. (4th) 193.

13 Peter Usher, "Environment, Race and Nation Reconsidered: Reflections on Aboriginal Land Claims in Canada," Wiley Lecture, *Canadian Geographer* 47, no. 4 (2003): 365-82.

14 Chris Tollefson and Karen Wipond, "Cumulative Environmental Impacts and Aboriginal Rights," *Environmental Impact Assessment Review* 18 (1998): 371-90, 389.

15 Russell Barsh, "Canada's Aboriginal Peoples: Social Integration or Disintegration?" *Canadian Journal of Native Studies* 14, no. 1 (1994): 1-46, 36.

16 *R. v. Sparrow*, [1990] 1 S.C.R. 1075.

17 Michael Coyle, *Addressing Aboriginal Land and Treaty Rights in Ontario: An Analysis of Past Policies and Options for the Future*, Ipperwash Inquiry Research Report, 2005, Ipperwash Inquiry, http://www.attorneygeneral.jus.gov.on.ca/inquiries/ipperwash/policy_part/research/index.html.

18 Tollefson and Wipond, "Cumulative Environmental Impacts," 383.

19 *Haida Nation v. British Columbia (Minister of Forests)*, [2004] 3 S.C.R. 511.

20 Coyle, *Addressing Aboriginal Land and Treaty Rights*, 23, 28.

21 Ibid., 57.

22 Ibid., 76.

23 Timothy McDaniels and William Trousdale, "Resource Compensation and Negotiation Support in an Aboriginal Context: Using Community-Based Multi-Attribute Analysis to Evaluate Non-Market Losses," *Ecological Economics* 55, no. 2 (2005): 173-86.

24 David C. Natcher, "Land Use Research and the Duty to Consult: A Misrepresentation of the Aboriginal Landscape," *Land Use Policy* 18, no. 2 (April 2001): 113-22.

25 Ibid., 121.

26 Charles Coffey, *The Cost of Doing Nothing: A Call to Action*, 1997, Royal Bank of Canada, http://www.rbcroyalbank.com/aboriginal/r_comm.html.

27 Susan Clairmont, "Focus on Fantino: OPP Chief Says They Are Peacekeepers Not Problem-Solvers in Caledonia," *Hamilton Spectator*, 12 November 2007, A6.

28 Ibid.

29 Ibid.

30 Evelyn Peters, "Aboriginal People and Canadian Geography: A Review of the Recent Literature," *Canadian Geographer* 44, no. 1 (2000): 44-55, 45.

31 Michael Coyle, "Claims Resolution: A Healing Process?" in Jill Oakes et al., eds., *Sacred Lands: Aboriginal World Views, Claims, and Conflicts*, 259-64 (Edmonton: Canadian Circumpolar Institute, 1996), 261.

32 *Declaration of Rights of Indigenous Peoples*, adopted by General Assembly Resolution 61/295, 13 September 2007, http://www.un.org/esa/socdev/unpfii/en/drip.html.

33 Indian and Northern Affairs Canada, "Canada Endorses the United Nations Declaration on the Rights of Indigenous Peoples," 12 November 2010, press release, Indian and Northern Affairs Canada, http://www.ainc-inac.gc.ca/ai/mr/nr/s-d2010/23429-eng.asp.

34 Royal Commission on Aboriginal Peoples (RCAP), *Royal Commission Report on Aboriginal Peoples* (Ottawa: Indian and Northern Affairs Canada, 1996), vol. 2, Indian and Northern Affairs Canada, http://www.ainc-inac.gc.ca/ap/rrc-eng.asp.

35 Celia Haig-Brown and David Nock, "Introduction," in Celia Haig-Brown and David Nock, ed., *With Good Intentions: Euro-Canadian and Aboriginal Relations in Colonial Canada*, 1-31 (Vancouver: UBC Press, 2006), 6.

36 Terre Satterfield, *Anatomy of a Conflict: Identity, Knowledge, and Emotion in Old-Growth Forests* (Vancouver: UBC Press, 2002), 7.

37 Andrew Woolford, *Between Justice and Certainty: Treaty Making in British Columbia* (Vancouver: UBC Press, 2005), 27-36.

38 David Rossiter and Patricia Wood, "Fantastic Topographies: Neo-liberal Responses to Aboriginal Land Claims in British Columbia," *Canadian Geographer* 49, no. 4 (2005): 352-67, 365.

39 Usher, "Environment, Race, and Nation Reconsidered," 381.

40 James (Sakéj) Youngblood Henderson, "Postcolonial Ledger Drawing: Legal Reform," in Marie Battiste, ed., *Reclaiming Indigenous Voice and Vision*, 161-71 (Vancouver: UBC Press, 2000), 169.

41 John Borrows, *Recovering Canada: The Resurgence of Indigenous Law* (Toronto: University of Toronto Press, 2002), 776.

42 Ibid., 115.

43 Ibid., 127.

44 *An Act to Amend and Consolidate the Laws Respecting Indians*, assented to on 12 April 1876, http://epe.lac-bac.gc.ca/100/205/301/ic/cdc/aboriginaldocs/stat/html/1876ap12.htm.

45 Will Kymlicka and Wayne Norman, "Citizenship in Culturally Diverse Societies: Issues, Contexts, Concepts," in Will Kymlicka and Wayne Norman, eds., *Citizenship in Diverse Societies*, 1-41 (New York: Oxford University Press, 2000), 39, as cited in Borrows, *Recovering Canada*, 156.

46 This massive and fascinating body of scholarship deserves much more attention than I am able to pay it within the constraints of this research. Since the legal terrain of Aboriginal rights and title is changing especially rapidly, I have chosen to focus mainly on relatively recent bodies of work in the Canadian context, concentrating on discussions of sovereignty and land rights as they might apply to the Haudenosaunee of the Six Nations.

47 Peter Russell, *Recognizing Aboriginal Title: The Mabo Case and Indigenous Resistance to English-Settler Colonialism* (Toronto: University of Toronto Press, 2005), 155.

48 Ibid., 335-46.

49 James Tully, *Strange Multiplicity: Constitutionalism in an Age of Diversity* (Cambridge: Cambridge University Press, 1995), 1 [emphasis in original].

50 Ibid., 2.

51 Ibid., 191.

52 Ibid., 202.

53 Matthias Koenig and Paul de Guchteneire, "Political Governance of Cultural Diversity," in Matthias Koenig and Paul de Guchteneire, eds., *Democracy and Human Rights in Multicultural Societies*, 3-17 (Aldershot: Ashgate, 2007), 4.

54 Tully, *Strange Multiplicity*, 39.

55 Dale Turner, *This Is Not a Peace Pipe* (Toronto: University of Toronto Press, 2006), 13.

56 Dale Turner, "From Valladolid to Ottawa: The Illusion of Listening to Aboriginal People," in Oakes et al., *Sacred Lands*, 53-68, 53.

57 Turner, *This Is Not a Peace Pipe*, 55.

58 Turner, "From Valladolid to Ottawa," 65.

59 Ibid., 63.

60 Gisday Wa and Delgam Uukw, Gitksan and Wet'suwet'en Hereditary Chiefs, *The Spirit in the Land: Statements of the Gitksan and Wet'suwet'en Hereditary Chiefs in the Supreme Court of British Columbia 1987-1990* (Gabriola Island: Reflections, 1992), 40-41.

61 *Constitution Act, 1982* (U.K.), 1982, c. 11, s. 59.

62 Mary Ellen Turpel, "Aboriginal Peoples and the Canadian Charter: Interpretive Monopolies, Cultural Differences," in Richard Devlin, ed., *First Nations Issues*, 40-73 (Toronto: Emond Montgomery, 1991), 42.

63 Ibid., 56.

64 Alan Cairns, *Citizens Plus: Aboriginal Peoples and the Canadian State* (Vancouver: UBC Press, 2000), 6.

65 Tom Flanagan, *First Nations? Second Thoughts* (Montreal and Kingston: McGill-Queen's University Press, 2000); Macklem, *Indigenous Difference*, 109.

66 RCAP, *Royal Commission Report on Aboriginal Peoples*, vol. 2.

67 Ibid.

68 Macklem, *Indigenous Difference*, 4.

69 Ibid., 189.

70 Patrick Macklem, "First Nations Self-Government and the Borders of the Canadian Legal Imagination," *McGill Law Journal* 36 (1990): 382-456, 445.

71 Kent McNeil, "Envisaging Constitutional Spaces for Aboriginal Governments," *Queen's Law Journal* 95 (1994): 95-137, 114-32.

72 Ibid., 136.

73 Emily MacKinnon, *The Nisga'a Final Agreement and Canadian Federalism: Asymmetrical Design* (Vancouver: Faculty of Law, University of British Columbia, 2010), 8 [unpublished paper].

74 Ibid., 9.

75 James (Sakéj) Youngblood Henderson, "The Context of the State of Nature," in Battiste, ed., *Reclaiming Indigenous Voice and Vision*, 11-38, 22.

76 Ibid., 33.

77 James (Sakéj) Youngblood Henderson, "Sui Generis and Treaty Citizenship," *Citizenship Studies* 6, no. 4 (2002): 415-42, 426.

78 Ibid., 422.
79 Ronald Niezen, "Recognizing Indigenism: Canadian Unity and the International Move-ment of Indigenous Peoples," *Comparative Studies in Society and History* 42, no. 1 (2000): 119-48, 133.
80 Ted Moses, as spoken at the Meeting on the United Nations Draft *Declaration on the Rights of Indigenous Peoples*, Sweden, June 1993, as cited in Niezen, "Recognizing Indigenism," 139.
81 Ibid., 142.
82 Ibid., 144.
83 RCAP, *Royal Commission Report on Aboriginal Peoples*, vol. 2.
84 Macklem, "First Nations Self-Government," 443.
85 McNeil, "Envisaging Constitutional Spaces," 133.
86 Cairns, *Citizens Plus*, 6.
87 Wayne Warry, *Ending Denial: Understanding Aboriginal Issues* (Toronto: Broadview Press, 2007), 45-59.
88 Flanagan, *First Nations?* 6.
89 Warry, *Ending Denial*, 44.
90 Flanagan, *First Nations?* 61.
91 Ibid., 194.
92 Borrows, *Recovering Canada*, 9.
93 Ibid., 10.
94 Warry, *Ending Denial*.
95 Frances Widdowson and Albert Howard, *Disrobing the Aboriginal Industry: The Decep-tion behind Indigenous Cultural Preservation* (Montreal and Kingston: McGill-Queen's University Press, 2008).
96 Ibid., 32.
97 Ibid., 23.
98 Ibid., 36.
99 Ibid., 89-100.
100 Ibid., 104.
101 Ibid., 105.
102 Ibid., 84-85.
103 Daniel Salée, "Indigenous Peoples and Settler Angst in Canada: A Review Essay," *International Journal of Canadian Studies* 41, no. 4 (2010): 315-33, 320.
104 Ibid., 321.
105 However, the borders of this specific chunk were complicated by differences between land "granted" in the Haldimand Proclamation and the subsequent Simcoe Patent.
106 These specific claims are filed as such, according to Canada's terminology, which dif-ferentiates between smaller, more quantifiable grievances (specific claims) and broader claims to address larger, possibly less specifically defined territories, as well as areas where no treaties were made (comprehensive claims).
107 Coyle, "Claims Resolution," 17-18.
108 Marcus Lane, "The Role of Planning in Achieving Indigenous Land Justice and Com-munity Goals," *Land Use Policy* 23 (2006): 385-94, 386.
109 Claudia Notzke, "A New Perspective in Aboriginal Natural Resource Management: Co-Management," *Geoforum* 26, no. 2 (1995): 187-209.
110 Patrick Wilson, "Native Peoples and the Management of Natural Resources in the Pacific Northwest: A Comparative Assessment," *American Review of Canadian Studies* 32, no. 3 (2002): 397-414.

111 Robert Anderson, Leo-Paul Dana, and Theresa Dana, "Indigenous Land Rights, Entre-preneurship, and Economic Development in Canada: 'Opting-In' to the Global Economy," *Journal of World Business* 41, no. 1 (2006): 45-55.
112 *Places to Grow Act*, S.O. 2005, c. 13.
113 Deborah Jean Doxtator, "What Happened to the Iroquois Clans? A Study of Clans in Three Nineteenth Century Rotinonhsyonni Communities" (Ph.D. dissertation, University of Western Ontario, London, 1997), 326; Christopher Alcantara, "Certificates of Possession and First Nations Housing: A Case Study of the Six Nations Housing Program," *Canadian Journal of Law and Society* 20, no. 2 (2005): 183-205.
114 Susan Hill, "'Traveling Down the River of Life Together in Peace and Friendship, Forever': Haudenosaunee Land Ethics and Treaty Agreements as the Basis for Restructuring the Relationship with the British Crown," in Leanne Simpson, ed., *Lighting the Eighth Fire: The Liberation, Resurgence and Protection of Indigenous Nations*, 1-34 (Winnipeg: Arbeiter Ring, 2008), 33.
115 Ibid., 34.
116 Ibid.

Conclusion

1 *Places to Grow Act*, S.O. 2005, c. 13.
2 James Clifford, *The Predicament of Culture: Twentieth-Century Ethnography, Literature, and Art* (Cambridge, MA: Harvard University Press, 1988), 8.
3 Jim Windle, "Mixed Emotions over Caledonia Couple's Settlement," *Tekawennake*, 6 January 2010, 2.
4 Erin Tully-Musser, "Judge Arrell Ruled with a Heavy Hand against Six Nations," *Tekawennake*, 7 October 2009, 1.
5 Jim Windle, "Doering in the Hot Seat at Haldimand Council Chambers," *Tekawennake*, 18 November 2009, 7.
6 Erin Tully-Musser, "Elected Chief Bill Montour Looks towards 2010," *Tekawennake*, 30 December 2009, 1.
7 Erin Tully-Musser, "Cabinet Shuffle, Was Duguid Too Good?" *Tekawennake*, 20 January 2010, 1.
8 Christie Blatchford, *Helpless: Caledonia's Nightmare of Fear and Anarchy, and How the Law Failed All of Us* (Toronto: Doubleday Canada, 2010), viii.
9 *An Act to Amend and Consolidate the Laws Respecting Indians*, assented to 12 April 1876, http://epe.lac-bac.gc.ca/100/205/301/ic/cdc/aboriginaldocs/m-stat.htm.
10 Royal Commission on Aboriginal Peoples, *Royal Commission Report on Aboriginal Peoples* (Ottawa: Indian and Northern Affairs Canada, 1996), Indian and Northern Affairs Canada, http://www.ainc-inac.gc.ca/ap/rrc-eng.asp.

Bibliography

Primary Sources

Appleby, Timothy. "Mayor Hangs on Despite Caledonia." *Globe and Mail*, 14 November 2006, A18.

Bailey, Sue. "Politicians Point Fingers, Dodge Duties, Critics Say." *Brantford Expositor,* 21 April 2006, C2.

Ball, Vincent. "Confederacy Objects to City's Land Deal." *Brantford Expositor,* 7 May 2007, A1.

Barrett, Toby. "Dispute Is Talk of the Land." *Grand River Sachem,* 25 August 2006, 4.

–. "Government Can't Ignore Its Role." *Grand River Sachem,* 13 July 2007.

–. "One Law for All – Period." *Grand River Sachem,* 3 August 2007, 10.

–. "A Plan for Land Dispute." *Grand River Sachem,* 5 May 2006, 8.

–. "Unhappy Anniversary Caledonia – February 28." *Grand River Sachem,* 23 February 2007, 8.

–. "What's on Negotiating Table?" *Grand River Sachem,* 28 July 2006, 14.

Bauslaugh, Cheryl. "'It Was Pretty Hot and Heavy': Haldimand Mayor Still Hopes for Peaceful Resolution to Protest." *Brantford Expositor,* 21 April 2006, C3.

–. "Safety Measures Eyed for Caledonia School." *Brantford Expositor,* 17 August 2006, A1.

–. "Six Nations Protesters Reopen Part of Highway 6." *Brantford Expositor,* 16 May 2006, A4.

Bonnell, Gregory. "Police Presence, Court Order Fail to Deter Protesters." *Brantford Expositor,* 30 March 2006, A4.

Bradshaw, James. "Six Nations to 'Consider' $26-Million Offer in Welland Dispute." *Globe and Mail,* 13 December 2007, A16.

Brant Riding Intergovernmental Committee. "Meeting Minutes," 17 March 2007 [used with permission; on file with author].

Brown, Dana. "Henco Gets $12.3 Million for Land: McGuinty Implores Native Protesters to Leave Douglas Creek Estates Property." *Hamilton Spectator,* 23 June 2006, A5.

–. "Montour Vows New Era of Communication." *Hamilton Spectator,* 20 November 2007, A6.

–. "OPP Stop Flap over Flags in Caledonia." *Hamilton Spectator,* 4 December 2006, A9.

Campbell, Murray. "A Standoff by the Numbers." *Globe and Mail,* 1 March 2007, A14.

Canadian Press. "Developer Says He's 'Done Nothing Wrong' as Native Protesters Occupy Subdivision." *Brantford Expositor,* 2 March 2006, A4.

–. "Finley Floats a Suggestion." *Brantford Expositor,* 5 April 2007, A15.

–. "GRCA Projects Moving Forward without Six Nations Consultation." *Brantford Expositor,* 15 November 2006, A4.

–. "Native Protesters Remove Barricade in Caledonia." *Brantford Expositor,* 12 July 2006, A5.

–. "Peterson to Help Solve Land Dispute: Former Premier Says He Can't Guarantee He'll Have Success." *Brantford Expositor,* 1 May 2006, A1.

–. "Six Nations Protesters Occupy Home Building Site in Caledonia." *Brantford Expositor,* 1 March 2006, A5.

Clairmont, Susan. "Focus on Fantino: OPP Chief Says They Are Peacekeepers Not Problem-Solvers in Caledonia." *Hamilton Spectator,* 12 November 2007, A6.

Corporation of Haldimand County. "A Message to the Citizens of Haldimand County Regarding the Current Demonstration at Douglas Creek Estates in Caledonia." 22 April 2006. Press release, Haldimand County, http://www.haldimandcounty.on.ca/MediaReleases.aspx.

–. "A Message to the Citizens of Haldimand County Regarding the Current Demonstration at Douglas Creek Estates in Caledonia." 23 April 2006. Press release, Haldimand County, http://www.haldimandcounty.on.ca/MediaReleases.aspx.

–. "A Message to the Citizens of Haldimand County Regarding the Demonstration at Douglas Creek Estates in Caledonia." 26 April 2006. Press release, Haldimand County, http://www.haldimandcounty.on.ca/MediaReleases.aspx.

–. "A Message to the Citizens of Haldimand County Regarding Recent Local Calls for Action Regarding the Demonstration at Douglas Creek Estates in Caledonia." 24 April 2006. Press release, Haldimand County, http://www.haldimandcounty.on.ca/MediaReleases.aspx.

–. "A Message from Haldimand County Council Regarding Remarks Made by the Mayor on Tuesday Morning April 25, 2006." 25 April 2006. Press release, Haldimand County, http://www.haldimandcounty.on.ca/MediaReleases.aspx.

–. "Caledonia Land Dispute." 19 January 2007. Press release, Haldimand County, http://www.haldimandcounty.on.ca/MediaReleases.aspx

–. "County Establishes Emergency Shelter and Emergency Telephone Number." 23 May 2006. Press release, Haldimand County, http://www.haldimandcounty.on.ca/MediaReleases.aspx.

–. "Douglas Creek Estates Demonstration Chronology of Events." 30 January 2007. Press release, Haldimand County, http://www.haldimandcounty.on.ca/MediaReleases.aspx.

–. "For Immediate Release." 13 October 2006. Press release, Haldimand County, http://www.haldimandcounty.on.ca/MediaReleases.aspx.

–. "Haldimand County Caledonia Centre Remains Open to Everyone." 7 June 2006. Press release, Haldimand County, http://www.haldimandcounty.on.ca/MediaReleases.aspx.

–. "Haldimand County Council Passes Two Motions Regarding Douglas Creek Estates Issue." 9 May 2006. Press release, Haldimand County, http://www.haldimandcounty. on.ca/MediaReleases.aspx.

–. "Haldimand County Council Statement re: Douglas Creek Estates Occupation." 16 May 2006. Press release, Haldimand County, http://www.haldimandcounty.on.ca/MediaReleases.aspx.

–. "Haldimand County Opens Local Business Emergency Relief Assistance Office." 29 May 2006 [used with permission; on file with author].

–. "Mayor Declares 'State of Emergency.'" 22 May 2006. Press release, Haldimand County, http://www.haldimandcounty.on.ca/MediaReleases.aspx.

–. "Mayor Marie Trainer Declares an End to State of Emergency in Haldimand County." 8 June 2006. Press release, Haldimand County, http://www.haldimandcounty.on.ca/MediaReleases.aspx.

–. "News Release from the Council of the Corporation of Haldimand County." 9 July 2007. Press release, Haldimand County, http://www.haldimandcounty.on.ca/MediaReleases.aspx.

–. "Power Restored in Haldimand County." 24 May 2006. Press release, Haldimand County, http://www.haldimandcounty.on.ca/MediaReleases.aspx.

–. "Province Commits to Communications and Business Assistance." 1 May 2006. Press release, Haldimand County, http://www.haldimandcounty.on.ca/MediaReleases.aspx.

–. "Province Offers Assistance to Haldimand County." 28 April 2006. Press release, Haldimand County, http://www.haldimandcounty.on.ca/MediaReleases.aspx.

–. "Province Provides Local Businesses with Emergency Financial Relief Program." 26 May 2006. Press release, Haldimand County, http://www.haldimandcounty.on.ca/MediaReleases.aspx.

–. "Re: CaledoniaWakeUpCall.com Website Misrepresentation." 6 November 2006. Press release, Haldimand County, http://www.haldimandcounty.on.ca/MediaReleases.aspx.

–. "State of Emergency Due to the Power Outage Remains in Effect." 25 May 2006. Press release, Haldimand County, http://www.haldimandcounty.on.ca/MediaReleases.aspx.

Coyle, Michael. *Results of Fact-Finding on Situation at Caledonia* (Ottawa: Government of Canada, 7 April 2006).

Dawson, Katie. "Finley Meets with Rotary Club." *Grand River Sachem*, 16 March 2007, 3.

–. "March Back at DCE." *Grand River Sachem*, 13 October 2006.

–. "McHale Leads March." *Grand River Sachem*, 20 October 2006, 1.

–. "Natives Shout 'Go Home Gary.'" *Grand River Sachem*, 26 January 2007, 1.

–. "'Remember Us' March Leads to One Arrest." *Grand River Sachem*, 12 October 2007, 3.

–. "Six Nations Responds to Government." *Grand River Sachem*, 26 October 2007, 1.

Department of Justice Canada. "Canada's Position on the History of the Surrender of the Plank Road Lands (including the Douglas Creek Estates): Summary of the Narrative Presented by Michael McCulloch to the Plank Road Lands Side Table." 3 November 2006, 1 [used with permission; on file with author].

Dobrota, Alex, and Hayley Mick. "Caledonia Tensions Heat Up as Judge Orders End to Talks: Ontario Court Orders Natives Off Disputed Land to Restore 'the Rule of Law.'" *Globe and Mail*, 9 August 2006, A1.

Doering, Ronald. "Letter to Chief Allen MacNaughton." 13 June 2007 [used with permission; on file with author].

–. "Re: Plank Road Side Table." Letter. 18 September 2006 [used with permission; on file with author].

–. "Senior Federal Negotiator's Speaking Points: Welland Canal Flooding." 12 December 2007 [used with permission; on file with author].

Dring, Neil. "Natives Stall Another Housing Project." *Grand River Sachem*, 25 May 2007, 1.

Editorial. "Caledonia Protesters Target Osgoode Hall, Say Claims Money Used to Construct Building." *Hamilton Spectator*, 22 August 2007, A10.

Finley, Diane. "Governments Working Hard for Resolution." *Brantford Expositor*, 24 April 2006, A9.

–. "No Need for Rally Says MP." *Grand River Sachem*, 13 October 2006, 4.

Freeze, Colin, and Oliver Moore. "Caledonia Tensions Reach Boiling Point." *Globe and Mail*, 23 May 2006, A1.

Gamble, Susan. "City Breaking the Law: Protesters." *Brantford Expositor*, 4 August 2007, A3.

–. "Dispute Is Dividing Community: Mayor." *Brantford Expositor*, 25 April 2006, A7.

–. "Haldimand Mayor Pins Vandalism on Natives: Damage to Power Station Could Reach $2 Million: Trainer." *Brantford Expositor*, 27 May 2006, A1.

–. "Ontario Still Wants to See Negotiated Settlement: Minister." *Brantford Expositor*, 21 April 2006, C2.

–. "Protesters Stand Firm: Deadline Passes to Leave Caledonia Construction Site." *Brantford Expositor*, 23 March 2006, A1.

–. "Some 'Divine Intervention.'" *Brantford Expositor*, 31 August 2006, A5.

–. "Whose Land Is It, Anyway?" *Brantford Expositor*, 8 May 2006, A1.

Government of Canada. "Federal Legal Response to Haudenosaunee/Six Nations' Presentation of November 14, 2006." 25 January 2007 [used with permission; on file with author].

Graham, Jennifer. "Talks on Caledonia Occupation on Hiatus." *Brantford Expositor*, 24 April 2006, A1.

Green, Wilma. "Road to the Reclamation." CD and accompanying transcript. Ohsweken: CKRZ FM, 21 December 2007.

Grice, Craig. "Spotlight on Caledonia." *Grand River Sachem*, 7 December 2007, 6.

Harries, Kate. "Records Show Caledonia Land Never Given Up, Natives Say: On Anniversary of Occupation, Chiefs Contend Confederacy Leaders in Past Only Leased Areas." *Globe and Mail*, 1 March 2007, A14.

Haudenosaunee Development Institute. "Haudenosaunee Development Protocol." 1 September 2007 [used with permission; on file with author].

Haudenosaunee Men's Council of the Grand River. "Six Nations: How We Got Here." Undated [used with permission; on file with author].

Healey, Deirdre, and Barb McKay. "Natives Disregard Judge's Decision: Vow to 'Maintain Position' for Now." *Hamilton Spectator*, 9 August 2006, A1.

Hemsworth, Wade. "'Everybody's Watching'; Six Nations Residents Blame All Levels of Government for Not Stepping Forward and Resolving Land Claims." *Hamilton Spectator*, 21 April 2006, A8.

Henco Industries Limited v. Haudenosaunee Six Nations Confederacy Council, (2006) 82 O.R. (3d) 721, 277 D.L.R. (4th) 274, 240 OAC 119 (ON C.A.).

Henco Industries Ltd v. Haudenosaunee Six Nations Confederacy Council, [2006] OJ No. 3285 (QL), (Ontario Superior Court of Justice).

Hill, Hazel. "Grand River Update from Hazel Hill, March 10, 2007." 10 March 2007. Mass e-mail [used with permission; on file with author].

–. "Hazel's Update." 23 April 2007. Mass e-mail [used with permission; on file with author].

–. "Hazel's Update of April 12, 2007." 12 April 2007, 1. Mass e-mail [used with permission; on file with author].

–. "Hazel's View from the Table." *Tekawennake*, 27 June 2007.

–. "Update from Grand River." 18 July 2006. Mass e-mail [used with permission; on file with author].

–. "Update from Grand River." 25 September 2007. Mass e-mail [used with permission; on file with author].

–. "Update from Grand River October 19, 2006." 19 October 2006. Mass e-mail [used with permission; on file with author].

–. "Update from Grand River November 16, 2006." 16 November 2006, 1. Mass e-mail [used with permission; on file with author].

–. "Update from Grand River: Hazel Hill." *Tekawennake*, 14 November 2007.

Hill, Leroy. "Canada Owes Us Millions." *Brantford Expositor*, 11 January 2007, A10.

"Honour Six Nations Land Claims: Do Not Buy or Sell Unsettled Land." Information pamphlet, 2006 [used with permission; on file with author].

Howlett, Karen. "Ottawa Accepts Leadership Role in Effort to Quell Caledonia Dispute." *Globe and Mail*, 15 November 2006, A7.

–. "Standoff at Caledonia: McGuinty Comes under Fire in Legislature as Natives Resist Predawn OPP Raid." *Globe and Mail*, 21 April 2006, A1.

Indian and Northern Affairs Canada. "Barbara McDougall Appointed as Federal Representative in Caledonia Talks." 3 May 2006. Press release, Department of Indian and Northern Affairs, http://www.ainc-inac.gc.ca/ai/mr/nr/m-a2006/2-02763-eng.asp.

–. "Canada Endorses the United Nations Declaration on the Rights of Indigenous Peoples." 12 November 2010. Press release, Department of Indian and Northern Affairs, http://www.ainc-inac.gc.ca/ai/mr/nr/s-d2010/23429-eng.asp.

–. "Exploration Resolution Process: Joint Statement of Canada, Ontario, and Six Nations." 5 April 2006. Press release, Department of Indian and Northern Affairs, http://www.ainc-inac.gc.ca/ai/mr/nr/j-a2006/snjs-eng.asp.

–. "Frequently Asked Questions – Canada's Offer to Six Nations Welland Canal Flooding Claim." 21 January 2008. Press release, Department of Indian and Northern Affairs, http://www.ainc-inac.gc.ca/ai/mr/nr/s-d2007/2-2980-faq-eng.asp.

–. "Michael Coyle Appointed to Undertake a Fact-Finding Initiative in Relation to the Situation in Caledonia." 24 March 2006. Press release, Department of Indian and Northern Affairs, http://www.ainc-inac.gc.ca/ai/mr/nr/j-a2006/2-02758-eng.asp.

–. "Statement by Canada's New Government Regarding the United Nations Declaration on the Rights of Indigenous Peoples." 12 September 2007, 1. Press release, Department of Indian and Northern Affairs, http://www.ainc-inac.gc.ca/ai/mr/nr/s-d2007/2-2936-eng.asp.

–. "Statement from Canada's Representatives in Six Nations Talks." 12 December 2007. Press release, Department of Indian and Northern Affairs, http://www.ainc-inac.gc.ca/ai/mr/nr/s-d2007/2-2980-eng.asp.

Indian and Northern Affairs Canada and Ontario Secretariat of Aboriginal Affairs. "Joint Statement by Minister Jim Prentice and Minister David Ramsay." 11 June 2006. Press

release, Secretariat of Aboriginal Affairs, http://www.aboriginalaffairs.gov.on.ca/
english/news/2006/news_060611.asp.

"Indians at San Francisco." *Brantford Expositor,* 27 April 1945.

Knisley, Jim. "County Seeks Answers." *Grand River Sachem,* 12 May 2006, 5.

–. "Developers Cautious." *Grand River Sachem,* 4 August 2006, 9.

–. "Doering Says Negotiations Can't Go On Forever." *Grand River Sachem,* 7 December 2007, 3.

–. "Marie Muzzled." *Grand River Sachem,* 28 April 2006, 3.

–. "Provincial Negotiator Reports Progress in Land Talks." *Grand River Sachem,* 15 September 2006, 3.

Kruchak, Matt, Barb McKay, and Marissa Nelson. "Caledonia Erupts: Emergency Declared, Schools Closed: Fists Fly as Natives and Non-Natives Take to the Streets." *Hamilton Spectator,* 23 May 2006, A1.

Legall, Paul. "Builder Calls Natives' Fees 'Mafia Shakedown.'" *Hamilton Spectator,* 14 September 2007, A1.

–. "Judge Continues Hearing: Protester Claims His Land Ownership Constitutes Conflict of Interest." *Hamilton Spectator,* 17 March 2006, A4.

–. "Natives Vow to Continue Protest after Court Blow." *Hamilton Spectator,* 10 March 2006, A8.

–. "Police Cars in Hagersville Put Natives on 'High Alert.'" *Hamilton Spectator,* 4 March 2006, A5.

–. "Six Nations Warns of Legal Action over Permits." *Hamilton Spectator,* 10 October 2007, A1.

Legall, Paul, and Daniel Nolan. "Mayor Lands in Hot Water: Apologizes to Natives." *Hamilton Spectator,* 26 April 2006, A1.

Leslie, Keith. "Caledonia Talks Back On." *Brantford Expositor,* 14 June 2006, A1.

–, and Tobi Cohen. "Prentice Cancels Meeting on Caledonia Standoff." *Brantford Expositor,* 1 November 2006, A1.

Livingston, Gillian. "Ontario Considers Financial Help in Native Occupation." *Brantford Expositor,* 13 April 2006, A5.

MacNaughton, Allen. "Confederacy Optimistic, but Wants Halt to Development on Crown Lands within Track." *Grand River Sachem,* 14 September 2007, 7.

–. "Feds and Provinces Leave Table." *Grand River Sachem,* 21 September 2007.

–. "Press Release from Six Nations Confederacy Council." *Grand River Sachem,* 10 November 2006, 4.

–. "Statement: Chief Allen MacNaughton Six Nations Confederacy Council Negotiating Team Response to Canada." 5 December 2006, 1. Press release [used with permission; on file with author].

–, Barbara McDougall, and Jane Stewart. "Negotiation Framework." 22 June 2006 [used with permission; on file with author].

Marion, Michael-Allen. "City Can't Comply with Protocol: Mayor. Municipalities Must Follow Ontario Laws in Granting Permits to Developers." *Brantford Expositor,* 13 September 2007, A4.

–. "City Rejects Playing Host to Meeting, Lack of Native Representation Cited as Concern." *Brantford Expositor,* 15 June 2006, A1.

–. "Confederacy Chiefs Call for Talks on Land Claims: Throw Support behind Caledonia Housing Development Occupation." *Hamilton Spectator,* 28 March 2006, A1.

–. "Conservative MPP Lays Blame for Standoff with Liberals." *Brantford Expositor,* 21 April 2006, C3.

–. "Hundreds Protest Government Inaction over Native Occupation in Caledonia." *Brantford Expositor,* 16 October 2006, A1.

–. "Six Nations Offered $26M to Settle One Land Claim." *Brantford Expositor,* 13 December 2007.

Martin-Hill, Dawn. *Sewatokwa'tshera't: The Dish with One Spoon* (Brantford: Lock3 Media, 2008).

Maughan, Christopher. "Caledonia Offer 'a Slap in the Face.'" *Brantford Expositor,* 1 June 2007, A1.

McArthur, Greg. "Caledonia Natives Set to Remove One Blockade." *Globe and Mail,* 22 May 2006, A1.

McKay, Barb. "Land Negotiators Join Talks." *Hamilton Spectator,* 4 May 2006, A8.

Mick, Hayley. "Polarizing Figure Takes on Native Protesters: Caledonia Fight Becomes Full-Time for Christian with Troubled Background." *Globe and Mail,* 20 January 2007, A15.

Monture, Phil. "Hamilton/Port Dover Plank Road Update." 6 December 2006, Caledonia Wakeup Call, http://www.caledoniawakeupcall.com/updates/061206mnn.html.

Morse, Paul. "Court Orders Protesters Out: Natives Must Leave by Thursday." *Hamilton Spectator,* 22 April 2006, A3.

Muse, Sandra. "2006: Janie Jamieson Looks Back on History." *Tekawennake,* 3 January 2007, 7.

–. "CHTV Scolded by Indian Affairs Minister." *Tekawennake,* 9 August 2006, 1.

–. "Haldimand Council Can't Seem to Muzzle Mayor Trainer." *Tekawennake,* 31 May 2006, 1.

–. "Haldimand Deputy Mayor Wants Healing to Begin." *Tekawennake,* 31 May 2006, 4.

–. "Judge Playing Dangerous Game, Says Janie Jamieson." *Tekawennake,* 31 May 2006.

–. "Numerous Events Lead to Escalation of Racial Tensions." *Tekawennake,* 24 May 2006, 17.

Nelson, Marissa. "Clan Mothers Seek UN's Help; Doreen Silversmith Says 'Genocidal Practices' of Canada Must Stop." *Hamilton Spectator,* 3 May 2006, A6.

–. "Local Folk Broker Barricade Deal: A Small Group of Caledonia and Native Residents Take Charge and Find a Way to Move Ahead." *Hamilton Spectator,* 24 May 2006, A6.

–. "Protesters Observe Raid Anniversary: Natives Challenged OPP and Retained Position on Occupied Site." *Hamilton Spectator,* 20 April 2007, A12.

–. "Rude Awaking for Young Protester." *Hamilton Spectator,* 21 April 2006, A1.

–, and Joan Walters. "RCMP Specialists at Land Dispute: Spectator Exclusive." *Hamilton Spectator,* 2 August 2006, A1.

Nolan, Daniel. "Caledonia Convoy Set to Roll Today." *Hamilton Spectator,* 2 May 2007, A10.

–. "Caledonia Negotiations Near Turning Point." *Hamilton Spectator,* 23 February 2007, A10.

–. "E-mail Threatens Lacrosse Game; Caledonia Citizens Are Being Called on to 'Restrict Access' to Six Nations Match." *Hamilton Spectator,* 6 June 2006, A2.

–. "Finley: Send Cops to Clear Out Natives: MP Wants Caledonia Returned to 'Normalcy.'" *Hamilton Spectator,* 9 June 2006, A9.

–. "Mayor Urges Organizer to Cancel Second Caledonia March." *Hamilton Spectator,* 14 December 2006, A14.

–. "McDougall, Stewart Join Team: Peterson Suggests Province Buy Protest Site," *Hamilton Spectator*, 11 May 2006, A6.

–. "Ottawa Offers $26m for Claims; Welland Feeder Canal/Dunnville Dam." *Hamilton Spectator*, 13 December 2007, A7.

–. "Six Nations Evidence Due." *Hamilton Spectator*, 21 October 2006, A15.

Office of the Premier of Ontario. "Ontario Premier Dalton McGuinty Today Issued the Following Statement Regarding the Events in Caledonia." 22 May 2006. Press release, Office of the Premier of Ontario, http://www.premier.gov.on.ca/news/event.php?ItemID=4699&Lang=EN.

Oliviera, Mike, and Steve Erwin. "Ontario Buys Out Caledonia Developer." *Brantford Expositor*, 17 June 2006, A1.

Ontario Ministry of Aboriginal Affairs. "Statement by Ontario's Principal Representative Regarding Provincially Owned Lands near Six Nations Reserve." 27 October 2007. Press release, Ministry of Aboriginal Affairs, http://www.aboriginalaffairs.gov.on.ca/english/news/2007/oct26nr_07.asp.

Ontario Ministry of Economic Development. "Ontario Provides Financial Assistance Program for Caledonia Area Businesses." 16 June 2006. Press release, Caledonia Wakeup Call, http://www.caledoniawakeupcall.com/updates/060616omedt.html.

Ontario Ministry of Public Infrastructure Renewal. *Growth Plan for the Greater Golden Horseshoe* (Toronto: Ministry of Public Infrastructure Renewal, 2006), Places to Grow, https://www.placestogrow.ca.

Ontario Provincial Police. "Canada Day Celebrations." 29 June 2006. Press release, Caledonia Wakeup Call, http://www.caledoniawakeupcall.com/OPPRelease.html.

–. "First Nations Land Claim Dispute: Caledonia." 3 April 2006. Press release, Caledonia Wakeup Call, http://caledoniawakeupcall.com/OPPRelease.html.

–. "Key to Successful Negotiations and Community Safety: Understanding, Mutual Respect and Meaningful Dialogue." 23 September 2006. Press release, Caledonia Wakeup Call, http://www.caledoniawakeupcall.com/OPPRelease.html.

–. "Protesters Removed from Caledonia Housing Development." 20 April 2006. Press release, Caledonia Wakeup Call, http://caledoniawakeupcall.com/OPPRelease.html.

–. "Rally Is Irresponsible." 18 January 2007. Press release, Caledonia Wakeup Call, http://www.caledoniawakeupcall.com/OPPRelease.html.

–. "Tolerance Encouraged in Caledonia." 8 August 2006. Press release, Caledonia Wakeup Call, http://www.caledoniawakeupcall.com/OPPRelease.html.

Ontario Secretariat of Aboriginal Affairs. "Haudenosaunee/Six Nations-Canada-Ontario Main Negotiation Table Update." 27 July 2006. Press release, Secretariat of Aboriginal Affairs, http://www.aboriginalaffairs.gov.on.ca/english/news/2006/news_060727.asp.

–. "Media Advisory – Minister Responsible for Aboriginal Affairs and Haldimand County Mayor Available to Media." 25 September 2006. Press release [used with permission; on file with author].

–. "Progress Being Made on Caledonia Situation." 28 April 2006. Press release, Secretariat of Aboriginal Affairs, http://www.aboriginalaffairs.gov.on.ca/english/news/2006/news_060428_2.asp.

–. "Province Appoints David Peterson to Help Resolve Caledonia Situation." 29 April 2006. Press release, Secretariat of Aboriginal Affairs, http://www.aboriginalaffairs.gov.on.ca/english/news/2006/news_060429.asp.

–. "Significant Progress Made in Caledonia Dispute." 16 June 2006. Press release, Secretariat of Aboriginal Affairs, http://www.aboriginalaffairs.gov.on.ca/english/news/2006/news_060616.asp.

–. "Six Nations (Caledonia) Costs to Date." 16 February 2007. Press release, Secretariat of Aboriginal Affairs, http://www.aboriginalaffairs.gov.on.ca/english/news/2006/news_061102.asp.

–. "Statement from Minister Ramsay – Minister Responsible for Aboriginal Affairs." 31 October 2006. Press release, Secretariat of Aboriginal Affairs, http://www.aboriginalaffairs.gov.on.ca/english/news/2006/news_061101.asp.

Pacienza, Angela. "Premier to Caledonia Residents: Be Patient: Asks for More Time to Resolve Dispute." *Brantford Expositor,* 11 May 2006, A1.

Pearson, Mike. "Anger, Frustration Lead to Revolt." *Grand River Sachem,* 28 April 2006, 9.

–. "Arrest Warrants to Be Addressed." *Grand River Sachem,* 7 July 2006, 1.

–. "Barricades Down, Negotiations Set for Thursday." *Grand River Sachem,* 16 June 2006, 11.

–. "Contempt Charges Unclear." *Grand River Sachem,* 28 July 2006, 1.

–. "Fact Finder Arrives." *Grand River Sachem,* 31 March 2006, 1.

–. "Feds Working to Resolve Standoff: Finley." *Grand River Sachem,* 12 May 2006, 3.

–. "Moratorium Shocks Henco Lawyer." *Grand River Sachem,* 26 May 2006, 18.

–. "Natives Committed to Land Rights." *Grand River Sachem,* 23 June 2006, 9.

–. "Natives Defy Arrest Warrant." *Grand River Sachem,* 24 March 2006, 1.

–. "Natives Rally for Sovereignty." *Grand River Sachem,* 28 July 2006, 1.

–. "Natives Shut Down Home Construction." *Grand River Sachem,* 3 March 2006, 1.

–. "Natives Staying the Course." *Grand River Sachem,* 10 March 2006, 1.

–. "Six Nations Protesters Hold Information Picket." *Grand River Sachem,* 17 August 2007, 1.

–. "A State of Emergency Declared after Town Left in the Dark." *Grand River Sachem,* 26 May 2006, 3.

–. "Talks Fail to End Protest; Henco Industries Considering Legal Action against OPP." *Grand River Sachem,* 21 April 2006, 7.

Powless, Lynda. "Six Nations at the Cross Roads: Douglas Creek Reclamation – A Pictorial History." Ohsweken, ON: Turtle Island News Publications, 2006.

Prentice, Jim. "Letter to Six Nations 'Iroquois' Confederacy." 17 April 2006 [used with permission; on file with author].

Puxley, Chinta. "Bill for Caledonia Standoff at $55 Million: PC Leader." *Brantford Expositor,* 27 September 2006, A1.

–. "Caledonia Braces for Showdown." *Brantford Expositor,* 14 October 2006, A1.

–. "Caledonia Judge Overruled." *Brantford Expositor,* 15 December 2006, A1.

–. "Caledonia Visit Top Priority: Bryant." *Brantford Expositor,* 1 November 2007, A1.

–. "McGuinty Wants Ottawa to Pay Up." *Brantford Expositor,* 21 October 2006, A1.

–. "Protesters Intimidating Caledonians, says MP." *Brantford Expositor,* 29 August 2006, A1.

–. "Resolving Caledonia Dispute Requires 'Patience.'" *Brantford Expositor,* 26 February 2007, A1.

–. "Standoff Taught Police, Province." *Brantford Expositor,* 25 August 2006, A1.

–. "'Too Many Voices' Hindering Caledonia Talks: Six Nations Chief." *Brantford Expositor,* 14 March 2007, A1.

–, and Jennifer Ditchburn. "Stop Acting Like Kids, Politicians Scolded." *Brantford Expositor,* 2 November 2006, A1.

Ramsay, David. "Letter from David Ramsay to Haudenosaunee Six Nations Confederacy Council." 17 May 2006 [used with permission; on file with author].

Six Nations Band Council. "Backgrounder: Six Nations Plank Road Claim in Brief." n.d. [used with permission; on file with author].

Six Nations Council. "Six Nations of the Grand River Community Profile." 2007. Six Nations Council, http://www.sixnations.ca/CommunityProfile.htm.

Six Nations "Iroquois" Confederacy. "Land Rights Statement as Adopted in Council." 4 November 2006. Published in full in *Tekawennake*, 22 November 2006, Turtle Island Native Network, http://www.turtleisland.org/news/news-sixnations.htm.

–. "Rotienneson Urge the Public to Keep the Peace." 17 October 2007 [used with permission; on file with author].

"Six Nations of the Grand River: Land Rights, Financial Justice, Creative Solutions." November 2006. Booklet handed out by Six Nations Lands and Resources Department, http://www.hamilton.ca/NR/rdonlyres/0FCA0BC2-A78F-47AC-9577-016BB397F1D7/0/SixNationsClaimsBooklet.pdf.

Sloat, Buck. "Problems Are Far from Over." *Grand River Sachem*, 30 June 2006, 4.

Smith, Scott. "Townsfolk Getting Testy over Blockades." *Tekawennake*, 26 April 2006, 2.

Tully-Musser, Erin. "Cabinet Shuffle, Was Duguid Too Good?" *Tekawennake*, 20 January 2010, 1.

–. "Elected Chief Bill Montour Looks towards 2010." *Tekawennake*, 30 December 2009, 1.

–. "Judge Arrell Rules with a Heavy Hand against Six Nations." *Tekawennake*, 7 October 2009, 1.

Van Driel, Frederieka. "Ontario's Approach to Land Claims." *Tekawennake*, 1 November 2006, 2.

Wallace, James. "Documents Obtained by Osprey News Puts Price Tag on Settling Caledonia Dispute: Ottawa to Offer $125 Million." *Brantford Expositor*, 31 May 2007, A1.

Windle, Jim. "Bryant Brings His Wallet to Caledonia – Rejects HDI." *Tekawennake*, 28 November 2007, 1.

–. "Developers Disappointed at Onondaga Longhouse." *Tekawennake*, 5 September 2007, 2.

–. "Doering in the Hot Seat at Haldimand Council Chambers." *Tekawennake*, 18 November 2009, 7.

–. "John Tory's 'Friendly but Firm' Comments Draw Ire." *Tekawennake*, 12 September 2007, 7.

–. "Mayor Hancock Set to Protect Relationship with Six Nations/New Credit." *Tekawennake*, 6 December 2006, 1.

–. "McHale's Flag Flap Flops." *Tekawennake*, 24 January 2007, 1.

–. "Mixed Emotions over Caledonia Couple's Settlement." *Tekawennake*, 6 January 2010, 1.

–. "Optimism for Christmas Settlement." *Tekawennake*, 5 December 2007, 10.

–. "Progress at the Table Slow but Showing Fruit." *Tekawennake*, 24 October 2007, 4.

–. "St. Amand Says Talks Must Continue." *Tekawennake*, 16 August 2006, 3.

–. "Talks End – Negotiations Finally Begin: Money Not the Issue, Land Should Be Returned." *Tekawennake*, 6 June 2007, 1.

–. "Tensions at the Negotiations Noticeable." *Tekawennake*, 24 October 2007, 5.

–. "Trainer Wants to Meet with PM Harper on Land Claims Resolution." *Tekawennake*, 11 July 2007, 2.

Zronik, John Paul. "12 Months Later, There Is No End in Sight to the Dispute over Native Land Claims. 'This Is Going to Take a Long Time,' Says a Federal Negotiator." *Brantford Expositor,* 24 February 2007, A1.

–. "All Quiet at Occupation Site, but Protest Takes Personal Toll." *Brantford Expositor,* 24 February 2007, A12.

–. "Brant Expansion Influenced by Others." *Brantford Expositor,* 8 July 2006, A12.

–. "Haldimand Held Hostage: Trainer." *Brantford Expositor,* 10 July 2007, A1.

–. "Inside the Occupation." *Brantford Expositor,* 5 May 2006, A1.

–. "Levac Takes Shot at Tory Rival." *Brantford Expositor,* 4 October 2007, A4.

–. "Natives Remove Main Barricade: Protesters Put Focus on Land Claims." *Brantford Expositor,* 24 May 2006, A1.

–. "Six Nations Not Being Notified of Development in Brant County, Complains Confederacy Chief." *Brantford Expositor,* 20 December 2006, A3.

Secondary Sources

Alcantara, Christopher. "Certificates of Possession and First Nations Housing: A Case Study of the Six Nations Housing Program." *Canadian Journal of Law and Society* 20, no. 2 (2005): 183-205.

Alfred, Gerald (Taiaiake). *Heeding the Voices of Our Ancestors: Kahnawake Mohawk Politics and the Rise of Native Nationalism.* Don Mills: Oxford University Press, 1995.

–. *Peace. Power. Righteousness: An Indigenous Manifesto.* Don Mills: Oxford University Press, 1999.

Anderson, Robert, Leo-Paul Dana, and Teresa Dana. "Indigenous Land Rights, Entrepreneurship, and Economic Development in Canada: "Opting-In" to the Global Economy." *Journal of World Business* 41, no. 1 (2006): 45-55.

Asch, Michael, and Norman Zlotkin. "Affirming Aboriginal Title: A New Basis for Comprehensive Claims Negotiations." In Michael Asch, ed., *Aboriginal and Treaty Rights in Canada: Essays on Law, Equity, and Respect for Difference,* 208-29. Vancouver: UBC Press, 1997.

Barsh, Russell. "Canada's Aboriginal Peoples: Social Integration or Disintegration?" *Canadian Journal of Native Studies* 14, no. 1 (1994): 1-46.

Battiste, Marie. "Introduction." In Marie Battiste, ed., *Reclaiming Indigenous Voice and Vision,* xvi-xxx. Vancouver: UBC Press, 2000.

Becker, Mary. "Iroquois and Iroquoian in Canada." In Bruce Morrison and Roderick Wilson, eds., *Native Peoples: The Canadian Experience,* 229-47. Don Mills: Oxford University Press, 2004.

–. "We Are an Independent Nation: A History of Iroquois Sovereignty." *Buffalo Law Review* 46 (1998): 981-1001.

Blatchford, Christie. *Helpless: Caledonia's Nightmare of Fear and Anarchy, and How the Law Failed All of Us.* Toronto: Doubleday Canada, 2010.

Blommaert, Jan, and Chris Bulcaen. "Critical Discourse Analysis." *Annual Review of Anthropology* 29 (2000): 447-66.

–, and Jef Verschueren. *Debating Diversity: Analysing the Rhetoric of Tolerance.* London and New York: Routledge, 1998.

Bobiwash, Rodney. "The Sacred and the Profane: Indigenous Lands and State Policy." In Jill Oakes et al., eds., *Sacred Lands: Aboriginal World Views, Claims, and Conflicts,* 203-13. Edmonton: Canadian Circumpolar Institute Press, 1996.

Bogart, William. *Good Government? Good Citizens? Courts, Politics, and Markets in a Changing Canada*. Vancouver: UBC Press, 2005.

Borrows, John. *Recovering Canada: The Resurgence of Indigenous Law*. Toronto: University of Toronto Press, 2002.

Bourgeois, Donald. "The Six Nations: A Neglected Aspect of Canadian Legal History." *Canadian Journal of Native Studies* 6, no. 2 (1986): 252-70.

Bramsted, Ernest, and K.J. Melhuish, eds. *Western Liberalism: A History in Documents from Locke to Croce*. London: Longman, 1978.

Braun, Bruce. "'On the Raggedy Edge of Risk': Articulations of Race and Nature after Biology." In Donald Moore, Anand Pandian, and Jake Kosek, eds., *Race, Nature, and the Politics of Difference*, 175-203. Durham, NC: Duke University Press, 2003.

–. *The Intemperate Rainforest: Nature, Culture, and Power on Canada's West Coast*. Minneapolis: University of Minnesota Press, 2002.

Cairns, Alan. *Citizens Plus: Aboriginal Peoples and the Canadian State*. Vancouver: UBC Press, 2000.

Carpenter, Roger. *The Renewed, the Destroyed, and the Remade: The Three Thought Worlds of the Huron and the Iroquois, 1609-1650*. East Lansing, MI: Michigan State University Press, 2004.

Carroll, William, and Robert Ratner. "Master Frames and Counter-Hegemony: Political Sensibilities in Contemporary Social Movements." *Canadian Review of Sociology* 33, no. 4 (1996): 407-35.

Clark, Bruce. *Native Liberty, Crown Sovereignty: The Existing Aboriginal Right of Self-Government in Canada*. Montreal and Kingston: McGill-Queen's University Press, 1990.

Clayton, Daniel. "Captain Cook and the Spaces of Contact at 'Nootka Sound.'" In Jennifer Brown and Elizabeth Vilbert, eds., *Reading beyond Words: Contexts for Native History*, 95-123. Peterborough, ON: Broadview, 1996.

Clifford, James. *The Predicament of Culture: Twentieth-Century Ethnography, Literature, and Art*. Cambridge, MA: Harvard University Press, 1988.

Coffey, Charles. *The Cost of Doing Nothing: A Call to Action*. Royal Bank of Canada, 1997. http://www.rbcroyalbank.com/aboriginal/r_comm.html.

Coyle, Michael. *Addressing Aboriginal Land and Treaty Rights in Ontario: An Analysis of Past Policies and Options for the Future*. Ipperwash Inquiry Research Report, Toronto, 2005. http://www.attorneygeneral.jus.gov.on.ca/inquiries/ipperwash/policy_part/research/index.html.

–. "Claims Resolution: A Healing Process?" In Jill Oakes et al., eds., *Sacred Lands: Aboriginal World Views, Claims, and Conflicts*, 259-64. Edmonton: Canadian Circumpolar Institute, 1996.

Clyne, Michael. "Establishing Linguistic Markers of Racist Discourse." In Christina Schaffner and Anita Wenden, eds., *Language and Peace*, 111-18. Amsterdam: Harwood, 1999.

Cunnean, Chris. "The Criminalization of Indigenous People." In Tania Das Gupta et al., eds., *Race and Racialization: Essential Readings*, 266-74. Minneapolis: University of Minnesota Press, 2007.

de la Salette Correia, Maria. "Peace, Order, and Good Government at Oka 1990: A Limited Anthropological Analysis." In Jill Oakes et al., eds., *Sacred Lands: Aboriginal World Views, Claims, and Conflicts*, 69-76. Edmonton: Canadian Circumpolar Institute, 1996.

Delgado, Richard. "Storytelling for Oppositionists and Others: A Plea for Narrative." In Richard Delgado and Jean Stefancic, eds., *Critical Race Theory: The Cutting Edge*, 60-70. Philadelphia: Temple University Press, 2000.

Derrida, Jacques. *Specters of Marx: The State of Debt, the Work of Mourning, and the New International*, translated by Peggy Kamuf. London and New York: Routledge, 1994.

Doxtator, Deborah Jean. "Inclusive and Exclusive Perceptions of Difference: Native and Euro-based Concepts of Time, History, and Change." In Germaine Warkentin and Carolyn Podruchny, eds., *Decentring the Renaissance: Canada and Europe in Multi-disciplinary Perspective 1500-1700*. Toronto: University of Toronto Press, 2001.

–. "What Happened to the Iroquois Clans? A Study of Clans in Three Nineteenth Century Rotinonhsyonni Communities." Ph.D. dissertation, University of Western Ontario, London, 1997.

Escobar, Arturo. *Encountering Development: The Making and Unmaking of the Third World*. Princeton: Princeton University Press, 1995.

Fairclough, Norman. *Analysing Discourse: Textual Analysis for Social Research*. London and New York: Routledge, 2003.

Flanagan, Tom. *First Nations? Second Thoughts*. Montreal and Kingston: McGill-Queen's University Press, 2000.

Foucault, Michel. *The Archaeology of Knowledge*. London: Tavistock, 1972.

–. *Discipline and Punish*. London: Lane, 1977.

–. *L'Ordre du Discours*. Paris: Gallimard, 1971.

Francis, Daniel. "The Imaginary Indian: The Image of the Indian in Canadian Culture." In Tania Das Gupta et al., eds., *Race and Racialization: Essential Readings*, 234-39. Minneapolis: University of Minnesota Press, 2007.

Furniss, Elizabeth. "Challenging the Myth of Indigenous Peoples' 'Last Stand' in Canada and Australia: Public Discourse and the Conditions of Silence." In Annie Coombes, ed., *Rethinking Settler Colonialism: History and Memory in Australia, Canada, Aotearoa New Zealand, and South Africa*, 172-92. Manchester: Manchester University Press, 2002.

Gee, James Paul. *An Introduction to Discourse Analysis: Theory and Method*. London and New York: Routledge, 2005.

Gisday Wa, and Delgam Uukw, Gitksan Hereditary Chiefs. *The Spirit in the Land: Statements of the Gitksan and Wet'suwet'en Hereditary Chiefs in the Supreme Court of British Columbia 1987-1990*. Gabriola Island: Reflections, 1992.

Haig-Brown, Celia, and David Nock. "Introduction." In Celia Haig-Brown and David Nock, eds., *With Good Intentions: Euro-Canadian and Aboriginal Relations in Colonial Canada*, 1-31. Vancouver: UBC Press, 2006.

Hale, Horatio. *The Iroquois Book of Rites*, edited by William Fenton. Toronto: University of Toronto Press, 1963.

Hall, Stuart. "Cultural Identity and Diaspora." In Jonathan Rutherford, ed., *Identity, Community, Culture, Difference*, 222-37. London: Lawrence and Wishart, 1990.

Harding, Robert. "Historical Representations of Aboriginal People in the Canadian News Media." *Discourse and Society* 17, no. 2 (2006): 205-35.

Harring, Sidney. *White Man's Law: Native People in Nineteenth-Century Canadian Juris-prudence*. Toronto: University of Toronto Press, 1998.

Harris, Cole. "How Did Colonialism Dispossess? Comments from an Edge of Empire." *Annals of the Association of American Geographers* 94, no. 1 (2004): 165-82.

–. *Making Native Space: Colonialism, Resistance, and Reserves in British Columbia.* Vancouver: UBC Press, 2002.

Henderson, James (Sakéj) Youngblood. "The Context of the State of Nature." In *Reclaiming Indigenous Voice and Vision,* 11-38. Vancouver: UBC Press, 2000.

–. "Postcolonial Ghost Dancing: Diagnosing European Colonialism." In Marie Battiste, ed., *Reclaiming Indigenous Voice and Vision,* 57-76. Vancouver: UBC Press, 2000.

–. "Postcolonial Ledger Drawing: Legal Reform." In Marie Battiste, ed., *Reclaiming Indigenous Voice and Vision,* 161-71. Vancouver: UBC Press, 2000.

–. "Sui Generis and Treaty Citizenship." *Citizenship Studies* 6, no. 4 (2002): 415-42.

Hill, Susan. "The Clay We Are Made Of: An Examination of Haudenosaunee Land Tenure on the Grand River Territory." Ph.D. dissertation, Department of Native Studies, Trent University, Peterborough, 2006.

–. "'Traveling Down the River of Life Together in Peace and Friendship, Forever': Haudenosaunee Land Ethics and Treaty Agreements as the Basis for Restructuring the Relationship with the British Crown." In Leanne Simpson, ed., *Lighting the Eighth Fire: The Liberation, Resurgence and Protection of Indigenous Nations,* 1-34. Winnipeg: Arbeiter Ring, 2008.

Hobbes, Thomas. *Leviathan.* Indiana: Hackett, 1651. http://oregonstate.edu/instruct/phl302/texts/hobbes/leviathan-contents.html.

Hylton, John. *Aboriginal Self-Government in Canada: Current Trends and Issues.* Saskatoon: Purich, 1999.

Indian and Northern Affairs Canada. "Background to the Grand River Notification Agreement." *Ontario Region – Agreements.* Ottawa: Indian and Northern Affairs Canada, 2005. http://www.lmtac.com/handbook2006/Example%2023.pdf.

Johnston, Charles. "The Six Nations in the Grand River Valley, 1784–1847." In Edward Rogers and Donald Smith, eds., *Aboriginal Ontario: Historical Perspectives on the First Nations.* Toronto: Dundurn, 1994.

–, ed. *The Valley of the Six Nations: A Collection of Documents on the Indian Lands of the Grand River.* Toronto: Champlain Society for the Government of Ontario, University of Toronto, 1964.

Johnston, Hank, Enrique Larana, and Joseph Gusfield. "Identities, Grievances, and New Social Movements." In Hank Johnston, Enrique Larana, and Joseph Gusfield, eds., *New Social Movements: From Ideology to Identity,* 3-35. Philadelphia: Temple University Press, 1994.

Katz, Cindi. "On the Grounds of Globalization: A Topography for Feminist Political Engagement." *Signs* 26, no. 4 (2001): 1213-34.

Kobayashi, Audrey, and Linda Peake. "Racism Out of Place: Thoughts on Whiteness and an Antiracist Geography in the New Millennium." *Annals of the Association of American Geographers* 90, no. 2 (2000): 392-403.

Koenig, Matthias, and Paul de Guchteneire. "Political Governance of Cultural Diversity." In Matthias Koenig and Paul de Guchteneire, eds., *Democracy and Human Rights in Multicultural Societies,* 3-17. Aldershot: Ashgate, 2007.

Kymlicka, Will, and Wayne Norman. "Citizenship in Culturally Diverse Societies: Issues, Contexts, Concepts." In Will Kymlicka and Wayne Norman, eds., *Citizenship in Diverse Societies,* 1–41. New York: Oxford University Press, 2000.

Lane, Marcus. "The Role of Planning in Achieving Indigenous Land Justice and Community Goals." *Land Use Policy* 23 (2006): 385-94.

Lawrence, Bonita. "Gender, Race, and the Regulation of Native identity in Canada and the United States: An Overview." *Hypatia* 18, no. 2 (2003): 3-31.

Leroy Little Bear. "Jagged Worldviews Colliding." In Marie Battiste, ed., *Reclaiming Indigenous Voice and Vision*, 77-85. Vancouver: UBC Press, 2000.

Li, Tania Murray. "Masyarakat Adat, Difference, and the Limits of Recognition in Indonesia's Forest Zone." In Donald Moore, Jake Kosek, and Anand Pandian, eds., *Race, Nature, and the Politics of Difference*, 380-406. Durham, NC: Duke University Press, 2003.

Lyons, Oren. "The American Indian in the Past." In Oren Lyons and John Mohawk, eds., *Exiled in the Land of the Free: Democracy, the Indian Nations, and the U.S. Constitution*, 13-42. Santa Fe, NM: Clear Light, 1991.

–. "The Seventh Generation Yet Unborn." *Futurist* 22, no. 2 (1988): 60.

Lyons, Oren, and John Mohawk. "Introduction." In Oren Lyons and John Mohawk, eds., *Exiled in the Land of the Free: Democracy, the Indian Nations, and the U.S. Constitution*, 2-12. Santa Fe, NM: Clear Light, 1991.

MacKinnon, Emily. *The Nisga'a Final Agreement and Canadian Federalism: Asymmetrical Design*, Vancouver, UBC Faculty of Law, 2010 [unpublished].

Macklem, Patrick. "First Nations Self-Government and the Borders of the Canadian Legal Imagination." *McGill Law Journal* 36 (1990): 382-456.

–. *Indigenous Difference and the Constitution of Canada*. Toronto: University of Toronto Press, 2001.

–. "What's Law Got to Do with It? The Protection of Aboriginal Title in Canada." *Osgoode Hall Law Journal* 35, no. 1 (1997): 125-37.

Manning, Erin. *Ephemeral Territories: Representing Nation, Home, and Identity in Canada*. Minneapolis: University of Minnesota Press, 2003.

Martindale, Barbara. *Caledonia: Along the Grand River*. Winnipeg: Natural Heritage Books, 1995.

McCarthy, Theresa. "'It Isn't Easy': The Politics of Representation, 'Factionalism,' and Anthropology in Promoting Haudenosaunee Traditionalism at Six Nations." Ph.D. dissertation, Department of Anthropology, McMaster University, 2006.

–. "Mobilizing the Metanarrative of Iroquois Factionalism and the Kanonhstaton Land Reclamation in the Grand River Territory." Unpublished paper, University of Buffalo, 2008 [used with permission; on file with author].

McDaniels, Timothy, and William Trousdale. "Resource Compensation and Negotiation Support in an Aboriginal Context: Using Community-Based Multi-Attribute Analysis to Evaluate Non-Market Losses." *Ecological Economics* 55, no. 2 (2005): 173-86.

McMillan, Alan, and Eldon Yellowhorn, eds. *First Peoples in Canada*. Vancouver: Douglas and McIntyre, 2004.

McNeil, Kent. "Envisaging Constitutional Spaces for Aboriginal Governments." *Queen's Law Journal* 95 (1994): 95-137.

Mehmet, Ozay. *Westernizing the Third World: The Eurocentricity of Economic Development Theories*. London and New York: Routledge, 1999.

Memmott, Paul, and Stephen Long. "Place Theory and Place Maintenance in Indigenous Australia." *Urban Policy and Research* 20, no. 1 (2002): 39-56.

Moore, Donald, Anand Pandian, and Jake Kosek. "The Cultural Politics of Race and Nature: Terrains of Power and Practice." In Donald Moore, Jake Kosek, and Anand Pandian, eds., *Race, Nature, and the Politics of Difference*, 1-70. Durham, NC: Duke University Press, 2003.

Nader, Laura. "Controlling Processes: Tracing the Dynamic Components of Power." *Current Anthropology* 38, no. 5 (1997): 711-37.

–. "Current Ilusions and Delusions about Conflict Management: In Africa and Elsewhere." *Law and Social Inquiry* 27, no. 3 (2002): 573-94.

Natcher, David C. "Land Use Research and the Duty to Consult: A Misrepresentation of the Aboriginal Landscape." *Land Use Policy* 18, no. 2 (April 2001): 113-22.

Niezen, Ronald. "Recognizing Indigenism: Canadian Unity and the International Movement of Indigenous Peoples." *Comparative Studies in Society and History* 42, no. 1 (2000): 119-48.

Noon, John. *Law and Government of the Grand River Iroquois.* New York: Viking Fund, 1949.

Notzke, Claudia. "A New Perspective in Aboriginal Natural Resource Management: Co-management." *Geoforum* 26, no. 2 (1995): 187-209.

Ofner, Patricia. "The Indian in Textbooks: A Content Analysis of History Books Authorized for Use in Ontario Schools." MA thesis, Lakehead University, 1983.

Olwig, Kenneth. "Landscape as a Contested Topos of Place, Community, and Self." In Paul Adams, Steven Hoelscher, and Karen Till, eds., *Textures of Place: Exploring Humanist Geographies,* 93-119. Minneapolis: University of Minnesota Press, 2001.

–. *Landscape, Nature, and the Body Politic: From Britain's Renaissance to America's New World.* Madison, WI: University of Wisconsin Press, 2002.

Peters, Evelyn. "Aboriginal People and Canadian Geography: A Review of the Recent Literature." *Canadian Geographer* 44, no. 1 (2000): 44-55.

Porter, Robert. "Building a New Longhouse: The Case for Government Reform within the Six Nations of the Haudenosaunee." *Buffalo Law Review* 46 (1998): 805-945.

Razack, Sherene. *Looking White People in the Eye: Gender, Race, and Culture in Courtrooms and Classrooms.* Toronto: University of Toronto Press, 1998.

–. *Race, Space, and the Law: Unmapping a White Settler Society.* Toronto: Between the Lines, 2002.

Reid, Jennifer. *Louis Riel and the Creation of Modern Canada: Mythic Discourse and the Postcolonial State.* Albuquerque, NM: University of New Mexico Press, 2008.

Rogers, Edward. "The Algonquian Farmers of Southern Ontario." In Donald Smith and Edward Rogers, eds., *Aboriginal Ontario: Historical Perspectives on the First Nations.* Toronto: Dundurn, 1994.

Ross, Michael Lee. *First Nations Sacred Sites in Canada's Courts.* Vancouver: UBC Press, 2005.

Rossiter, David, and Patricia Wood. "Fantastic Topographies: Neo-liberal Responses to Aboriginal Land Claims in British Columbia." *Canadian Geographer* 49, no. 4 (2005): 352-67.

Royal Commission on Aboriginal Peoples. *Royal Commission Report on Aboriginal Peoples.* Ottawa: Indian and Northern Affairs Canada, 1996. http://www.ainc-inac.gc.ca/ap/rrc-eng.asp.

Russell, Peter. *Recognizing Aboriginal Title: The Mabo Case and Indigenous Resistance to English-Settler Colonialism.* Toronto: University of Toronto Press, 2005.

Said, Edward. *Culture and Imperialism.* New York: Vintage, 1994.

Salée, Daniel. "Indigenous Peoples and Settler Angst in Canada: A Review Essay." *International Journal of Canadian Studies* 41, no. 4 (2010): 315-33.

de la Salette Correia, Maria. "Peace, Order, and Good Government at Oka 1990: A Limited Anthropological Analysis." In Jill Oakes et al., *Sacred Lands: Aboriginal World Views, Claims, and Conflicts,* 69-76. Edmonton: Canadian Circumpolar Institute Press, 1996.

Satterfield, Terre. *Anatomy of a Conflict: Identity, Knowledge, and Emotion in Old-Growth Forests*. Vancouver: UBC Press, 2002.

Six Nations Lands and Resources. "Six Nations of the Grand River: Land Rights, Financial Justice, Creative Solutions." Claims Summary. Ohsweken: Six Nations of the Grand River, 2006.

Smith, Linda Tuhiwai. *Decolonizing Methodologies: Research and Indigenous Peoples*. London and New York: Zed Books, 1999.

Sundberg, Juanita. "Placing Race in Environmental Justice Research in Latin America." *Society and Natural Resources* 21, no. 7 (2008): 569-82.

Surtees, Robert. "Land Cessions, 1763-1830." In Donald Smith and Edward Rogers, eds., *Aboriginal Ontario: Historical Perspectives on the First Nations*. Toronto: Dundurn, 1994.

–. "The Iroquois in Canada." In Francis Jennings, ed., *The History and Culture of Iroquois Diplomacy: An Interdisciplinary Guide to the Treaties of the Six Nations and Their League*, 67–83. Syracuse: Syracuse University Press, 1985.

Titley, E. Brian. *A Narrow Vision: Duncan Campbell Scott and the Administration of Indian Affairs in Canada*. Vancouver: UBC Press, 1986.

Tollefson, Chris, and Karen Wipond. "Cumulative Environmental Impacts and Aboriginal Rights." *Environmental Impact Assessment Review* 18 (1998): 371-90.

Tully, James. *Strange Multiplicity: Constitutionalism in an Age of Diversity*. Cambridge: Cambridge University Press, 1995.

Turner, Dale. "From Valladolid to Ottawa: The Illusion of Listening to Aboriginal People." In Jill Oakes et al., eds., *Sacred Lands: Aboriginal World Views, Claims, and Conflicts*, 53-68. Edmonton: Canadian Circumpolar Institute Press, 1996.

–. *This Is Not a Peace Pipe*. Toronto: University of Toronto Press, 2006.

Turpel, Mary Ellen. "Aboriginal Peoples and the Canadian Charter: Interpretive Monopolies, Cultural Differences." In Richard Devlin, ed., *First Nations Issues*, 40-73. Toronto: Emond Montgomery, 1991.

Usher, Peter. "Environment, Race and Nation Reconsidered: Reflections on Aboriginal Land Claims in Canada." Wiley Lecture. *Canadian Geographer* 47, no. 4 (2003): 365-82.

Usher, Peter, Frank Tough, and Robert Galois. "Reclaiming the Land: Aboriginal Title, Treaty Rights, and Land Claims in Canada." *Applied Geography* 12 (1992): 109-32.

–. *Elite Discourse and Racism*. Newbury Park: Sage, 1993.

Varadharajan, Asha. "The 'Repressive Tolerance' of Cultural Peripheries." In Marie Battiste, ed., *Reclaiming Indigenous Voice and Vision*, 142-49. Vancouver: UBC Press, 2000.

Venne, Sharon. "Understanding Treaty 6: An Indigenous Perspective." In Michael Asch, ed., *Aboriginal and Treaty Rights in Canada: Essays on Law, Equality, and Respect for Difference*, 173-207. Vancouver: UBC Press, 1997.

Voice of the Grand, *Talk of the Nation*. Ohsweken: CKRZ FM Radio, 1999.

Warry, Wayne. *Ending Denial: Understanding Aboriginal Issues*. Toronto: Broadview Press, 2007.

Weaver, Sally. "The Iroquois: The Consolidation of the Grand River Reserve in the Mid-Nineteenth Century, 1847–1875." In Edward Rogers and Donald Smith, eds., *Aboriginal Ontario: Historical Perspectives on the First Nations*, 182-212 (Toronto: Dundurn, 1994).

–. "The Iroquois: The Grand River Reserve in the Late Nineteenth and Early Twentieth Centuries, 1875-1945." In Edward Rogers and Donald Smith, eds., *Aboriginal Ontario: Historical Perspectives on the First Nations*, 213-57. Toronto: Dundurn, 1994.

Widdowson, Frances, and Albert Howard. *Disrobing the Aboriginal Industry: The Deception behind Indigenous Cultural Preservation.* Montreal and Kingston: McGill-Queen's University Press, 2008.

Williams, Paul, and Curtis Nelson, "Kaswentah," January 1995, research report prepared for the Royal Commission on Aboriginal Peoples, *For Seven Generations: An Information Legacy of the RCAP,* CD-ROM, Libraxus, 1997.

Wilson, Patrick. "Native Peoples and the Management of Natural Resources in the Pacific Northwest: A Comparative Assessment." *American Review of Canadian Studies* 32, no. 3 (2002): 397-414.

Winant, Howard. *The World Is a Ghetto: Race and Democracy since World War II.* New York: Basic Books, 2001.

Woolford, Andrew. *Between Justice and Certainty: Treaty Making in British Columbia.* Vancouver: UBC Press, 2005.

Index

LAW AND
SOCIETY

Lesley Erickson
Westward Bound: Sex, Violence, the Law, and the Making of a Settler Society (2011)

David R. Boyd
The Environmental Rights Revolution: A Global Study of Constitutions, Human Rights, and the Environment (2011)

Elaine Craig
Troubling Sex: Towards a Legal Theory of Sexual Integrity (2011)

Jocelyn Downie and Jennifer J. Llewellyn (eds.)
Being Relational: Reflections on Relational Theory and Health Law (2011)

Grace Li Xiu Woo
Ghost Dancing with Colonialism: Decolonization and Indigenous Rights at the Supreme Court of Canada (2011)

Fiona Kelly
Transforming Law's Family: The Legal Recognition of Planned Lesbian Motherhood (2011)

Colleen Bell
The Freedom of Security: Governing Canada in the Age of Counter-Terrorism (2011)

Andrew S. Thompson
In Defence of Principles: NGOs and Human Rights in Canada (2010)

Aaron Doyle and Dawn Moore (eds.)
Critical Criminology in Canada: New Voices, New Directions (2010)

Joanna R. Quinn
The Politics of Acknowledgement: Truth Commissions in Uganda and Haiti (2010)

Patrick James
Constitutional Politics in Canada after the Charter: Liberalism, Communitarianism, and Systemism (2010)

Louis A. Knafla and Haijo Westra (eds.)
Aboriginal Title and Indigenous Peoples: Canada, Australia, and New Zealand (2010)

Janet Mosher and Joan Brockman (eds.)
Constructing Crime: Contemporary Processes of Criminalization (2010)

Stephen Clarkson and Stepan Wood
A Perilous Imbalance: The Globalization of Canadian Law and Governance (2009)

Amanda Glasbeek
Feminized Justice: The Toronto Women's Court, 1913-34 (2009)

Kim Brooks (ed.)
Justice Bertha Wilson: One Woman's Difference (2009)

Wayne V. McIntosh and Cynthia L. Cates
Multi-Party Litigation: The Strategic Context (2009)

Renisa Mawani
Colonial Proximities: Crossracial Encounters and Juridical Truths in British Columbia, 1871-1921 (2009)

James B. Kelly and Christopher P. Manfredi (eds.)
Contested Constitutionalism: Reflections on the Canadian Charter of Rights and Freedoms (2009)

Catherine Bell and Robert K. Paterson (eds.)
Protection of First Nations Cultural Heritage: Laws, Policy, and Reform (2008)

Hamar Foster, Benjamin L. Berger, and A.R. Buck (eds.)
The Grand Experiment: Law and Legal Culture in British Settler Societies (2008)

Richard J. Moon (ed.)
Law and Religious Pluralism in Canada (2008)

Catherine Bell and Val Napoleon (eds.)
First Nations Cultural Heritage and Law: Case Studies, Voices, and Perspectives (2008)

Douglas C. Harris
Landing Native Fisheries: Indian Reserves and Fishing Rights in British Columbia, 1849-1925 (2008)

Peggy J. Blair
Lament for a First Nation: The Williams Treaties of Southern Ontario (2008)

Lori G. Beaman
Defining Harm: Religious Freedom and the Limits of the Law (2007)

Stephen Tierney (ed.)
Multiculturalism and the Canadian Constitution (2007)

Julie Macfarlane
The New Lawyer: How Settlement Is Transforming the Practice of Law (2007)

Kimberley White
Negotiating Responsibility: Law, Murder, and States of Mind (2007)

Dawn Moore
Criminal Artefacts: Governing Drugs and Users (2007)

Hamar Foster, Heather Raven, and Jeremy Webber (eds.)
Let Right Be Done: Aboriginal Title, the Calder Case, and the Future of Indigenous Rights (2007)

Dorothy E. Chunn, Susan B. Boyd, and Hester Lessard (eds.)
Reaction and Resistance: Feminism, Law, and Social Change (2007)

Margot Young, Susan B. Boyd, Gwen Brodsky, and Shelagh Day (eds.)
Poverty: Rights, Social Citizenship, and Legal Activism (2007)

Rosanna L. Langer
Defining Rights and Wrongs: Bureaucracy, Human Rights, and Public Accountability (2007)

C.L. Ostberg and Matthew E. Wetstein
Attitudinal Decision Making in the Supreme Court of Canada (2007)

Chris Clarkson
Domestic Reforms: Political Visions and Family Regulation in British Columbia, 1862-1940 (2007)

Jean McKenzie Leiper
Bar Codes: Women in the Legal Profession (2006)

Gerald Baier
Courts and Federalism: Judicial Doctrine in the United States, Australia, and Canada (2006)

Avigail Eisenberg (ed.)
Diversity and Equality: The Changing Framework of Freedom in Canada (2006)

Randy K. Lippert
Sanctuary, Sovereignty, Sacrifice: Canadian Sanctuary Incidents, Power, and Law (2005)

James B. Kelly
Governing with the Charter: Legislative and Judicial Activism and Framers' Intent (2005)

Dianne Pothier and Richard Devlin (eds.)
Critical Disability Theory: Essays in Philosophy, Politics, Policy, and Law (2005)

Susan G. Drummond
Mapping Marriage Law in Spanish Gitano Communities (2005)

Louis A. Knafla and Jonathan Swainger (eds.)
Laws and Societies in the Canadian Prairie West, 1670-1940 (2005)

Ikechi Mgbeoji
Global Biopiracy: Patents, Plants, and Indigenous Knowledge (2005)

Florian Sauvageau, David Schneiderman, and David Taras,
with Ruth Klinkhammer and Pierre Trudel
The Last Word: Media Coverage of the Supreme Court of Canada (2005)

Gerald Kernerman
Multicultural Nationalism: Civilizing Difference, Constituting Community (2005)

Pamela A. Jordan
Defending Rights in Russia: Lawyers, the State, and Legal Reform in the Post-Soviet Era (2005)

Anna Pratt
Securing Borders: Detention and Deportation in Canada (2005)

Kirsten Johnson Kramar
Unwilling Mothers, Unwanted Babies: Infanticide in Canada (2005)

W.A. Bogart
Good Government? Good Citizens? Courts, Politics, and Markets in a Changing Canada (2005)

Catherine Dauvergne
Humanitarianism, Identity, and Nation: Migration Laws in Canada and Australia (2005)

Michael Lee Ross
First Nations Sacred Sites in Canada's Courts (2005)

Andrew Woolford
Between Justice and Certainty: Treaty Making in British Columbia (2005)

John McLaren, Andrew Buck, and Nancy Wright (eds.)
Despotic Dominion: Property Rights in British Settler Societies (2004)

Georges Campeau
From UI to EI: Waging War on the Welfare State (2004)

Alvin J. Esau
The Courts and the Colonies: The Litigation of Hutterite Church Disputes (2004)

Christopher N. Kendall
Gay Male Pornography: An Issue of Sex Discrimination (2004)

Roy B. Flemming
Tournament of Appeals: Granting Judicial Review in Canada (2004)

Constance Backhouse and Nancy L. Backhouse
The Heiress vs the Establishment: Mrs. Campbell's Campaign for Legal Justice (2004)

Christopher P. Manfredi
Feminist Activism in the Supreme Court: Legal Mobilization and the Women's Legal Education and Action Fund (2004)

Annalise Acorn
Compulsory Compassion: A Critique of Restorative Justice (2004)

Jonathan Swainger and Constance Backhouse (eds.)
People and Place: Historical Influences on Legal Culture (2003)

Jim Phillips and Rosemary Gartner
Murdering Holiness: The Trials of Franz Creffield and George Mitchell (2003)

David R. Boyd
Unnatural Law: Rethinking Canadian Environmental Law and Policy (2003)

Ikechi Mgbeoji
Collective Insecurity: The Liberian Crisis, Unilateralism, and Global Order (2003)

Rebecca Johnson
Taxing Choices: The Intersection of Class, Gender, Parenthood, and the Law (2002)

John McLaren, Robert Menzies, and Dorothy E. Chunn (eds.)
  Regulating Lives: Historical Essays on the State, Society, the Individual, and the Law (2002)

Joan Brockman
  Gender in the Legal Profession: Fitting or Breaking the Mould (2001)